Energy and Society

THE RELATION BETWEEN ENERGY, SOCIAL CHANGE, AND ECONOMIC DEVELOPMENT

Fred Cottrell

PROFESSOR OF GOVERNMENT AND SOCIOLOGY
MIAMI UNIVERSITY, OXFORD, OHIO

GREENWOOD PRESS, PUBLISHERS
WESTPORT, CONNECTICUT

To
ANNICE, BILL,
BOB, AND COLLEEN

Foreword

This work traces man's use of energy, from readily available but low-yield sources, such as plant life and draft animals, to more complicated but high-yield forms, such as steam power and electricity, and indicates broadly the influences on social interrelations. The thesis is that the amounts and types of energy employed condition man's way of life materially and set somewhat predictable limits on what he can do and on how society will be organized.

The influence of energy is seen to be ubiquitous, with economic, political, social, psychological, and ethical consequences intermeshed. The study thus follows no established academic field exclusively. As a result, concepts (both elementary and more advanced) are taken from various disciplines.

It is this interdisciplinary orientation, centering upon the easily understood and measurable concept of energy (in terms of calories and horsepower), which the present writer wishes particularly to stress and commend. Having himself been interested in interdisciplinary questions for more than a quarter of a century, and finding the problem of synthesis an increasingly difficult one in the face of ever more minute specialization, he feels that the author's unique and significant approach to the dynamics of social change will find many welcome users among those of like interests in the various social fields.

Not the least of the contributions of the book is the light it throws upon certain controversial issues which are as a rule thought of as belonging to one specialized social discipline alone but which in fact represent border-line problems involving two or more disciplines. This question will be touched upon again later, following a resumé of the work, which is given below.

Since man, like other animals, originally depends largely on plants to secure the physical energy he himself employs, the study opens with an examination of the limits under which this sun-plant-man or sun-plant-animal-man system operates. From his food man can convert into various forms of energy no more than about 3,500 calories a day; nor can he survive and remain productive on an average daily food consumption of much less than 2,000 calories. Under average conditions about 20 per cent of this converted energy can be used for mechanical work, the equivalent roughly of from $\frac{1}{2}$ to 1 hp-hr per day per man. Put otherwise, in a 10-hour working day a man can deliver from 1/10 to 1/20 as much mechanical power as a horse, but his caloric intake and thus his dependence on plants is also only about 1/10 to 1/20 as much. Where land is plentiful, population sparse, and draft animals available, there may be an economy in substituting draft animals for manpower; but with increased population and competition of land for the production of food and feed, the situation may be reversed, the survival of man being more important than the feeding of work animals.

It is pointed out that where manpower alone is available for tilling the soil man's social behavior is relatively narrow and one's ability to predict his conduct is relatively high. These factors are modified in some degree with the introduction of draft animals, since man now has more surplus time and energy in which to develop other activities. Social and trading relations become somewhat more complex where the energy of the flowing stream (which has its own peculiar limitations) is used for transportation purposes and thus modifies the relations between those sharing the stream and others not so favored. All such energy utilization, however, including the use of the windmill and water wheel, is of a relatively low order and continues to set rather severe limits on social behavior and organization. These limitations are illustrated from various sources, particularly from the changes wrought in the culture of the Plains Indians with their redomestication of horses brought in earlier by the Spanish, and from the civilization of the Egyptians living on the reoccurring bounties of the Nile during the reign of the pharaohs.

The introduction of the sailing ship brought more drastic changes. A much greater specialization of labor and exchange of products became possible. Important shifts of power occurred, favoring certain occupations, classes, and regions. New forms of thought and behavior developed. The relatively great power of Phoenicia, Greece, and Rome, as contrasted with neighboring countries with a much wider agricultural base, can be traced to the influence of the sailing ship, as can also the later civilizations of the Mediterranean basin and along the west coast of Northern Europe. In England, the protection of the sea and the use of sail permitted the rise of sea lords to challenge the land lords of

Continental Europe with its continuance of feudalism. This made possible the later use of steam as an adjunct of sail and the creation of still larger surpluses of energy, greatly expanding the range of choices on the part of those in control of the surplus energy. The basis was thus laid for the effective use of the still greater energy of coal, oil, and falling water, the rise of England as the workshop of the world together with her great development as a trading nation, and the pervasive spread of English law and social and political institutions.

The more complicated converters of energy, the steamship, stationary engine, and locomotive, led to further significant changes in economic, political, and social organization, favoring those regions possessing the high energy of coal, oil, gas, and falling water as against areas confined to the use of energy gained primarily from organic or other low-energy converters. The opportunities and limits of social organization based on the exploitation of high-energy fuels are shown to be quite different from those based primarily on the sailing ship, the domesticated animal, or the human being working unaided with the soil.

Although the more advanced energy converters have been introduced at different times to different peoples with different social backgrounds, and the consequences of the new technology among them have varied considerably, a number of limits may nevertheless be observed and certain generalizations may be made about the direction of the changes accompanying the shift to high-energy technology. These the author then proceeds to outline.

First, there are certain physical or mechanical limitations which are generally applicable. Experience demonstrates that in many instances the yields per acre in hoe culture are as high or higher than those in plow culture. Thus the amount of food secured by introducing tractors or draft animals may not only be no greater than that presently available but it may actually be smaller. Coupled with this is the fact that the mechanical energy expended in producing a given amount of food mounts with increasing farm mechanization. The saving is of course in terms of output per man-hour, but unless the hours saved can be profitably employed in other activities the results may be actually detrimental rather than beneficial to the indigenous population. Industrialization is as a rule a gain to food raisers themselves only where there is land not presently in use for their sustenance or where they can add nonagricultural activities to their present farm labor. Elsewhere such industrialization can be secured only by coercing those living on the land to reduce their claims on the farm product or by forcing some of them to move elsewhere. Either contingency presents a bleak prospect today for the great masses living in such regions as India or China. Furthermore, where industrialization has occurred, not only is there additional need for food to take care of those working in the factories but also those left behind on the farms tends to multiply to the point where they continue to require for themselves all the food the land will provide.

This continuing or reoccurring population pressure is a second major limiting factor. In the early period of the industrial revolution, it was possible for great numbers of resolute and trained people to emigrate from overcrowded areas to relatively empty continents. In certain of these sparse settlements, Christian fortitude, the horse and plow, the steam engine and the railroad not only increased output per man-hour on the farms but also enabled factories and cities to develop with great rapidity, population to expand at an accelerated pace, and high-energy resources (coal and oil and gas) to be increasingly exploited for the purpose of supplying fuel for an ever advancing technology. This was the course followed particularly in the United States.

In the mother countries, however, population pressures were only temporarily eased. Moreover, other nations (such as Germany, Italy, and Japan) attempting later to develop the new technologies were finally faced not only with heavy population pressures at home but with a dearth of favorable population outlets abroad. Thus they embarked on military conquest to secure their "places in the sun." In the meantime, also, newly industrialized countries, such as the United States and Germany, had enacted restrictive measures to protect their growing industries from the sometimes ruthless methods employed by England, which had to keep expanding her markets for manufactured goods in return for food and raw materials to take care of continuing population pressures at home. Despite two world wars, the population problems in the older countries and in some of the newer ones have nowhere been solved and their outside sources of food and other primary supplies are now being increasingly curtailed. The same cycle of problems is apparent in the Communist states, which are attempting industrialization in forced marches, starting with small stocks of capital goods and huge and rapidly growing populations. In addition, these states are pushing out and infiltrating into already overpopulated agricultural areas.

Another major limitation to high-energy development is the inertia and resistance of long-established customs and ideologies to changes necessitated by its introduction. Such changes disrupt closely knit kinship groups, substitute the role of the market with its broad instabilities for the direct hand-to-mouth arrangements of low-energy societies.

necessitate modifications in the property institution through such developments as corporate organization, and require an expansion of the powers of the state, both to regulate the market and to attempt responsibilities which the market strips from the family and the village but which the state finds it very difficult if not impossible to assume.

The resultant apathy, anxiety, insecurity, and hostility to Western colonialism and imperialism render certain areas of the world today an easy prey to the propaganda of the Communists with their rosy promises to correct such difficulties despite their complete inability to do anything about them. Soviet imperialism, based on the establishment and maintenance of a high-energy technology in the mother country, can be no different from, and must operate under the same set of limitations as, any other type of modern imperialism.

Politically, high-energy technology has operated (or failed to operate) under practically all forms of government. The limitations mentioned above are always present. Geography, energy resources, climate, population, and scientific and related ideology must apparently continue to be mixed in certain right proportions for such technology to continue to develop. There is evidence that a wider regionalism than the traditional national state is now required in some areas. Other factors regarding future requirements have not yet been clearly delineated. A continuing analysis of the relationships between energy and society should provide fruitful answers to some of the insistent questions already in evidence.

A few additional comments are here added from the point of view of the present author. It is of course not to be assumed (nor does the author of this book assume) that, given certain "right" conditions, high-energy technology will necessarily and automatically emerge, unless one semantically includes in the concept "right" important libertarian forces which materialistic determinism does not include.

The perennial problems of value theory are particularly highlighted by this book, especially in their implicit ethical aspects. The market if freely operating is supposed in classical theory to bring value in exchange or price down to a reasonably fair level—that level being visualized in terms of the labor and other sacrifices or human costs that are involved. Utility and the free gifts of nature are assumed to be neutralized and generalized through the marketplace and the competitive process. Thus the physical energy of unaided man and a thousand times that energy in a machine would exchange on even terms if the labor and other sacrifice involved in making them available were the same. Neoclassical or utility theory is thought to achieve the same ethical objective by way of marginalism, also assuming a freely operating competitive process. In the past century or more both classical and neoclassical value theories have come under severe attack; but marginal-utility rationalization is still dominant, although some economists believe they can escape certain implications (in the comparison of desires and thus utilities) by substituting "indifference" for "measurement."

In utility theory, nevertheless, one implication cannot be escaped, whether utility is cut marginally or indifferently. Utility or usefulness to man includes the free gift of nature, whether this is little, as in lowly plant life, or energy-wise ten thousand times as much, as in a pool of petroleum. For which of these is man "willing" to pay more, from the standpoint of utility? And since utility necessarily contains a free gift (of a variable and unmeasurable amount), should man "have" to pay for the free-gift portion? This impasse between economic-utility and ethical theory, while not pretending to be resolved by the analysis undertaken in this book, is at least set forth in a new and significant perspective.

This is also true in regard to classical and neoclassical value theory in general, which is highly unrealistic in a historical, political, and socio-logical frame of reference. In its compartmentalized ivory-tower development, economic theory has usually assumed that there once was a time (in an "early and crude" state of society) when competition was freely and fairly operating and that only in relatively recent centuries have predatory and oligopolistic tendencies crept in to create the currently recognized problems of monopoly, administrated prices, and business depression.

As seen in proper evolutionary and social perspective, predatory conditions are nothing new. Shrewd, ambitious, unscrupulous men have from time immemorial secured power for themselves and have monopolized human and other energy resources, much more under "early and crude" conditions than at present. Subjugation of peoples, exactions of tribute, reaping the benefits of slavery and serfdom, and charging what the traffic will bear have been dominant factors in enriching and maintaining dictatorships and oligarchies as civilization has developed. Freely operating markets, where each participant has equal power, have existed mainly in the hopes and aspirations of moralists and utopian dialecticians. It is with such hopes and aspirations as one looks to the future, however, that value theories in economics and ethics are being brought closer together, and with the aid of the other social disciplines also, not in any nostalgic return to a past golden age of harmonies which never existed in fact.

Out of severe predatory conditions, law and order and fair play are gradually emerging. The fact that we think today in terms of broad social objectives, of ethical codes and trade practices, of minimum wages and full employment indicates the relatively high moral level of social organization thus far attained. The kind of broad inter-disciplinary perspective provided by such studies as *Energy and Society* should not only do much to keep our thinking straight, as we move still further along the road of harmonizing economic, ethical, sociological, political, and other social objectives but also keep us aware of the limitations and problems to be faced in further techno-logical development.

JOSEPH MAYER, *Chairman*
Department of Economics,
Miami University, Oxford, Ohio

Preface

The inspiration for this book came initially from the enthusiasm with which some of my students received the ideas here set forth as they were presented in my lectures. At first the ideas were no more than brief suggestive propositions. Under the stimulus of the interest they evoked, sentences developed into paragraphs and, later, into the chapters of a short paper, which was mimeographed for use in class sessions. But graduates continued to ask for more complete formulation than they had received in class, and it was in discussions with them that many aspects of my thesis were modified and elaborated.

So the brief mimeographed statement eventually became a book. In the early stages of the writing I was particularly sustained, encouraged, and guided by my colleagues Read and Florence Bain, Paul Hatt, Sigmund and Maxine Nosow, Edith Foth Puff, David and Jeanette Lewis, George and Johanne Fathauer, Alver Jacobson, Julianna and Homer Schamp, Michael Eckstein, and Alfred Schnurr. I was also encouraged to complete the writing by Professor William Form of Michigan State University.

To complete the work I was given a sabbatical leave by Miami University during the summer and fall of 1952. I was privileged at this time to work in the libraries of the Hoover Institute and the Stanford Food Research Institute at Stanford University and the Giannini Foundation at the University of California. Dr. Warren Thompson of the Scripps Foundation for Population Research was kind enough to read the manuscript and to aid in its completion by providing housing and clerical assistance. I was also greatly aided by the enthusiastic backing and trenchant criticism of Donald Bogue, whose research supported some of my hypotheses and demonstrated the invalidity of others I had formulated. Through the courtesy of the Scripps Foundation, Mary Jane Tunnell, with the assistance of her engineer husband John, gave editorial help.

The reader also owes more than he knows or I can acknowledge to the work of the editors. Dr. Richard T. LaPiere encouraged and participated in a stylistic revision which was largely completed by Ruth Eisenstein.

At every step I was encouraged and aided by my wife in the rewriting of the manuscript.

I wish also to acknowledge the help provided by Mrs. Meredith Farmer, who, under great pressure of time, did the job of typing the final manuscript.

FRED COTTRELL

Contents

Foreword vii

Preface xv

CHAPTER 1. THE NATURE AND CHARACTERISTICS OF ENERGY . . . 1

The Problem Stated 2
Energy Defined 5
Measurements of Energy 6
The Energy Field 9
Conversion Rate or Gradient 10
Surplus Energy 11

CHAPTER 2. ORGANIC ENERGY AND THE LOW-ENERGY SOCIETY . . 15

Plants as Converters 16
Animals as Converters 19
Food-gathering Societies 23
Food-raising Societies 28
Surplus and Civilization 32
Current Low-energy Societies 35

CHAPTER 3. INORGANIC ENERGY SOURCES: WIND AND WATER . . 39

The River as Transport 39
The River as Source of Mechanical Energy 42
Limitations of Water Wheel and Windmill 43
The Sea and the Ship 46
The Sailing Ship: Revolution in Energy Source 50

CHAPTER 4. SAIL, TRADE, AND MERCANTILISM 52

The Concept of "Opportunity Cost" 53
Prerequisites to Trade 57
Changes Wrought by the Ship 62

Sail and Stream in Antiquity 66
The Sailing Ship and the Colonial System 68
The Sailing Ship and the Mercantilistic Society 72

CHAPTER 5. STEAM: KEY TO THE INDUSTRIAL REVOLUTION . . . 79

The Steamship 79
The Locomotive 81
British and European Railroad Usage 88
Use of the Railroad in America 91
Petroleum 93
Nuclear Fuel 97
Electricity 98
Characteristics of Electricity 99
Hydroelectric Power 105
The Internal Combustion Engine 106

CHAPTER 6. THE HISTORICAL CIRCUMSTANCES 110

The Assumption that Progress is Inevitable 110
The Population Factor 117
The Prospects for Asia 128
Communism Versus Capitalism 132

CHAPTER 7. THE INDUSTRIALIZATION OF AGRICULTURE 134

Hoe Versus Plow 135
Horse Versus Tractor 138
Where the Hoe is Indispensable 142
Energy Costs of Industrial Farming 148
Distribution of Energy Surpluses 152
Restraints on the Diffusion of Industrial Agriculture 155
Problems of Agriculture in the High-energy Society 158

CHAPTER 8. CAPITALISM IN THEORY AND IN FACT 166

The Controlled Population 167
Price-measured Cost Versus Energy Cost 173
Social Organization 179
The Theory of Capitalism 182
Comparisons and Contrasts 190
Marxian Theory and Communist Practice 194
Modern Technology and International Disequilibrium 198

CHAPTER 9. THE ORGANIZATION OF PRODUCTIVE EFFORT 200

Requirements of the Ship 200

Technique and Organization 204
The "Curse" of Bigness 206
Specialization and Division of Labor 209
Changing Property Rights 213
Ownership: Past and Present 216
Collectivism Versus Individualism 219
The Corporation 222

TER 10.   THE DISTRIBUTION OF CONSUMERS' GOODS 232

The High-energy Consumption Unit 235
The Market Place 243
Instability of the Free Market 248
The Businessman Versus the Politician 252

TER 11.   THE ENLARGEMENT AND CONCENTRATION OF POLITICAL
          POWER   256

Expanding Functions of the State 259
War and the Modern State 267
Political Bureaucracy 269
The Future of Government 271

TER 12.   NOT ONE WORLD, BUT MANY 278

Energy and International Position 278
The World State 284
Ideological Unification 286
Regional Bases of Energy Use 287
Geography and Regionalism 294
Ideological Unity and Economic Regionalism 298
Undeveloped Areas and the Welfare State 301
Regional High-energy Systems 304
Short-term and Long-term Prospects 309

          References 313

          Index 325

The Nature and Characteristics
of Energy

The discovery and development of atomic power have led to a rash of speculation about the influence which this new source of energy will have on the future of mankind. The prophets of doom say that it will condemn man to a return to the cave. There is no way scientifically to refute this position—here we can consult only hopes and fears. On the other hand, there are those who see in atomic energy the basis for a brave new world, in which war is impossible and men are freed from the necessity to work. This claim can be tested on the basis of man's past experience.

In peacetime, atomic energy will compete with other sources of energy. In the past man has abandoned one source of energy for another only because of the prospect of overwhelming advantage, and then with reluctance. So to predict where and how atomic energy will influence the future we must know not only its costs and the gains to be made through its use, but also the costs and advantages of the forms of energy now in use. The same kind of speculation as has accompanied the rise of atomic power was associated with the introduction of new energy sources in the past, but in the past we did not have the store of scientific knowledge that we have today. This work is an effort to bring together and examine some of this knowledge so that we may increase our ability to foresee the future effects of energy, and so avoid some of the pitfalls into which we might otherwise stumble.

THE PROBLEM STATED

The thesis of the book is simple. It is that the energy available to man limits what he *can* do and influences what he *will* do. It will not be easy to establish, for the energy converters man uses are embedded in a social matrix in which it is difficult to distinguish the relationships primarily connected with technical operations from those primarily of social origin. Nevertheless the effort must be undertaken, because only if we can separate the effects of the two types of controlling factor can we know how much of what men strive to do is possible of achievement.

Conflict between communism and social organization in the patterns found in the Free World shapes our day. Free enterprisers hold that the political and economic ideas developed largely in the British Commonwealth, the United States, and Northwest Europe have demonstrated their capacity to deal with industrial society. Communists, on the other hand, believe that only through use of the Marxian model can man fully realize the potentialities of modern technology. Each school holds that if its system is adopted, eventually all the world will share a standard of material well-being equal or superior to that now enjoyed in the wealthiest states. Each is expected by its proponents to bring into being a society largely free from toil and poverty, without reference to the geographic and demographic facts or the technological propositions faced by a particular people. Now if the thesis here presented is substantiated, it will be up to these ideologists to show how the systems they propose will convert and distribute energy so that man everywhere *will* do what they hold he *will be able to* do, and also to prove that nothing involved in the process of producing and using more energy is likely to influence men to distribute it unequally—or, more specifically, to deny to great areas of the world the wealth it would be possible for them to have if energy were "properly" distributed.

Thus the thesis offered here is likely to raise questions about the reliability of certain propositions which are basic to the policies of both the Communist and the Free World. Some of the makers of these policies will be unwilling to accept its implications. In anticipation of such resistance, our argument has been built upon widely accep   rinciples of natural science rather than "self-evident" truths   out human nature.

The scientist's contribution can be summed up in the formula: If you do thus and so, this will follow. In other words, science prescribes the conditions necessary to bring about change and predicts its consequences. Whether or not human beings can be influenced deliberately to perform or to eschew certain acts in order to achieve or to avoid predicted consequences cannot be learned from the scientific position itself. If we are to predict whether or not a given group will wish to change in the manner required to make use of new fuels and converters, we shall have to know what, in the particular situation envisaged, has to be changed so that these fuels and converters can be used. This means that a careful effort must be made to distinguish between the social relationships that are dependent upon the use of present converters and those that may be expected to continue even though new sources of power energize them. Only to the degree that we know what must be changed can we know the costs of change and so estimate man's willingness to alter his society.

There are and have been many kinds of labels used in explaining why man persists in or modifies his behavior. He has been variously classified as primarily a power-seeking or political animal, a money-seeking or economic being, a being endowed by blood and soil with racial instincts which guide his choices, the helpless puppet of physical or biological forces which move him, an anarchistic element in time and space guided only by his will, and many other kinds of creature. The makers of these labels, having endowed man with a basic nature, then proceed to infer how such a creature should act and predict how in fact he will act. Here we provide no such grand scheme. We are trying to discover the relations between the energy converters and fuel men use and the kinds of societies they build.

The methods involved in trying to arrive at the truth in regard to these relationships are varied. The physical and biological sciences can tell us the nature and amount of energy that can be secured from a given fuel or converter. Examining this evidence enables us to form an idea of the way man would act if limited by this particular source of energy. We can also estimate how he might act if he were to seek to make the most efficient * possible use of this source.

Turning from this ideal, we shall examine historic evidence to see how in fact people confined to the use of given energy sources have acted. This will indicate the degree to which their behavior has corresponded with that required ideally to exploit th ir energy sources.

Changes in values and social structure which have accompanied alteration in energy sources will also be examined, along with evidence as to whether or not such changes reveal a common pattern. Analysis of this evidence will provide a means of finding out why some people did not take advantage of known sources of energy by some standards clearly superior to sources they did use.

We make no a priori assumption as to the part that energy plays in man's behavior. We shall make an effort to discover what part it does play, in the belief that by so doing we can help to bring about a closer correspondence between the expectations of men and what is likely to happen.

Even the most elementary knowledge of physiology and of thermodynamics makes it clear that man can exist only where he is able to replace the energy which he uses up in the process of living. He must regularly be in control of energy equal to or in excess of this minimum. A permanent deficit makes life impossible.

Beyond this biologically set minimum the amount of energy required by man is set by the goals he seeks. There are few, if any, societies in which men choose to exert no more energy than is required to maintain a supply of food, protection from the elements, and procreation. Rather, there is a wide range of values which induce man to strive for a large number of goals requiring for their achievement control over varying forms and amounts of energy. The preservation of a system of values requires a continuous supply of energy equal to the demands imposed by that system of values. Conversely, as we shall later show, changes in the amount or form of energy available give rise to conditions likely to result in changes in values, for men who share common values make similar changes in choice when faced with similar changes in the consequences of their acts. These changes in choice are influenced

* See page 8 for a definition of "efficient" as used in this book.

not only by the values they have learned but by changed limits as to what it is physically possible for them to do. Thus the possibility of predicting change depends as much on a knowledge of the physical potentialities in a situation as it does on a knowledge of the values men hold.

Probably as a result of the errors of the physical determinists and the Marxists, there has in the United States particularly been a marked hesitancy to examine the social consequences of the physical arrangements by which men live. There have, however, been a number of fruitful investigations. Among the social scientists, W. F. Ogburn, Lewis Mumford, George K. Zipf, John Q. Stewart, Leslie White, Hornell Hart, and numerous others have given particular attention to the social implications of technology and of the energy it makes available. This book starts with a somewhat different type of investigation from theirs and arrives at somewhat different conclusions, and no attempt will be made generally to discuss their contributions.

The approach here used cuts across many of the traditional lines of division of labor among social scientists. This gives rise to some of the same kinds of difficulties as have confronted other scientists using energy as a common denominator. Many things which are elementary to the specialist in one field must be said for the sake of the reader who is not trained in that field. Thus readers sophisticated in any of the areas covered will find the work a mixture of elementary and more advanced levels. This difficulty may be illustrated by the concept of *energy*.

ENERGY DEFINED

Energy must be defined in terms of the ways in which it manifests itself. It is variously classified as heat, light, sound, radio, radar, TV, electricity, magnetism, mechanical energy, growth, and even "matter." At one time it was difficult for the layman to accept the fact that these fields represent different manifestations of the same thing, and even today in the face of "the bomb" and of the everyday miracle by which electricity is converted in the average household into many other forms of energy, conversion of energy from one form to another is not yet a commonplace. To do justice to the concept of energy would require treating each of its manifestations as it is treated by experts in that particular field. We must ignore the somewhat variant meaning of the concept to experts in various scientific pursuits; a common core of meaning as shared by layman and expert is the most that we can deal with in these pages.

Energy Converters

It is apparent that, as a means to convert energy, man can be measured like any other converter. This is not to say that in every situation the most significant thing about a man is that he is a converter—even though when he ceases so to be he is dead. It is to say that, significant or not, it is a fact that if man acts, his activities can be measured in physical terms.

Man also makes use of converters other than his own body to achieve his ends, and the energy these converters make available to him is also measurable. Thus wherever other converters can be used to replace or supplement the energies of man, the relative advantage, in energy terms, of using them over using his own physical effort can be calculated. However, such calculations will not alone serve to indicate whether the more or the less efficient converter as so measured will, in fact, be used. One of the problems incidental to this study will be to discover some of the conditions under which man will be likely to continue to pursue a course demonstrably "wasteful" of energy in preference to a more efficient way. Man seems frequently to follow such a course. For this reason we do not here accept Zipf's [1] conclusion that inevitably man will "in the long run" modify his culture in the direction of making life physically less difficult. In fact, there are some very old practices which are deliberately continued in use as if in response to an urge to do things "the hard way."

MEASUREMENTS OF ENERGY

To calculate the costs and gains of any action requires the use of common measures and accepted concepts. For convenience some of those frequently used in this book are presented in this chapter. Newtonian physics assumes that material objects will keep their existing relationships unless acted upon by an outside force. In other words, *work* is defined as a factor responsible for

[1] See References cited by chapter in full at the end of this book.

some sort of change in physical relationships. This may be a change of form, time, or place. Energy, in turn, since it is defined as the ability to do work, is involved in any change in physical relationship. A good deal of the time we shall be dealing with the *potential energy* to be derived from a change in a given source of energy. Such energy as is actually involved in doing work is called *kinetic energy*. Kinetic energy takes many forms, each of which can be measured. For example, mechanical energy is measured by setting up an arbitrary unit to measure force and another to measure distance. These two measurements are multiplied to give a composite figure. So, for example, a force adequate to lift one pound a distance of one foot is a *foot-pound*; that capable of lifting one kilogram a distance of one meter is a *kilogram-meter*, etc. These measurements have in turn been converted into other convenient units. Thus when Watt was attempting to sell his steam engines he found it necessary to state the relative capacity of his engine as compared with that of the horse, which the engine was often expected to replace. Watt set out to determine the strength of his engines as compared with that of the horses then in use in England. By testing them he discovered that the average horse could do 22,000 foot-pounds of work per minute for as long as 10 hours a day. In fixing on a unit to state the power of the steam engine, he arbitrarily increased the figure based on the horse by one-half, to ensure that the purchasers of his engines would get full measure, making the horsepower equal to a rate of 33,000 foot-pounds of work per minute, or 550 foot-pounds per second. This measure came into wide use with the adoption of the steam engine.

It may be well to state here the equivalence of some measures of heat and mechanical power that will be used. One kilowatt-hour is equivalent to 1.34 horsepower-hours and to 860 Calories; 1 horsepower-hour equals about 641.56 Calories. (Technically the great calorie, or the kilogram-calorie, this is the unit in which diets are commonly stated; it will be referred to throughout simply as the Calorie.)

Acceleration

It was stated above that mechanical energy is calculated in terms of motion, force and distance being used as parameters.

However, force itself was arbitrarily described in terms of pounds, a measure commonly used to express weight. To measure force in motion we must add a new dimension. This is *acceleration*, the rate of change of speed of movement. The specific relationship between rate of motion and energy required to produce it has been established empirically: the energy is equal to one-half the mass times the velocity squared. If the mass remains unchanged, it is clear that to increase the rate of motion of an object requires energy in proportion to the square of the velocity. Thus, at high speeds fairly large increments of energy may have only slight effects in altering the rate of motion.

Another of the laws of physics with which we shall be concerned is the principle of the conservation of energy. Newtonian physics holds that the amount of energy in the universe is a constant, and thus energy is never lost or gained. Man never creates energy or destroys it. These words have meaning only in terms of human values. What we mean when we say man creates energy is that he increases its supply at the time and place and in the form in which he needs it. He consumes energy when he makes it less available to serve his purposes. The efficiency of a converter is a measure of the proportion of the energy fed into it which is converted into the form desired. It is not only a physical measurement; it is also a social estimate. For example, blood sugar is converted into various forms of energy by the human body. Winter or summer, muscular exertion requires chemical change in that sugar, which also results in the giving off of heat. In winter the heat is often desirable, and exercise may be indulged in for the simple purpose of warming the body, whereas in summer the heat is frequently an undesired concomitant of exercise and its reduction would be welcome. Thus the efficiency of the body in converting food into energy would vary from season to season with the change in the ends desired. Usually the engineer simply assumes the social objective of the system in which he is working and measures in terms of it without further concern. If he is designing a light bulb he seeks to minimize heat; in a heating element he reduces to the lowest possible point the proportion of light rays being generated. But without a knowledge of the forms of energy being sought he has no means of determining efficiency.

THE ENERGY FIELD

There are a number of other concepts with which we shall have to work. The thesis that the energy available to man determines what man *can* do means that energy sets a limit. The idea that energy influences what man *will* do implies that within the limits so set the supply of energy is also a factor at work influencing choice. This kind of situation involves what is termed a *limited field*. The concept of limit is one very familiar to us. As applied to the discovery and measurement of energy, it is the point at which the energy being discovered ceases to have an effect upon the instrument used to discover and measure it. A Geiger counter shows the presence of radioactive substances; when it ceases to manifest any change in the presence of a substance we say we are outside the field of any radioactive substance, or beyond the limits of such a field. A battery yields a flow of electricity; when it ceases to affect an instrument designed to reveal a flow of current, we say that so far as the instrument is concerned the battery no longer creates a field, that the instrument is beyond the limits of the initial supply of energy the battery was capable of generating. If a thermometer placed in or near a furnace shows no perceptible change from the temperature which it exhibited at a more distant point, we say that the fuel which the furnace contained has been exhausted or the fire extinguished. Perhaps nothing more need be said about this familiar aspect of the concept, which relates to the total amount of energy. However, there is often another type of limit involved: the rate at which a converter can change energy. Enlarging the gas tank will not make a car go faster. A man who can easily lift a thousand bricks one at a time may find himself totally incapable of lifting all of them at once. Obviously the factors limiting the *rate* of conversion are other than those controlling the total amount of energy yielded. Since we are so frequently confronted with limits—on the amount we can lift at one time, on the speed at which we can run, on the amount of light yielded by a bulb, on the distance we can go in a given time in a car—this form of limit needs no further amplification.

The concept of the field, already in part described, is a little more difficult. The *field* is the sphere of an operation, that is, it is the range within which what is being observed retains its identity and affects an instrument in a manner significant to the observer. Fields are often recognized as a consequence of the pattern which they reveal. If a stone is dropped into still water, concentric circles spread across the surface, revealing the way the energy derived from the falling stone is being dispersed in the water. Most of us have seen how iron filings, sprinkled on a sheet of paper spread over a magnet, reveal the magnetic lines of force which constitute the field of the magnet. The converters which man uses have similar patterns. To use them most efficiently requires variation—in the way farms, roads, and streets are laid out, buildings are erected, and other structures are placed. The shape of the pattern existing in a man-made structure demonstrates whether or not it was constructed in such a way as to use a given converter efficiently. Such patterns give some evidence of past effects of the use of energy. Ecological study of man thus provides a means of showing what values have been operative in the past and also of indicating to a certain extent the changes which will be required if new converters with different fields come into operation.

CONVERSION RATE OR GRADIENT

Aside from this type of concept which deals with structure and form, we need a concept which will deal with the dynamics involved, that is, something to make it possible for us to measure the rate of conversion in one situation as compared with that in another. The rate of conversion can be expressed in terms of time or of distance. It can also be expressed as a fraction of the initial supply of available energy, a quantity of fuel consumed in a specific period of time or distance, or in some other manner. This is usually done by setting up a pair of coordinates, measuring on one axis some attribute such as the energy available and on the other time or distance, thus showing graphically how the two factors are related. For example, a graph may be set up showing, on one axis, the total gasoline in an automobile tank in terms of gallon units and, on the other, distance in terms of miles. Such a graph may be used to demonstrate the difference between two cars as to gasoline consumption. One of the coordinates might represent time rather than distance, in which case the graph would show how fast the consumption of the gasoline was taking place, or perhaps the difference in gasoline consumption of the same car at different speeds. The graph may be constructed from a known rate of consumption or may represent empirical observations (actual distance traveled and actual quantity of gas in the tank). Such graphs are very familiar. Commonly they are so constructed that the slope of the line joining the coordinate points becomes a significant indicator of the facts which are being portrayed, and a calculation of that slope can be made in terms of a mathematical equation. Since the slope of the line resembles an inclined plane, or what we call when we are climbing a hill a "grade," many sciences use the word *gradient* to indicate this relationship. Usually a rapid rate of consumption of energy is represented by a steep grade and a slower rate by a gentler grade.

A single line serves to show the particular gradient of a specific operation, but to represent the potential effects of an action, or the range of possible actions, another kind of representation is necessary. If, let us say, our automobile was in the middle of a perfectly flat plane (for example, the Utah salt flats), so that it could equally well move in all directions, in order to show all of its potential movement (assuming in each case that the path taken would be a straight line), we would have to revolve our single line, marked off into segments showing the rate of energy use, about the point of departure. We would thus generate a series of concentric circles. To show high energy consumption we would construct one set of circles close together, and to show a field with gentler gradient we would draw the circles farther apart. The outermost circle would represent the point of exhaustion of our original supply of energy, and the others would show the proportion of energy which would be consumed by the car in reaching that series of points represented by a particular circle. So we could visualize the whole potential field. As we shall see, the comparison of the gradients and the fields of different converters gives us a means of discovering the degree to which actual behavior conforms to optimum behavior in energy terms.

SURPLUS ENERGY

There is one other general concept used throughout the work which should be defined here—the concept of *surplus energy* (often shortened to *surplus*). This is the energy available to man in excess of that expended to make energy available. Like the concept "efficiency," surplus energy represents a social estimate of a physical fact. Like efficiency, it has sometimes been a source of error because it has been taken to be exclusively a physical fact rather than a concept involving the process of valuation. To be sure that there will be no question as to what is meant by the term, we shall elaborate on our definition. At any given moment of time a man, a group, or any other socially functioning unit has available a limited supply of energy. This can be utilized immediately in its present form. It can also be used in an operation designed to increase the future supply of available energy. The simplest example would be seed grain, which may be eaten or planted. It is obvious that if the planter does not even get his seed back from the harvest, he has less energy at his disposal than he previously had: he has incurred a deficit. On the other hand, if he harvests enough grain to replace the seed, to supply the amount of energy expended in planting, cultivating, and harvesting his crop, and to get something more, he has gained energy beyond that which was previously his to command: he has surplus energy. A stroller eating blackberries growing wild along the road expends in the operations necessary to secure the berries only a small part of the energy he receives from them. He has gained surplus energy. On the other hand, a man who runs down a jack rabbit in an 80-acre field will probably expend more energy than he will gain from the operation.

In the more complex activities of modern society it is sometimes extremely difficult to discover all the costs and all the gains, energywise, which are involved; yet it is clear that the same propositions about energy hold for complex actions as hold for the simplest examples given above. The continual undertaking of projects that produce less energy than they consume inevitably leads to a deficit, and this must be made up from other operations in which there is a surplus if the society is not to find itself with less energy than it had before the projects in question were begun. As will be shown, in the older societies deficits were rather quickly detected. Either steps designed to correct energy deficits were taken quickly or the culture soon disintegrated. In more modern societies the facts are extremely difficult to come by. The struggle to determine the point where output exceeds input, or to assure that surplus energy from some operations can be depended upon to supply the deficits from others, is inconclusive and is usually prolonged until some crisis forces recognition of the deficit or results in collapse of the system.

It is assumed here that the value of energy in the situation in which it is being expended to create new energy is unchanged when, in turn, surplus energy becomes available, and hence the quantities of energy can be compared. In other words, the assumption is that there is no qualitative change in energy input and output. For example, it is assumed that energy in the form of seed can be treated as being, energywise, the same commodity as results from the harvest—or, again, that kilowatts of electricity going into the mining of coal are comparable to kilowatts of electricity manufactured by means of the mined coal. We here treat energy as being so easily converted from one form to another that it can for some purposes of calculation be considered neutral as a commodity and therefore capable of treatment on a strictly quantitative basis. The inconvertibility of other fuels into food makes a significant exception to this proposition, and we shall later have to deal with that difference at length. Throughout our discussion we must keep clear the distinction between the operations that produce surplus energy, and determine its amount and form, and those that determine the social claims placed upon it.

Some economists have attempted to deal with the problem of surplus energy on the basis of moral and religious propositions derived from man's experience of an earlier day. The fact is that the struggle to create morals which will furnish a rationale for the disposition of surplus energy is probably one of the crucial points of conflict in modern society. It is obvious that since the amount of surplus is clearly related to the social system under which it is being produced the two activities are not entirely separable, but it *is* possible to measure the first of these sets of facts with tools that are not dependent for their reliability upon assumptions peculiar to the situation in which they are being used. The possibility of doing this represents a real advantage.

To recapitulate, we shall be constantly using concepts and measurements taken from various sciences. They will be used with exactly the same denotations that they carry in these sciences. It is hoped that certain new connotations of some of them as they relate to social phenomena will be seen to be necessary attributes of their use in real situations. Among the concepts are those of kinetic and potential energy; field, limit, and gradient; and such measures as the Calorie, the kilowatt and the kilowatt-hour, the horsepower and the horsepower-hour. We shall assume a knowledge of the concepts of mass, acceleration, distance, and the energy relationships that exist between them, of the law of the conservation of energy, and of the concepts of efficiency and surplus energy. If they are kept clearly in mind and reexamined from time to time, it will add to the book's readability and serve to keep the reader on his guard against the errors that inevitably creep into a work of this kind.

Other concepts, particularly some from social science, will be brought in as needed. It seemed advisable to define them as we go along, in the context in which they are used, rather than to introduce them here.

CHAPTER 2

Organic Energy and the Low-energy Society

With only insignificant exceptions, such as the limited amount of energy available on earth from lunar gravitation and from cosmic rays, the energy that is available to man has come, or currently comes, from the sun. Uranium and other possible sources of atomic energy were created as the gases from which the earth was derived combined to form solids. Coal and oil, peat and gas are accumulations stored in the earth's crust from past operations of plant and animal life that have converted the radiant energy of the sun into energy-laden substances. We shall treat these resources as if they were of a different type from those that make use of the recurring presence of the sun. While they represent only a tiny accretion as compared with their original source, they currently provide man with his major sources of energy. This is primarily due to the fact that one of the still unsolved problems of science is how to take full advantage of the sun's energy.

It is obvious that it is not lack of a source of energy which limits man's activities. The amount of sunlight falling upon the earth's surface is so great that it is almost incomprehensible.[1] An acre receives about 20 million Calories per day, and the amount of solar heat that falls on only 1½ square miles in a day is equivalent to that generated by an atom bomb such as that used at Hiroshima. Thus the amount of radiant energy is so far in excess of man's present ability to convert it that it cannot be considered to limit human behavior. Energy-imposed limits stem from the particular means by which energy is converted into the particular forms desired by man at a particular time and place.

PLANTS AS CONVERTERS

Man has learned to convert radiant energy into other forms in only tiny amounts at a relatively high cost.[2] He has depended upon the action of plants to make the original synthesis and has proceeded from there to convert the resultant energy for his own purposes. His simplest method has been to eat plants, thus making some of their energy available to him. This system requires only a knowledge of what is edible. The converters automatically divert energy in sufficient quantities to ensure their own reproduction. This plant-man system is the prototype of all the systems of converters man uses; however, since man very early undoubtedly also ate animals, the plant-animal-man system is not much newer.

Plants vary in their capacity to survive in various soils and climates, and we can through the study of plant and animal ecology discover the limits within which the survival of various plants is possible. Plants also vary in their capacity to convert the energy of the sun into plant structure; Willcox [3] has shown that "the fixation of the calorific energy of the sun is variable with the species." The limits of the use of radiant energy by plants are fixed by the nature of photosynthesis itself.[4] It has been well established that only a small fraction of sunlight can ever be converted into other forms of energy by plant life. For example, it is estimated that only about 3⅓ per cent of the sunlight falling on the United States as a whole could be so converted. As a matter of fact, no crop grown in this country even approaches such a figure. Here corn is the crop that probably yields the largest heat-energy return, and a bumper corn crop returns only about 0.3 per cent of the radiant energy falling upon the land on which it is grown. This return includes the heat which can be obtained by using the cobs, stalks, and leaves as well as the edible kernels. Such a return is exceptional. "Corn belt" corn is the product of extremely favorable geographic conditions, aided by scientific agriculture. In areas where the land is poorer and farming practices are less efficient the returns are very much smaller.

The amount of energy each plant can convert is specific to that plant. Willcox [5] gives the simple formula worked out by acrobiologic science for ascertaining what it is: "Divide 318 by the normal percentage nitrogen content of whatever agrotype is being considered; the quotient is the theoretical absolute maximum number of pounds of dry vegetable substance which that agrotype can yield on one acre of ground in one crop cycle." Now since a plant also consistently yields a given quantity of energy per pound of dry weight, it is possible to discover the limits that are self-imposed on a people who choose a given crop as their basic diet. Rice apparently comes closest to yielding the various food elements in the proportion required by the human body; but Indian corn, soya beans, millet, rye, and wheat have become the basic diet in some areas, as have potatoes, sweet potatoes, and other crops in other areas. The particular crop which would provide the largest energy return in a given area is not necessarily the one used there. Factors other than energy efficiency affect the choice of foods made by man, and in a given instance the preference may be for a food that is less efficient than some other known and available food source. The total energy available to the people of a given area is thus determined by the inherent efficiency of the particular plant they have chosen to make their basic source of food.

Plants have in addition to their inherent efficiency another characteristic of great social significance. With few exceptions they are rooted in one place; thus the field in which a plant can act as a converter is the area which the plant itself occupies. Concentration of the energy which they produce involves the energy costs of harvesting them. Moreover, any mechanical energy which is derived from using them must involve another converter.

Where the only converters available consist of plants, animals used solely for food, and man, not only is man the controller and director of available energy, but his muscles provide all the mechanical energy he commands. And all operations which require the use of mechanical energy are limited to such as can be carried out by human beings.

Although man is a chemical-energy machine, his efficiency can be measured in terms of the heat value of the food he consumes as contrasted with the heat value of the mechanical energy he can deliver. Part of what a man consumes is utilized in such functions as respiration and the circulation of the blood. Part is given off as heat, and part is indigestible and leaves the body as waste product. Some energy is lost during sleep, and some is converted in the activity of the nervous system. So, as in the case of other engines, the total heat value of the fuel consumed can never be recovered in the form of mechanical energy. The average efficiency of the human being is about 20 per cent. This means that for each 100 Calories consumed as food the average man can deliver mechanical energy equivalent to 20 Calories of heat.

Physiologists are generally agreed that to maintain efficiency the average daily consumption of food should not be less than about 2,600 Calories per person per day. It is improbable that any population with a normal number of children and old people in it could consume more than 3,000 Calories per day per capita without producing excessive fat, which actually reduces the capacity to work. Three thousand Calories average intake and 20 per cent average efficiency provide mechanical energy equivalent to 600 Calories per person per day. This is a little less than one horsepower-hour (about 641.56 Calories).

No society keeps its members steadily employed at converting food into economically productive mechanical energy, and many societies have never supplied their members with as much as 3,000 Calories per day. Thus in many societies there is available considerably less than 1 horsepower-hour per day of mechanical energy per capita. Part of this mechanical energy must be used to produce or gather food. The remainder may be used for other pursuits. But no matter how little is used in procuring food the sum of the two cannot exceed the very modest total set by man's capacity as a mechanical-energy converter. Thus, regardless of the food supply, the difference per capita between the most and the least fortunate of societies, both using only men as mechanical energy converters, is not very great. The average consumption cannot fall very much below 2,000 Calories per day per person and, as we have seen, it cannot rise much above 3,000 Calories. So even taking the maximum difference in food consumption between the lowest and the highest to be as much as 1,000 Calories, at an efficiency of 20 per cent there is a difference in total mechanical energy available equivalent to about ⅓ horsepower-hour per day per person. Nor is this fact significantly affected by the use of animals rather than, or in addition to, plants for food.

ANIMALS AS CONVERTERS

The differences between those who consume plants only and those who make use of animals as well as plants for food are probably significant rather for the pattern than for the limits of the field generated. Man usually adds meat to his diet if he can, and under some circumstances his chances for survival may be tremendously affected by his ability and willingness to provide himself with animal food. The chief significance of the use of animals lies in the fact that some edible animals can assimilate plants—and parts of plants, such as bark—which man cannot directly digest. Many of the grasses which are not directly consumable grow in areas where it is not possible for man unaided by other sources of energy to replace them with edible plants. Since sheep, goats, and cattle on the hoof can be driven over distances much greater than it is possible for a man to carry or drag the meat of their carcasses, man is able by following or driving livestock to consume the plant products of an area enormously more extensive than he could otherwise make use of. Similarly, man is able to live in climates where plants are not available the year round, partly by using the energy of plants stored in the form of animal products during the months when no plant food is available. Occasionally even carnivores are used to promote man's survival. The Plains Indians sometimes lived through a hard winter by eating the dogs which had shared their kill during the summer months.

The use of animals for food is subject to the limitation that the animals so used are in competition with men for plants. The number of plants in an area sets the limit on the food available both for man and for other animals. If man permits animals to eat plants which he otherwise might himself eat, or permits land to be used to raise plants for feed which could be used to raise plants for human food, he limits the number of men who can be fed from that land. Wheat, which is very widely used as a foodstuff, will serve as an illustration of this relationship. The amounts of energy made available to man through the use of wheat in the form of bread and in the form of animal products are shown in the table on page 20.

Since other feed crops can usually be grown more advantageously, wheat is only rarely raised to feed animals. However, other

100 LB OF WHEAT CONSUMED AS	YIELD IN CALORIES
Bread	120,000
Chicken	9,625
Eggs	30,000
Pork	38,700
Milk	25,230
Beef	11,500

plants edible by human beings exhibit the same pattern of loss as does wheat. Man gains through eating animals only a fraction of the energy contained in the plants eaten by those animals.

Nevertheless, in many areas people permit animals to survive even though this results in reducing the number of human beings who can live there. The case of the sacred cattle of India, which are permitted to eat food which would lengthen the life span of a large part of the population, is an example. Elsewhere animals are kept for the enjoyment of a particular class, as were the deer of the English forests. Sometimes, too, an inefficient use of animals is required by religious belief, as in the case of the Jews and the Mohammedans, who are prohibited from eating the flesh of swine, which happen to be more efficient converters of plants than are cattle. But in certain large areas such as China, in some parts of Eastern Europe, and in Southeast Asia, men are unable to eat meat simply because the plants which animals might consume go directly to human consumption. In these areas a return to the consumption of meat could come about only with widespread reduction of the population or enormous increase in the available plant food supply, or both. In 1940 about 55 per cent of the world's population had a daily intake of 2,000 Calories or less; 30 per cent had 3,000 or more, and 15 per cent had about 2,500. The world average was about 2,400 Calories per day.[6] Asia, where the population presses most closely on the food supply, produces about 49 per cent of the plant foods but only about 16 per cent of the meat, dairy, and poultry products. With the world's population increasing steadily, it is unlikely that in most areas there will be any large general increase in the use of animals for food.

The domestication of *draft* animals greatly increases the *mechanical energy* available to those who possess them. There are many varieties of animals used for draft, and in order to be exact it would be necessary to calculate the costs and output of each kind. However, since the horse is so widely used it will serve to illustrate the energy gains to be made through the use of draft animals. As we have already indicated, Watt found that the horses in use in England in his day produced the energy equivalent to about ⅔ horsepower, or about 6 horsepower-hours per 9-hour day. Morrison [7] says that a modern horse weighing 1,500 to 1,600 pounds can convert about 1 horsepower steadily for 10 hours a day, and that the average horse is about 20 to 25 per cent efficient. However, since horses in the United States today work only 800 to 1,000 hours a year, they deliver only 6 to 7 per cent of the heat value of their average annual food consumption. A man working 50 hours a week for 50 weeks a year delivers, then, only ¼ as much energy as a horse, but the heat energy consumed by the horse is 10 times as great as that consumed by the man. Compared strictly on the basis of energy, under these conditions man is 2½ times as efficient as the horse.

The great value of the horse lies in the rate at which it is able to deliver energy. During a limited plowing season, for example, a man and a team can prepare a very much larger area for planting than can a man alone. Outside the tropics only a limited number of days can be spent in preparing the seedbed and planting. Crops require a minimum growing season, and the total planting time is the difference between the length of the growing season and the interval from the time when the ground can be worked to the time when frost sets in. Where the limit on the size of the crop that can be raised is found in the length of the period during which land can be prepared, the horse, by permitting a great increase in the amount of land plowed, may more than compensate for the days when it is idle.

It must not be forgotten, however, that the efficient use of draft animals takes place within distinct limits. In the first place, arable land is not always available in such quantities that plowing or harvesting is the limiting factor on the crop raised. Frequently the number of persons who have a right to share in the product of the land is great enough to make it possible for them to plant and harvest all the available land in the time permitted by the growing season. In such cases the net cost of using the horse would be greater than the increase in the energy returned. Furthermore, in many cases land that cannot be cultivated by the use of the horse exists interspersed with land fit for horse cultivation and land fit only for pasture. Where this is so, an economy that made use of the hoe could support a larger population than could an economy that used only such land as could be cultivated by horses.

Because man's skill, intelligence, and dexterity enable him to do many things not possible to a horse, man can be employed many more hours of the year than the horse can. His efficiency rises proportionately. Thus those who control the method of cultivation may choose to rid themselves of horses in order to employ men. This might take place in an area dominated by the family as an economic unit because it would obligate family members to work for the food they had a right to share anyway. In a feudal or slave system the value of men as a source of military power and prestige or as contributors to the bodily comfort of the landlord or slave-owner often resulted in the displacement of horses by men. Where other values and social structures prevail, the relative efficiency of men as compared with draft animals in securing the desired results has determined the choice as to which would be permitted to survive.

One of the early evidences of population pressure is the reduction in the number of food animals, followed by the reduction of draft-and-food animals, such as cows and horses, in favor of those draft animals, such as the water buffalo, which can survive on the plant product of land which will not yield nearly as much energy in the form of humanly edible food. Thus many areas which once supported draft animals and food animals now make use of almost none. This tendency to regress has frequently been checked. The failure of a society to utilize its land in such a way that the land provides sufficient energy in the requisite form to maintain the population has often resulted in the society's being overrun by outsiders. If a society uses its land in such a way that it passes the point of diminishing energy returns, it may be conquered by a neighbor with greater surplus, who then may ruthlessly restore that land-to-population ratio which will yield maximum surplus. Feudal landlords who permitted the population to grow to the point where they had no horses were often defeated in battle by their horse-riding neighbors. The exploits in India and China of such horse-riding herders as Genghis Khan give evidence of some of the dangers of overpopulation.

The difference between the maximum and minimum mechanical-energy surplus available to those using only plant and animal converters is by modern standards very small. But in the absence of other energy sources these differences have been very significant.

Today all but the more primitive societies supplement plants and animals with other sources of energy; and it is therefore necessary to turn to the data on such primitive societies provided by anthropologists, archaeologists, and historians to ascertain the relation between plant and animal use and social life. These data have not, however, been presented in terms of the analytical concepts used here, and ideally they should be reexamined in terms of these concepts. Practical considerations preclude our doing this, and what follows is based upon summaries of anthropological and other research into primitive peoples. The result is the use of analytical categories that are not entirely germane to the problems here under consideration, but no better alternative is at present available.

FOOD-GATHERING SOCIETIES

One method of classifying societies is that developed by Forde in his classic work *Habitat, Economy and Society*. He groups the societies he discusses in three categories: food gatherers, cultivators, and pastoral nomads. We have found it expedient to lump the two latter types under one heading, "food raisers." The data that Forde worked with were collected by men using various field categories that could conveniently be subsumed under his types. All the societies studied are primarily dependent upon the use of plants, men, and animals as converters. The differences that they exhibit give some evidence of the range of social relationships possible within the limits imposed by these energy sources; they also give evidence of the social consequences of even slight variations, by today's standards, in sources and amounts of available energy.

As Forde points out, food gatherers are for the most part without the accouterments of "civilized" man. The surplus energy gained under this system is very small on an annual basis, though it might temporarily be enormous during berry-picking time or the salmon run or after a buffalo hunt. The total energy annually available does not permit any great expansion of population, and thus food gatherers have frequently fallen victim to the more numerous and powerful food raisers. In point of fact, once domestication of plants and animals has developed, the food gatherer has tended to be driven away from the areas in which food raising was possible. As a result, he currently exists chiefly where food gathering actually yields a higher return from existing resources than would an available alternative land use. The precarious existence of such contemporary food gatherers as the Eskimo, the Athabascan hunter, and the Indians of the Orinoco suggests why food gatherers often fail to survive in the face of more effective systems of energy exploitation.

Since food rarely grows in such abundance that a group can long remain in one place, everything that food gatherers use must be transported. Their means of transportation are, characteristically, limited to human portage or sledge dogs. Consequently, tools must be simple and light in weight. Housing must either be improvised at many different sites or be very easily transportable. Clothing must be light and simple. No great energy can be devoted to the erection of shrines or otherwise expended in placating or worshiping the gods. The size of the social unit is necessarily small, for if any great number of people gather together, they soon exhaust the local supply of most of their energy sources and have to range far afield in the search for new sources. The resulting expenditure of time and energy in gathering and dispersing endangers rather than contributes to survival. At best the division of labor is limited, for almost everyone must spend a great deal of time and energy in the pursuit of food. Priests and other social functionaries who gather no food cannot contribute enough to food-gathering groups to offset the energy lost in supporting them. The kinship groups among food gatherers may carry on economic, political, and religious functions, but such small units are incapable of creating or transmitting any very large culture base; consequently tradition, law, and religion remain relatively simple,*

---

* Simple, that is, if the culture as a whole is compared with that of the large social units of urban society. Some single aspect, such as the kinship system itself, may be relatively complex, as in the case of the aborigines of Australia.

providing only a limited number of controls for the guidance of the head of the household.

The Paiute of the American West provides an example of the social simplicity of the life of the food gatherer. He lived principally upon a few types of seeds, such as the pine nut and acorn, upon lizards and snakes, grasshoppers and grubs, and the rabbits and the rare deer which he could kill. To get the latter, as Forde [8] puts it, "the deer hunter usually went out alone with his dog. Finding his quarry, he then had to run it down relentlessly, perhaps for several days, until he could get close enough to shoot it; he would then have to carry it painfully home on his back." And we may add that unless he was unusually lucky a good deal of the meat would spoil before it could be eaten. The Paiute clothed himself after a fashion in rabbit skins, piled up brush in a wickiup to shield himself from the storm, and usually died before he was twenty-five years old. Although he lived in an extremely adverse environment, which today does not support one person per square mile, he probably is more typical of the food gatherer than the romantic cares to admit. Bilby's account of the Eskimo in *Nanook of the North* describes another food-gathering people living under adverse conditions. The fact that Nanook, his chief informant and the central character of the book and the film, later died of starvation puts a fitting conclusion to the account.

The Horse and the Plains Indians

The Plains Indians, like some other food gatherers, lived in a more favorable environment. But because they had no draft animals they were unable to cultivate the land extensively and raise crops that could compete successfully with the buffalo grass. In those few areas where trees killed off the grass the Indian could in turn kill the trees and for a few years get a crop from the land so cleared. In most of the prairie such cultivation methods supported only small groups of food raisers. The chief source of energy was the buffalo, which was hunted afoot with the aid of the long bow and arrow. During the summer the Plains Indians gathered into large groups for the purpose of staging a drive in which the buffalo were driven to their deaths over a bluff or into a trap. Only thus could these Indians survive in groups larger than a few households. Continuous hunting would have disturbed the grazing herds; this would have meant continuous movement of the tribe, which in turn would have led to further disturbance of the buffalo. Hence the social, economic, and political units had to be small. The physical accouterments of life were few, though more numerous than in the case of the Paiute. The "man of distinction" was the hunter. The ritual connected with coming of age was designed both to teach the arts, skills, and attitudes necessary for effective hunting and to glorify or even sanctify them.

This pattern was changed whenever these Indians captured and redomesticated the horses which had escaped from the early Spanish expeditions. The introduction of the horse into these cultures serves as an excellent illustration of the effects which the adoption of a new converter may have. It also shows how the existing culture limits the use to which a new converter will be put. Forde [9] says that "the introduction of the horse did not basically change the culture of the western Plains, but it widened the range of activities, greatly increased success in hunting and provided a wealth of food and leisure. . . ." It was also a "form of personal property which gave impetus to a wide range of modifications." As he points out, "the horse gave the ascendancy to the western nomadic hunting peoples, and the cultivators were either driven out or abandoned their more settled life and more advanced culture for the rich rewards of buffalo hunting."

Mishkin [10] goes further to show how the introduction of the horse changed what was regarded as the ideal man from one having those qualities of stoicism, patience, and skill which had characterized the hunter afoot with the long bow to one with the qualities of the daredevil rider, wielding a lance to hamstring his kill or using the short bow from horseback. In time the skilled horse thief and warrior was elevated to a position equal if not superior to that of the hunter. The size of the effective social unit changed as the advantage of the large group for protection in warfare more than offset any residual value which the small group originally had in hunting. Social organization became necessary to control these larger groups. Picked hunters frequently brought in game for the whole community. Unskilled, slow, or crippled heads of households were denied the right to hunt lest they endanger the source of food for the whole group. The relationship between responsibility for the family and ability to meet that responsibility was altered by social fiat. One squaw could not preserve all the meat or dress the hides of all the game killed by one horse-borne hunter. Since there was no change in the division of labor between the sexes, polygyny became the rule, and the accumulation of women, particularly by stealing, became a source of power and prestige.

Many of the pre-Columbian food-gathering tribes were confined to areas in which food raisers were unable to operate. As the Plains Indians acquired the horse, the energy available to them increased sufficiently to permit them to drive back the cultivators and thus extend their hunting grounds. The gain was, however, temporary. As the European settlers moved westward, bringing the harness and the plow, which enabled them to turn under the buffalo grass of the plains and replace it with crops that yielded a larger surplus, they relentlessly drove the food-gathering Indians from their ancestral homeland into less and less satisfactory areas. Here their culture was destroyed by their inability to get at the buffalo, whose energy had sustained it, and they survive today only as a colorful anachronism.

Most other food gatherers have met a like fate. Some have been able to maintain their existence by attaching themselves to agricultural regions, by gathering a product of desert, mountain, or forest to exchange for the products of a culture yielding more surplus energy. Some exist on sufferance, in areas unfitted for incorporation into dominant civilizations, as do the Seminoles of Florida, the Eskimo and isolated tribes in Alaska, Canada, and Greenland, and various native peoples in Africa, Asia, and South America. While anthropologists have discovered enormous differences among food gatherers, they have also shown that they operate within the limits which have been discussed above. These limits differ in some degree from those which characterize societies that Forde classifies as food gatherers. An unsatisfactory aspect of Forde's classification is that the transition from one to another means of securing food is in fact gradual. Many food gatherers raised some food or at least returned annually to the same areas where it grew naturally. Some promoted the growth of the edible plants by cutting down or killing trees whose shade reduced their fruitfulness, or by pulling weeds; these were in a limited sense food raisers. But even though what Forde called the food gatherer may not exactly typify any actual society, the "type" may serve to summarize the characteristics of those societies which modally resemble it.

FOOD-RAISING SOCIETIES

Forde's classifications apply not only to primitive or prehistoric peoples but also to modern farmers. For present purposes the category "food raiser" has most analytical significance when it is restricted to those people who are or have been almost completely dependent upon cultivated plants and/or domesticated animals for energy and those who, primarily dependent upon such sources, have secured supplementary energy through hunting wild animals and occasionally using wind or water power. Even when so restricted, "food raiser" is sometimes less useful than terms based upon other distinctions. For example, it is probable that there are more significant differences between people who are dependent primarily upon cereals grown on irrigated soil and nomadic herdsmen (who are also food raisers) than there are between those herdsmen and some of the hunters who occupy country where game is plentiful. Nevertheless, the significance of the domestication of plants and animals as contrasted with the use of these converters in the wild state is very great. Food raising represents an advance in the means regularly to provide and secure energy surpluses.

In his work *Social Evolution*, Childe takes the position that all civilizations derive from "the cultivation of the same cereals and the breeding of the same species of animals." Curwen has traced the use of some of the existing food plants back to very early man and has shown how the appearance of new plants causes new social relationships to emerge. We shall not here attempt either to review or to criticize the whole of the theories propounded, but the facts adduced will show both how greatly surplus can be increased through the introduction of a new plant and how greatly surplus can vary among food raisers who use the same plant.

Curwen [11] estimates that the yield in Norman England was only 6 bushels per acre from 2 bushels of seed, with a total production per person of only 15 bushels per year. On the other hand, Thurnwald [12] found that in ancient Sumeria the yield was 80 to 100 times the seed. The total amounted to "2,800 litres per hectare," or nearly 32 bushels per acre, which is not a bad yield by today's standards. It is apparent that such great variability in yield at least established great differences in the energy limits under which men lived, however they may have used the surpluses so established. The variations in environment to which cultivated plants are subjected are easily observable even in old and well-established agrarian societies. The yield from the same seed on various parts of the same field frequently varies greatly; between farmers, or more particularly between regions, there is even greater variation. The usual adverse factors take their toll in differing degrees: there may be a shortage of some of the nutrients required for optimum growth; during the growing season there may be either too little or too much total precipitation, or precipitation may come at the wrong time; there may be other organisms to contend with, both plant and animal; the very processes of cultivation may be such as to reduce rather than to increase yield. Recently it has been discovered that the presence or absence of tiny traces of such minerals as cobalt and copper result in huge differences in plant yield. Where low yields are a consequence of a deficiency in minerals, that fact can now be determined and corrected; but a people dependent solely upon the energy of plants and animals could never develop the scientific knowledge necessary for the correction of such soil deficiency.

It is evident, then, that the limits imposed by the nature of the plants rarely constitute the actual and effective limits confronting those who depend upon those plants for daily living. In the first place, the land available sets limits to the amount of plant life that can be developed, whatever the character of the plants used. That plant life, in turn, sets limits upon the size of the possible population. It is comparatively easy to show, for example, that when population increases much beyond 3 persons per acre the energy derivable from most plants will not provide the means to carry out the intensive cultivation and restorative fertilization which are the only methods by which so little land can be made to provide sufficient energy to ensure the survival of its cultivators. The highest average energy yields produced anywhere in the world are secured from the intense cultivation of rice by the Japanese. They produce about 2,200 pounds of rice per acre. This yields roughly 9,000 Calories per acre per day the year round.

Thus, ⅛ acre would yield an average of 3,000 Calories, about what an active 150-pound man requires the year round for an adequate diet. During the period of intense cultivation he will, of course, demand more than this, but he can conserve his strength at other times. The average return from rice in India is only 829 pounds (1931–1936 average) as compared with the 2,200-pound Japanese yield. Therefore, in India a reduction of the amount of land per person below ⅔ acre reduces the energy available to a point below that necessary for survival. Soya beans or sugar beets produce more than this per acre under specified conditions, but they require supplementation by other crops and do not yield more than rice does when all the necessary factors are taken into account.

For a long time economists have been pointing to the law of diminishing returns, which sets an outer limit on the amount of food that can be produced in a given area. While they have sometimes confused the physical product of plant life with the "economic" value thereof, and have sometimes extended the meaning of the law to cover all the economic effects of limited land, no matter what its use, in essence the argument really stems from the facts to which we have just alluded. It is true that after a given point is reached a specific plant on a given piece of land will yield only so much plant product, no matter what increases in expenditure of labor or what additions to it in the form of nutrient are made. Moreover, as that limit is approached it is highly probable that a great deal of what is done is not what is required to permit the plant to reach its maximum output. Therefore, most of what is done will not yield a commensurate return or even any return whatsoever in increased energy to compensate for the energy expended. This is true even where soil is fertile and good management and plant science are used extensively. Where magic and religion and other practices interfere, the loss of energy is no doubt excessive.

In dealing with food raisers it is, therefore, necessary to distinguish between the total energy surplus which might be achieved under optimum food-raising conditions and what is actually secured under the existing conditions of man-land ratio, cultivation techniques, etc. These existing conditions can usually be improved only by the adoption of some new energy converter. The probability that a food-raising people will adopt a new converter seems to depend in considerable part upon their current ability to produce an energy surplus. In other words, the presence of an energy surplus is favorable to the adoption of a converter that will enlarge that surplus.

As Forde [13] indicates, "the range of economic and social variation among cultivators is greater than among food-gatherers, and this variability is not related in any simple way with the physical conditions." As will be shown, it is generally true that as the energy available to man increases, the variety of his activities increases. Where the energy available is only slightly in excess of that required for survival, any very great variation in behavior among those situated in any one place is impossible. Thus, whereas the variability of food raisers is very great as compared with that of food gatherers, it is small as compared with the variability of those who have larger energy surpluses. Food raising permits variability, but it also imposes limits which are reflected in some generally predictable results. Food raising decreases the time and energy spent securing food and thus permits men to do other things, but the mechanical energy available each day is still no greater than that of the human beings and the domesticated draft animals present. Food raising permits an increase in the number of persons who can be supported from a given piece of land and thus permits an increase in the surplus locally available. The increased surplus may be used in a variety of ways. It may be widely dispersed and result only in a general increase in leisure. (However, such dispersal may, and often does, lead to an increase in population, so that the land available per person is decreased to the point where each unit of land is supporting all the population that it can; when this point has been reached, there is no surplus.) The increased surplus may be used merely to increase the amount of waste. Or it may be concentrated, and the concentrated product, too, may be used in a variety of ways. It may be sacrificed to the gods. It may be buried in a tomb or destroyed at the death of a landlord or other ruler. It may be expended in the military conquest of areas which themselves yield lower surpluses. It may create a leisure class that is devoted to the cultivation of knowledge and the arts or that simply demands the continuous use of surplus in the creation of goods and services that are not productive of new arts, or knowledge, or new fixed structures. But there must be a surplus before it can be devoted to any such use.

SURPLUS AND CIVILIZATION

Civilization waited on the appearance of such energy surpluses. As Childe [14] says, civilization meant "the aggregation of large populations in cities; the differentiation within these of primary producers. . . , full-time specialist artizans, merchants, officials, priests, and rulers; an effective concentration of economic and political power; the use of conventional symbols for recording and transmitting information (writing), and equally conventional standards of weights and of measures of time and space leading to some mathematical and calendrical science." All of which are impossible except where surplus energy exists in considerable quantity. As we have already indicated, Childe holds that in every case civilization grew out of the cultivation of the same plants and the breeding of the same animals. Thurnwald [15] emphasized the same general propositions. He was, however, primarily concerned with showing how such institutions as slavery and serfdom served to concentrate the surpluses of food-raising cultures in such manner as to permit the military protection of the land and the development of a class of skilled artisans and specialists, neither of which is possible where men must remain dispersed in order to gather the fruits of field and chase.

While there is considerable variation among food-raising peoples, there are also numerous likenesses among them as a consequence of the limits inherent in food raising. Among all food raisers the family is the basic consumption unit, and to a large extent it is also the production unit for much of the goods and services produced. Division of labor is limited and is primarily based on differences in skill and learning, sex, and size and muscular power. Since so large a part of what must be done requires merely brute strength, there are also likely to appear status differences which assign whole sections of the population to physical tasks without regard for the potential skill, intelligence, strength, or sex of individuals. If the emergence of complex institutions depends upon the development of a surplus, so too the development of a surplus depends upon the existence of such institutions. Once a balance is attained, however, it is difficult to upset.

The Egyptians: An Example

The Egypt of the age of the Pharaohs provides a good demonstration of the working of a balanced system in which a comparatively small energy surplus is utilized in such a way that there is no disturbance to the energy-producing procedures. The Egyptians left a durable record of their accomplishments, and these records have been subjected to a great deal of study. The Egyptian system operated, moreover, under unique physical circumstances which precluded a disturbance of the balance through soil exhaustion. The Nile regularly replaced the soil, and continuous cropping caused no depletion. The deserts, sea, and river cataracts formed barriers which could be crossed by an invader bent on conquest and plunder only with great expenditure of energy surpluses. The Egyptians were, under these favorable conditions, able to push food raising to a climactic * stage.

During long periods of its history the surpluses of Egypt were absorbed by the burial mounds or pyramids. These contain both direct and symbolic evidence of Egyptian accomplishments. During the reign of some of the Pharaohs almost the total surplus of the people was concentrated in the erecting and furnishing of the pyramid which was to honor the ruler upon his death. The ruling class was small and consumed no great amount of wealth, for the chief objective of its way of life was to accumulate surpluses to be taken into death. The population was held constant or even diminished, since men were worked to death about as fast as they could be brought to maturity. Even so, the surpluses were never great. The Cheops pyramid, together with its furnishings, absorbed all the surplus energy produced during the lifetime of about 3 million people. During a 20-year period 100,000 slaves are said to have worked to produce the tomb. This was about ½₅ of the total population. We can calculate, then, that those who supplied the food to keep the pyramid builders alive each contributed

---

* This word is applied here in much the same way that it is used by ecologists. It indicates the culminating stage of the possible development in a region, given a limited set of plants and animals to begin with and assuming no major alteration in geographic conditions. We imply that given sufficient time the use of low-energy converters results in a type of persistent equilibrium between men and their environment.

only about 100 to 150 Calories a day. Thus, although the Egyptians enjoyed most favorable geographic circumstances, the total energy available to them was by modern standards extremely low, however high it may have been in comparison with the energy production of other societies of the time.

At other periods in its history the surpluses enabled Egypt to engage in conquest of all its neighbors. At still other times the surplus was exhausted in conspicuous expenditure and display among the living; at those times when controls over population broke down, the surplus was completely exhausted in civil war or by the increase in the number of mouths to be fed from the land.

It is possible to calculate the distance from their base on the Nile that the Egyptians could have advanced had they been willing to devote all their surpluses to conquest of neighboring peoples. The size of the surplus was one limiting factor: the surplus had to be carried or pulled from Egypt by men or asses. At some distance from the Nile the energy costs of transportation would have reduced the surplus derived from Egypt to a point below that available to the people being invaded, and Egyptian expansion would at this point have been checked. The topography and the resources of the region invaded, the will to resist and the military technology, strategy, and leadership of its inhabitants also would have been involved in fixing the ultimate limit to which the Egyptians could have advanced. Similarly, the possible spread of Egyptian culture was limited by its capacity to yield surplus under the very different conditions that prevailed outside Egypt. Egyptian culture was adopted elsewhere only with great difficulty. When Egypt did conquer a people, it was seldom able to assimilate them. And when conditions in Egypt led to disorganization, the conquered people usually broke away and resumed their previous way of life. Such a resumption is reported in the Biblical story of the exodus of the Jews from Egypt.

The peoples of the Fertile Crescent contributed much to what we now regard as civilization. But the extent of their political holdings, the range over which they were able to secure and maintain cultural homogeneity, and the diversity of their skills and knowledge were slight by present standards. Their history shows cyclical variations within constant limits. The abuses of one system gave rise to another system, which in turn was defeated by its own weaknesses. None of these systems could, however, exceed the limits imposed by the basic converters, that is, plants and animals. And these same basic converters are depended upon by the greater portion of the people of the world today. Moreover, the cultures of the rest of the peoples of the modern world were developed in considerable part under the limitations imposed by the plant-animal-man system.

CURRENT LOW-ENERGY SOCIETIES

Societies such as those that now exist in India, Africa, and China have been greatly modified by the introduction of new converters but are still closely restricted by the limited energy which they have available. The population is in many of these areas so great that local resources will not supply an adequate diet. In Yünnan,[16] for example, about 100 families (500 to 600 people) share 150 acres. This is about all the people that plant life will support if the plants are eaten directly. Buck[17] found that in the 1930's nearly 90 per cent of the potential farm area of China was in crops, while only 1.1 per cent was in pasture. By comparison, in the United States 42 per cent is in crops and 47 per cent is being used to pasture animals. Moreover, in the United States much of the crop land is used for feed rather than for food. The energy available from animal power in China was and probably still is close to zero, and the limits on the mechanical energy available in many Chinese villages might be ascertained simply by multiplying the number of persons by 20 per cent of the heat value of the per capita food intake.

Under these circumstances the energy costs of transportation between village and field would cut deeply into the available surplus if the distances were great. Consequently villages are very small and located at frequent intervals. When the small surpluses available have been used to support centralization of control, the effect of that control on energy production has rarely been equivalent to its cost. Even the introduction of new sources of supply has tended to affect the old system adversely. For example, many Chinese villages had long paid their taxes and bought necessary imports by converting the leaves of the mulberry trees along the canal banks into silk. When the Central Government was forced by foreign powers to protect trade in Japanese silk, American cotton, and British Commonwealth wool, many villages lost this source of income and were confronted by a great change in their way of life. Often the land was sold to pay taxes, and city people gained control over it. The consequence here was a great increase in tension between town and country, absentee owner and tenant, and an intense effort to restore the earlier balance. The present turmoil in China evidences both the efforts of the Communists to achieve greater centralization, which upset the balance still further, and their efforts to restore to the peasant control over the land he cultivates and to the village the self-subsistent economy which trade upset.

India shows many of the same characteristics. The average net cultivated area per capita of agricultural population in Bengal in 1939 was less than 1 acre, and 46 per cent of farming families had less than 2 acres each.[18] The tillable land of India is supporting the maximum number of people which it can maintain with the energy that is obtainable from it with existing practices. If higher demands are made on the soil, it will pass the point of diminishing returns. Here also the village community serves as the predominant spatial and functional unit. It supplies almost no surplus beyond that required for the local institutions themselves. The energy costs of national government or more extensive social organization must be provided by other energy sources. In the past much of the energy used for these purposes was imported from Britain in the form of goods produced with British coal and water power.

In some areas that have used only organic sources for energy the population has been limited at a point short of that which characterizes the "overpopulated" parts of China and India. However, as land becomes scarce in relation to the population, the tendency has been for more and more intensive cultivation to be undertaken. This has frequently resulted in an effort on the part of each farmer to increase the only productive factor over which he himself has control, namely, children. As a consequence, even greater pressure has been put upon the soil and even less energy has been available to devote to the development of new agricultural techniques or the enlargement of the area under cultivation.

Among the Bantu in Africa [19] it is the labor of clearing the land that sets limits on cultivation. Every child thus becomes an economic asset, and there is continuous emphasis on increasing the size of the family. However, life is there so precariously balanced that a crop failure is likely to result in starvation and a reduction in the working population in the next crop cycle. This is also the case in at least some parts of China. In a village in Yünnan, Fei and Chiang found that the size of farm that can be worked by a man and his wife alone is too small to support a family. As a result children must work; in the absence of children the older adults will starve.

Economic reciprocity between parents and children tends to become a necessity in societies that are dependent on organic converters. Children supply in these areas what is secured in industrial societies through unemployment, health, and disability insurance, and old-age allowances. Parents develop in the child values that will ensure their own survival, and the commandment "Honour thy father and thy mother: that thy days may be long upon the land . . ." is a statement of a functional relationship.

Their Conservatism

Since the limits within which low-energy societies operate are so narrow, extensive conflict and its concomitant wastes cannot long be tolerated. Hence institutions develop which tend to reinforce rather than to weaken each other. The introduction of any new element is likely to be disastrous to one or more of the parts making up the web of the culture. When this happens, the traditional allocation of scarce resources is threatened, since men then no longer learn from all the sources of authority the same design for the "good life." As a consequence, resistance to change frequently mounts as the ramifications of change appear. Moreover, change is often introduced into low-energy societies by "outsiders" who have their own reasons for inducing it. Frequently such change provides a more satisfactory way of life for only a few of the "natives," while others are forced to bear costs which they consider totally disproportionate to any foreseeable gains. Those members of the society who value very highly certain of the gains to be made through the introduction of new converters, welcome change and encourage it. For others, whose pastoral and agricultural values are thereby destroyed, the "material benefits" which accompany the use of the new converters are not adequate compensation for the values lost, and they struggle to preserve the system that is jeopardized by the introduction of the new converters. Even in the highly industrialized United States of today there is great respect for the virtues of the husbandman and for the rural institutions which support and are supported by many American ideals. For example, the "family-sized farm" is widely held to be necessary to democracy, Christianity, and individualism.

Thus low-energy societies offer more barriers to change than just those imposed by the costs of securing the new converters needed to effect change. Added to these are the costs of social disorganization and of purposeful resistance. If these barriers are to be overcome, there must be considerable energy in the hands of those who seek to bring about change. Since, as we have indicated, most of the energy available in low-energy societies rests in the hands of those with traditional social claims to it—for example, peasants, landlords, and others who will not want such change— a great increase in energy is necessary in order to provide a surplus adequate to secure the introduction and use of new converters. In a low-energy society change must come slowly, for the range between the most and the least effective use is not, by modern standards, great. Therefore the conquest of users of low-energy converters has frequently meant that the surplus produced merely passed from the hands of one group to another, its size remaining relatively constant and the culture remaining basically unchanged. Such drastic changes as the engulfment of the Plains Indians in the United States have been possible only with the extensive use of converters that were far more effective in delivering surplus energy than those that existed prior to the conquest.

In the main, then, the low-energy system of a people dependent wholly on food raising is inherently self-perpetuating. It develops a balance between population numbers, social institutions, energy usages, and energy production which is exceedingly difficult to disturb and which, if disturbed, tends to reassert itself. As a consequence, the impact of modern industrial technology on peasant societies is far weaker than is generally assumed, and those who have endeavored to introduce new converters to such peoples have had limited success.

CHAPTER 3

Inorganic Energy Sources: Wind and Water

Man has long sought to harness wind and water power efficiently. He has been hampered in that effort by the nature of these forces, which makes the converters that use them comparatively costly. In many cases the kind of energy they delivered was not very useful in his culture.

THE RIVER AS TRANSPORT

The flowing stream was undoubtedly used as a means of transportation long before written records could testify to this use. The more complicated problems of delivering the energy of the stream at some fixed point were not solved until much later. The water wheel came into use where food raising made reciprocating or rotary motion a valuable adjunct to energy from the older converters.

Both the flowing stream, as a carrier, and the water wheel expanded the limits of the culture of the men using them. As an energy source the stream differs greatly from plants and animals. Within its ribbonlike field, energy is constantly available, but just beyond those limits the stream provides no energy. It thus sets a spatially defined pattern for those who use it. It can carry great loads cheaply but only within well-defined areas. Most of the great streams provide energy for only a small part of the inhabitable area adjoining them. So where great areas were engaged in food raising, only a few workers could deliver their surplus to the stream to be borne away without consuming a fairly large part of that surplus in the costs of transportation to the stream's edge.

39

In other words, the streams in areas predominantly agricultural provide an energy advantage for only a thin fringe of communities located along river banks. Beyond the points where it is advantageous to use the stream the centripetal effect which naturally arises from the use of plants becomes manifest, that is, there is the tendency, already noted, to limit the size of settlements by reason of the energy costs entailed in going to and coming from the fields, and to make settlements almost completely self-subsistent.

Moreover, the stream provides energy only in one direction, downstream. Thus it moves the product of surplus energy away from its original site. If reciprocity or some kind of equilibrium between downstream and upstream areas is to be established, energy must be expended in returning to upstream users goods in exchange for those received. If this round-trip relationship were to represent the exchange of equal masses of goods, the stream would cease to be a source of surplus, for at least as much energy must be expended in getting the goods upstream as was gained in floating an equal cargo downstream. Under such conditions the stream would become a highway rather than an energy source.

These physical facts limit the kinds of culture which can make effective use of the energy of the stream in transportation and also limit the effect which that energy can have when put into use.

We have already indicated that where fertile soil exists in sufficient quantity in proportion to the population which is used in tilling it, it is usually possible to recover considerably more energy in the form of plant product than goes into producing the plant. In many areas of the world where this situation obtains men tend to multiply until the proportion of land to population is such that the energy secured from food raising is equal only to that which is required to sustain the local population. This is not a cause of extinction for the self-subsistent community, but it destroys all basis for extramural trade. The flowing stream is thus most useful when some relationship serves at once to limit population to the point of maximum energy surplus and to concentrate control over that surplus so that the largest possible portion of it can be used to produce goods for trade. Slavery and serfdom offered this combination of circumstances. They usually resulted in limiting population, for the serf was, in return for certain duties, supplied with a fixed amount of goods, regardless of the number of mouths he was attempting to feed, and the slave was provided with only sufficient goods to supply the number of children required to serve the master. Slavery and serfdom likewise frequently resulted in a concentration of control over surplus, which was sometimes utilized in trade for luxuries. It was in fact as an adjunct to such systems that the stream made its original contribution to civilization. It is frequently true that such exploitative systems run contrary to values which recur in family and community life, so that if a breakdown in power occurs the upstream communities tend to restore local autonomy in the control of surpluses and reduce exports in favor of local use of those surpluses.

Only if some kind of reciprocity exists between those who accumulate at a downstream site the product of upstream cultivation and those who make such surplus available can the relationship be continued. The values of those upstream who control surpluses must be complementary to the values of those with whom they deal downstream. Such trade characteristically takes the form of the receipt, from upstream sites, of raw materials, particularly minerals, forest products, food, and fiber, which have considerable bulk and mass. In return the product of artisanship, or of special skill or knowledge, which weighs less, is delivered upstream. This arrangement effects transport upstream at considerably less energy cost than is involved in the downstream movement of goods. It also frequently encourages upstream landlords to continue in their exploitative position. Thus the downstream site is likely to produce luxury goods for a small ruling class upstream in return for goods which might have been essential to the survival of many upstream villagers had they not been taken for the benefit of the trader. The historic antagonism between downstream towns and those located in the hinterland thus has a very natural origin.

Early civilization developed along the Nile, the Tigris, and the Euphrates. Cities also developed on the rivers of India and China as the spread of cultivation there brought about sufficient increase in surplus energy. But before the rise of agriculture there was no similar early development on the great rivers of North and South America, Europe, South and Central Africa. Early transportation by stream is thus seen to have served primarily as a limited adjunct to food-raising societies with the cultural means to concentrate available surplus. It must be remembered, however, that the social conditions required for the maintenance of agriculture also set limits to the kinds of civilization which could grow up around the use of the stream as a source of energy.

THE RIVER AS SOURCE OF MECHANICAL ENERGY

The appropriation of the energy of the flowing stream through its delivery at a fixed site is a much more complicated matter than the use of water for transportation. The first of the limits on the generation of mechanical energy from the stream is to be found in the potential energy stored in the water. As was pointed out earlier, a horsepower is equivalent to the delivery of 550 foot-pounds per second. This amounts to 1,980,000 foot-pounds per horsepower-hour. In other words, if the converter used is 100 per cent efficient in turning the potential energy of the water into mechanical energy, a ton of water must fall about ¼ mile to deliver the equivalent of 1 kilowatt-hour. Now the great areas in which food raisers create their largest surpluses are old river deltas, areas of very low relief. The Mississippi, for example, falls only 322 feet between Cairo, Illinois, where it joins the Ohio, and the Gulf of Mexico, more than 600 miles away. It falls only about 800 feet between Minneapolis and the Gulf, a distance of over 1,000 miles. Great rivers are so huge in volume that their potential energy is enormous even with so slight a fall. But means of handling such quantities of water as would permit the delivery of any great amount of mechanical energy with only a slight fall are even today prohibitively expensive. Moreover, the flow in any of the major rivers varies greatly during the year, and any works set up to capture their energy must allow for variation in the depth of the stream. Dams and locks which will withstand the force of great depths of moving water are generally considered to be more costly than is justified by the returns, as compared with other alternatives. Consequently any use of the water wheel on large rivers is likely to be limited to temporary structures or floating mounts. But these create new problems involved in delivering mechanical energy to the river banks. On small streams, where the flow is more constant and the descent of water precipitous, water wheels have often provided an important adjunct to the power of limited areas.

LIMITATIONS OF WATER WHEEL AND WINDMILL

But here we encounter another characteristic of both water wheels and windmills. This is the character of the field of the converter. To transform the power of moving wind or water into a localized force, the weight or force of the water or wind, acting on a vane or cup, is converted into angular motion about the axle of the wheel. Thence it must be transmitted as reciprocating or rotary motion. The area over which it can be delivered efficiently is determined by the efficiency of moving cams, shafts, belts, or gears. Since such means of transmission quickly waste, in the form of heat generated through friction, much of the energy which they are intended to transmit, the gradient in the field of a converter using mechanical transmission is very steep. Now in food-raising areas there are few tasks in which rotary or reciprocating motion with a narrowly limited field are involved. The bulk of the energy required, at the time when energy is most scarce, is used in plowing or otherwise preparing the seedbed. In this task energy must be used over a large area, and thus the water wheel or windmill is ill-fitted to carry it out. It is true that at some other times of the year reciprocating or rotary motion can be used, as in separating grain from chaff and particularly in milling it, or in spinning and weaving fiber. But there are often many hands which are idle except in preparing the seedbed, harvesting, and perhaps irrigating. These hands are well fitted to carry out exactly the kind of task for which the windmill or water wheel is also fitted. We thus come to the same kind of competition that eliminated the use of animals for draft in large parts of the world. If energy is diverted into the building and maintenance of the wheel, but the wheel adds nothing to the total food supply, it provides no useful energy in addition to that which is otherwise available in the form of unemployed or underemployed persons. In such cases diversion of energy to create converters merely reduces the supply of energy which could otherwise be used to increase directly the supply of goods or services sought as ends.

For example, a woman may expend less energy in grinding meal in a hand mill or metate or in pounding it out with a pestle in a mortar than she would expend carrying the grain to the mill and paying for the service rendered there. It may take more energy to transport unthreshed grain to the power separator, pay for the service, and return the grain than to flail it out and allow the wind to separate it, or to use a draft animal to stamp it out on a threshing floor. Thus only on extremely fertile lands, producing large crops in a very small area, could a fixed-site threshing or grinding machine be supplied with work enough to keep it going much of the year. Transportation costs frequently preclude the economic operation of the mill elsewhere. Landlords sometimes used water- and wind-driven mills to increase their own supply of energy by forcing their tenants to use the mills, taking part of the grain or meal in return, but frequently this merely increased the "unemployed" time of the peasant and left him with less food to consume than would otherwise have been available to him.

Other operations using rotary and reciprocal motion common to agricultural communities are spinning and weaving. These are laborious, but again they are among the means by which the hands needed at plowing or harvest time are kept busy at other times of the year. They enable those who cannot labor in the field to establish a legitimate claim to a share of the product of the field. Except in hilly or mountainous areas the commonly used fibers are produced on land which can be used alternatively to raise food and fiber. Thus fiber may be locally produced if it can so be obtained at a lower cost than the value of the food which could be produced on the same land. A self-sufficient agricultural community may elect to establish reciprocal exchange with another area in which food can be produced only at a cost much higher than that of producing fiber. To mountain people, for example, the production of fiber such as wool may provide a means to secure food or other energy sources in amounts greater than could be directly secured from their land. But to the agricultural community trade is energywise a means of gain only if the food to be exchanged plus the energy involved in its transport and the transport of the fiber cost less to produce than the fiber to be secured in trade.

Given the presence of idle hands—which is characteristic of many food-raising areas—the energy costs of spinning and weaving are not as significant as the net loss in energy that would result if food were to be exchanged for fiber, since the fiber can be secured with less energy at home. In certain areas, such as Iran, there are highlands which will support sheep and goats in greater numbers than human beings, and these areas adjoin valleys in which food can be produced to exchange for cotton and other fiber with less land than would be required to raise the cotton or other fiber. Distances are short enough to make transportation costs low, and as a consequence fairly large groups subsist in these highlands primarily by producing fiber for exchange. Most generally, however, fiber can be produced as a side line of the self-contained agricultural area. Towns in which there is more work to be done in producing textiles than can be supplied by the idle hands are rare. It was only when transportation costs were radically reduced that converters to be used specifically for spinning and weaving became economical in terms of the values characteristic of the self-contained village or manor. The use of the water wheel for this purpose was thus very limited.

Special Characteristics of the Windmill

The windmill met with many of the same obstacles. While the wind does not fix the location of the windmill so exactly as water does that of the water wheel, the windmill, like the water wheel, delivers its energy in a limited field characterized by a steep gradient. So again the only economical use of its energy is in the form of reciprocating or rotary motion. There are also, however, differences between the use of the windmill and that of the water wheel which arise from the character of the sources of the energy. Wind is generated by changes in the heat reaching various parts of the earth and moves in somewhat predictable paths, but these exhibit none of the sharp boundaries which characterize streams. And though in some areas where basic crops can be grown the wind is fairly predictable, it is hardly ever constant. The average velocity of the wind in a place tells little about the actual power potential there. Wind blowing 12 hours at 60 miles an hour and falling to a dead calm during the next 12 hours has averaged 30 miles an hour, but the total energy delivered is not the same as it is in a place in which it has blown steadily at 30 miles throughout the day and the night.

The pattern of the winds, the periods of time both seasonal and other during which they blow, has much to do with the power that can be made available. Windmills are most useful, then, where the winds blow at such velocities and at such times that they neither allow the converters to stand idle nor submit them to damaging strain. Such sites are rare. In a few areas, such as Holland, where their use could be depended upon to keep water from inundating low fields, or in the American Far West, where sufficient water could be stored to last until the wind blew again, the windmill proved to be a valuable adjunct. In the West Indies wind provided the power to mill the great quantities of sugar cane which trade permitted to be grown there. With but a few such exceptions, however, the windmill altered none of the established ways of exploiting the energy of plants and animals.

So long as only mechanical means existed for the transmission of the power of the water wheel and the windmill, they remained incapable of producing any sweeping changes in society. For the power they deliver today the world had to await the development of electrical generating and transmitting equipment, which originally depended on the use of other converters such as the steam engine. Accordingly, this use of wind and water power will be discussed later.

THE SEA AND THE SHIP

When the flowing stream reaches sea level, the potential energy it carries is exhausted. Except in the ocean currents, oceans, seas, and lakes provide as such no energy to those who use them, though they serve as cheap highways in many cases. Thus boats and ships must be propelled by other sources. Those propelled by men or animals are subject to the limits of which we have hitherto spoken. The wind-driven vessel is another story. The advent of the sailing ship was potentially capable of working a revolution among all those societies located on navigable waters. Unlike the use of animals as a source of mechanical energy, the use of the wind does not diminish the energy available to man in the form of food. The energy costs of operating a ship are only those of building, maintaining, and manning it. The surplus energy derived from the sails is potentially enormous as compared with the cost of producing the sail and hoisting it. Thus, for the first time in man's history, men, using the sailing ship, came into control of very large amounts of power largely independent of plant life or of the number of persons in the population using it. Sailing vessels are confined to waters in which they can maneuver and in which the winds are such as to propel them. Within these limits upon the trackless seas the sailing ship delivered energy at a rate previously unimagined.

The gradient of the sailing ship is more gentle than that of any of the converters previously discussed. For example, the amount of food a man or an animal can carry on his back or pull behind him in a wheeled vehicle is tiny as contrasted with the amount of food a sailboat managed by one man can carry. In addition, the distance a sailing ship can cover in a day, under favorable conditions, may be much greater than the distance a man walking or riding an animal can cover in the same time. Moreover, and this became very important historically, the field of the sailing ship merges with that of the flowing stream at its mouth, and energy derived from one of these sources can be used to supplement that derived from the other in maintaining or creating desired relations between downstream cities and the interior. Before we examine the new sets of social relationships to which the sailing ship contributed, it may be wise to inquire into the physical characteristics of the sailing ship as a converter.

No ratings in modern terms of the various types of sailing ships exist. At the time they were built, no calculation of the horsepower required to move them was made: a ship that had a good record, that provided adequately for a cargo, and that had low operating expenses was simply copied when a ship that was likely to sail in the same waters and to carry a similar cargo was needed. Modifications to achieve other aims or correct weaknesses that became apparent in operation were made on a trial-and-error basis.[1] Today ship architects usually design and test models, determining which shapes are desirable on the basis of the energy required to pull the various models. They can then calculate the power which will be required to drive the full-sized ship at the speed sought. In the construction of smaller vessels, particularly, where allowing extra power to compensate for possible error involves less cost than does the constructing and testing of models, set formulas are used, but at best such formulas are somewhat inaccurate. It is thus difficult to calculate the power necessary to drive ships which have long since been sunk or dismantled. But for the most part there are exact figures on the size of those ships and the speed of which they were capable. The horsepower required to drive them can be roughly calculated by direct comparison with that used today to drive ships of similar size at comparable speeds. This method leaves much to be desired as to accuracy, but in view of the enormous difference between the surplus produced by the ship and that produced by earlier converters, whatever error creeps in is probably not great enough to affect our conclusions radically.

The efficient size of the ship at any time or place is determined by such factors as available materials, existing shipbuilding technology, nature of the cargo, means of loading and unloading, the ability of the crew to put on and take off sail (taking into account the winds to be encountered), the purpose for which the vessel is to be used, etc. At various times one or another of these factors historically constituted the ruling limit. On the other hand the size of the crew was related not only to the size of the ship but also to such conditions as whether she must be expected at times to depend upon oars, and whether she was to be a fighting ship. During long periods the right of transit was likely to be challenged by pirates, privateers, and "legitimate" operations of hostile navies. In these circumstances the crew could not be limited to what was technologically efficient, but was enlarged for purposes of defense. The surplus energy produced was correspondingly diminished. The Egyptians were able to design, build, and sail ships up to 150 tons.* [2] There is little direct evidence of the speed of which they were capable, but from some indirect evidence it appears that it was not more than 8 knots. A ship of this speed and displacement today requires engines that deliver about 80 horsepower. They carried a crew of about 40 men, so since each man consumed the equivalent of about 1 horsepower-hour per day, the surplus developed at a maximum was about 47 horsepower-hours per day per crew member when the ship operated round the clock. This is considerably in excess of anything earlier developed upon land. The Egyptians used the ship chiefly to gather such luxuries as myrrh from Somaliland.[3] Later, the Phoenicians developed the art and techniques of shipbuilding and navigation further,[4] but their ships,

* Tonnage figures used here represent the carrying capacity of the vessel. This is figured out by assigning 1 ton for each 100 cubic feet of usable space in the vessel.

though somewhat different from those of the Egyptians, were hardly larger.

The Greeks developed the ship considerably. However, they were never able to secure such control upon the sea that they could reduce the crew to the point technologically most efficient. Their sailing ships, therefore, were also powered by oarsmen to increase their battle strength. The Greek trireme was manned by as many as 170 oarsmen on a boat 150 feet long and 16 feet wide, and her sail was only a supplementary source of power.

The Romans, after the defeat of the Carthaginians and the suppression of Greek piracy, were able to build true merchant ships up to 250 gross tons with crews reduced to the size necessary to handle the sails.[5] At a speed of 8 knots these ships must have generated about 100 to 120 horsepower. With a crew of 10 or 12 they produced a maximum of 10 horsepower per crew man. Running 24 hours a day, this ship could thus generate about 240 horsepower-hours or 240 man-days per man per day. This maximum, of course, was rarely if ever realized. Contemporary Norsemen developed a ship of about 30 tons, 80 feet in length, which carried a crew of 90 men and made 10 knots.[6] For a short period an oarsman can produce about 1 horsepower, so under stress the oarsmen could develop about 90 horsepower. But the sails, which could be operated round the clock, developed only about 30 horsepower. Hence, the surplus available to the Norsemen was quite small in comparison with that of the Romans. A vessel duplicating one of the early Norse ships was sailed across the Atlantic in 1893 with a crew of 12. This demonstrates that the Norse ship was not stripped to her minimum crew but, since it was chiefly a fighting vessel, was made to carry all the men she could, together with their arms and supplies, including booty.

Extensive trade was not characteristic of the use of the vessel outside the Mediterranean until medieval times, though the Phoenicians made such expeditions as those into the Baltic for amber during Rome's era of greatness.[7] In the 1400's, increase in the surpluses available for trade, together with new navigational techniques and the invention of gunpowder, which permitted domination of coastal areas from the sea, led to the development of ships of 300 to 500 tons. The ships at 10 knots developed from 150 to 250 horsepower.

THE SAILING SHIP: REVOLUTION IN ENERGY SOURCE

The great transformation which came during the seventeenth and eighteenth centuries with Dutch and British exploitation of the sea was made with Indiamen of about a thousand tons. The rapidity with which the increase in the size of the ship took place can be seen from the fact that the flagships of both Columbus and Drake, a century earlier, were only about 100 tons. Indiamen at 10 or 11 knots developed 500 to 750 horsepower with a crew of about 80 hands.

The climactic development of sail came in the early nineteenth century. Its achievements brought a surplus greater than that of any other converter in any preceding age. From the point of view of the total energy generated, if not of the surplus per man-day, the clipper ships were paramount. The record run of 436 miles in 23½ hours for an average of 18.55 knots made by the *Lightning*, a ship of 2,084 gross tons carrying a cargo of 2,000 tons, is respectable even today. The *Sovereign of the Seas*, a ship of 2,421 tons, is said to have once made 411 miles in a day, and single-mile runs at 22 knots or better have been authenticated for several of the clippers. This compares with the 23 knots of which the *Empress of Japan*, fastest ship in the Pacific in 1942 was capable. Other, larger, sailing ships were built, such as the *Great Republic*, 4,555 tons, the *Maria Rickmers*, 3,822 tons, and the *Preussen*, 5,081 tons, which averaged 16 knots for 24 hours, but all these ships made use of steam winches for hoisting and trimming sail and are thus excluded from our consideration of the surpluses generated by wind power combined only with manpower. The *Sovereign of the Seas*, which used only men to handle the sails, carried a crew of 105 hands and was able to make a top speed of about 17 knots. Since this was of course possible only with favoring wind, a steamship of somewhat lower-rated top speed under similar favorable circumstances would be able to equal it. Now modern vessels of about 2,400 tons, rated at about 14 knots, deliver 1,200 to 1,400 horsepower. Using the higher figure, we estimate that the *Sovereign* must have produced about 12 horsepower per crew man, or about 287 man-days surplus per man per day.

The greater effort required to attain the higher speeds did not prove to be jusifiable except under unusual circumstances such as those surrounding the California gold rush or in the first voyages of a season, when such races as the Grain Races and the Tea Races were staged. The extra sails by which the clippers gained their speed, at the cost of a great increase in necessary crew, were discarded. The clippers were replaced by slower ships delivering a larger per capita, though a smaller total, surplus. The most efficient sailing ships were thus able to produce a maximum of 200 to 250 times the human energy required to operate them. The ideal limit was, of course, never realized for any very long period, owing to failure of winds, time in port, and other factors. Out of this operating surplus must come the amortization of capital costs, the development of necessary port facilities, etc. Nevertheless, the sailing ship was a source of surplus energy far in excess of that produced by any other known converter until well into the nineteenth century.

To repeat, the sailing ship produced large surpluses of energy and generated a field enormous in extent. Historically it was only the first of a number of such converters, all of which we shall call, in contrast to their organic prototypes, *high-energy converters*. Since it is obvious that sail offered tremendous advantages, it might be expected that every people living on the seasoast would have adopted and exploited it fully. Actually, very few areas did bring sail to any very high level of usage. This fact calls for further analysis.

CHAPTER 4

Sail, Trade, and Mercantilism

The failure of people to use available wind and flowing water offers a challenge to those who accept the idea that "in the long run" men will always make the most effective use of the economic assets they have. The people in some societies have continued throughout a very long history to ignore this pattern of what the West calls "economic" behavior.

To account for differences between the societies that did and those that did not make use of stream and sail, each case might be studied separately. It may, however, be possible to effect considerable saving over this method by analyzing the conditions under which these converters can be used and the effects which follow from their use. If the analysis is correct, any sample picked at random from history should fit the pattern so derived.

The sailing ship set the stage, so to speak, for the introduction of other converters in many parts of the world. Thus the effects of the sailing ship influenced the way in which these other converters later came to be adopted. On the other hand, some societies went directly from the use of low-energy converters to the use of high-energy converters other than the sailing ship. It can be shown that there are differences in the way that high-energy converters have been and are being used which derive from this fact. That is why the influence of stream and sail must be analyzed before this is done for other converters.

Some of the factors affecting the use of the ship and the stream also relate to the use of other high-energy converters. Other factors are peculiar to these agents of transportation, and these must be examined before the use of the ship is given further consideration. The factors influencing the adoption and limiting the use of the stream and the ship might be classified as technological, geographic, and economic. Agreement on the meaning of the first two of these words is sufficiently general to make it unnecessary to define them here. The meaning of "economic," however, is not a matter of equally general agreement. In self-subsistent low-energy societies the separation of values into categories—social, economic, political, aesthetic, moral, religious, etc.—was not frequently made. All "good" conduct was approved, all socially disapproved conduct was "bad." The degree to which approval or disapproval followed from an act was not determined by whether or not it involved material things. Some acts concerned with materials were of the greatest significance, some of no concern whatever. On the other hand, the violation of a sacred rule that related in no way to the disposition of materials might be of very great concern. The hierarchy of values which the child learned as he grew up put things in their socially approved order, and it served no purpose to separate economic from other goods.

THE CONCEPT OF "OPPORTUNITY COST"

Increased exchange of goods took place in the commercial societies which grew up around the use of the flowing stream and the sailing ship. Here choice had to be made between articles or services which were produced locally under the sanction of local values and the products of a distant land. Two articles otherwise identical might be offered: acceptance of one would perpetuate existing relationships, acceptance of the other might destroy them. In the West most attention has been given to the Greek explanation as to the nature of these new situations. For Aristotle economics meant something akin to what we mean when we say a man is "economical," that is, that he makes the most of resources. Thus, there was an economy of the household, of the state, and of the market place. The proper relation between the claims of these contending institutions was of great concern to him. For reasons we shall later develop more completely, the term economy slowly came to mean "efficiency" as measured only in the market in terms of price. Within a single cultural system, where there is agreement on the proper role of price and the proper sphere of the market, this situation produces no more than tolerable confusion.

But for trade between two or more civilizations which differ on these matters, the attempt to make price measure all the values involved when goods produced in one system are introduced into another has frequently produced intolerable confusion. Hence the definition used here assigns the terms *economic* and *economical* neither to production and consumption of material things nor to price phenomena nor to sustenance activities; rather it follows the usage of those economists who assign the term to the effort on the part of the individual to achieve as many of his values as possible with the least sacrifice to his other values. Thus, all costs become *opportunity costs* in the sense that the cost of anything is the values that must be sacrificed to obtain it.

With such a definition it is possible easily to see how goods from abroad which could be secured at a lower price might be avoided by men who would in buying them sacrifice other values—such as family ties, local pride, or national esteem—not measured in price terms, which were to them of greater significance.

Economics and the Morality of Low-energy Society

Low-energy society was characterized by codes of conduct which sanctioned the recurring relationships commonly persisting between groups. Producers and consumers, artisans and peasants, priests and warriors, hunters and witch doctors lived in a world wherein they learned codes of good and bad conduct as they learned the knowledge and skills which they used. If goods or services not produced under the sanctions of these codes were offered they threatened the continuity of the accepted way of life. Thus there was a strong probability that efforts would be made to prevent the further use of such goods or services. Even when new sources or methods meant increased product available to the consumer they were likely to be widely opposed because of the moral and social costs which accompanied them. Thus the introduction of new methods and sources of production set up conflict in the society which resulted either in reaction which prevented further use of the new sources or methods or in a change in the sanctioned way of doing things. If the former occurred the old ways continued. However, if the new source or method was continued it too became sanctioned behavior, new codes making such behavior moral were developed, and the difficulty of substituting new ways for this sanctioned behavior again became a factor limiting further change. Empirical evidence exists to show that in a great many cases "economically superior" methods and sources were repudiated and the older, socially sanctioned methods retained. It also shows how the resistance of those seeking to retain the old ways was broken by those seeking the benefits of the new. But whether "progress" or "reaction" triumphed, morals and religion were frequently as clearly causal in producing the end results as were judgments about the physical effectiveness of proposed means of production.

In the low-energy society, because of the limits of which we have spoken, almost all the factors involved in the lives of the people interacted in the local community, within a very limited geographic area. Thus equilibrium was a result of a stable set of claims on the recurring sources of energy. Such claims were likely to be established in a fairly short time as the various reactionary forces came into balance with those forces making for change. Even when superior military force required the regular payment of tribute, as in the empires of Genghis Khan and other conquerors, the amount which they could successfully extract was rather quickly set, and the rest of what was locally produced, which could be divided among the local populace, was distributed in such a manner as to result in a fairly stable relationship among the locally sharing groups. These arrangements usually came to be expected, if not fatalistically accepted, as being required by some higher order.

Economics and Morality in High-energy Society

It is a very different story in the high-energy society. Here the transition to the use of high-energy converters has required the creation of new social units. The social unit which carries out the functions of the family may occupy very restricted space as compared with the area required for the state. The production of some goods may be carried out by the family, while other goods are produced by large corporations. The unit based on religious belief may be entirely separate and distinct from that organized to handle military control or protection. Such diversified experience imbues individuals with a hierarchy of values in which the demands of the state, the market, the corporation, or the church are

made supreme, as opposed to those of the family or the local community. Moreover, the particular order in which one of these institutional claims follows the others in the hierarchy of values common to the people may vary greatly among areas functionally
connected but geographically remote from one another or among
groups geographically near but functionally remote from one
another. Under these circumstances, change results in no such
immediate and effective reaction as can take place in the local
community of the low-energy society. Reaction may be delayed
or distorted by the social structure through which it manifests
itself, by the lapse of time which is required before the full effect
of the change can be observed in all parts of the system in interaction, or by some other factor. Thus because the attainment of
equilibrium in the high-energy society is likely to require accom-
modations of an entirely different character from those required in
the low-energy society, rapid adjustment and the prompt establishment of social equilibrium are relatively rare.

Almost all societies have some outside contacts. Such contacts,
became more numerous as fairly large surpluses came to be regularly produced and were transported over great distances. This increase in contacts became more significant where the flowing
stream began to be used as a cheap means of transportation; it was
vastly accentuated by the use of the sailing ship. There was also a
great advance in the separation of production from transportation,
which was increasingly carried on regularly by specialists adhering to different codes and using different converters from those
who participated in production. To the woman carrying yams
from her garden, or the husbandman carting home harvest grain,
transportation and production were no more separable than planting and harvesting; to an oarsman manning the sweep on a barge
carrying stone to build a pyramid, transportation and production
were widely separated. The fact that the energy of the flowing
stream and the sailing ship were available primarily for transportation created a distinction between goods which had not previously existed. Some goods and services, such as garden produce
and child care, had necessarily to be provided with the aid of
locally produced energy. These could not be replaced by transported goods. Other locally produced goods were identical with
those which came from outside the community. Low-cost trans-

portation might lead to the introduction of identical products from another region, offering at a cost markedly lower than that sanctioned by the local values. Then it would become necessary to develop means by which goods produced outside a system could be evaluated in terms of the effects which their introduction would have on values current in the society receiving them.

PREREQUISITES TO TRADE

As has been indicated, we are here accepting the theory of opportunity costs, in which the fact of trade is taken as evidence that the goods chosen are considered by those who choose them to be more valuable than the goods sacrificed to secure them. The theory also implies that if trade which seemed initially to maximize the values of an individual had consequences such as to alter some of the values on whose account it was initiated, then trade might stop. For example, if as a result of trade a man found himself shunned by his neighbors, condemned by the church, punished by the state, or banished from his family, it is perfectly possible that contemplation of these costs might cause him to forswear such exchange as he might have carried on in ignorance the fact that it would entail such costs.

Cheap transportation makes possible a new and different order of energy costs. It thus introduces new variables for selection. When some goods can be reduced in cost by a lowering of the cost of transportation while at the same time the costs of other goods remain the same, competition and conflict take the place of sanctioned controls. Prediction as to the extent to which a particular society will permit alteration of sanctioned relationships therefore depends upon a knowledge of *all* the changes which will take place as a consequence of the use of new converters. The introduction of cheap transportation produces a strain leading toward the substitution of the less for the more costly good on the part of those who stand to gain by the substitution. But it must not be forgotten that it also leads to resistance on the part of those who will lose by the change.

To understand trade requires consideration of the conditions faced by all whose choices will affect it. Each category of such persons has alternatives available to it (to put it another way, we may say that persons are ordinarily classified in terms of their

alternatives). "Difference in cost" as between two areas potentially involved in trade as a result of decreased transportation
costs may represent several distinct kinds of costs. One such difference may reflect geographic characteristics which affect the
amount of energy required to secure a given good. Thus, for
example, less energy is required to secure a given quantity of
commercially pure iron from the rich ores of the Mesabi than from
the low-grade ores that exist in many other places. This geographic advantage can be altered only by exhaustion of the rich
ores. Similarly, the long growing season in Florida makes it possible to utilize farm land and machinery more effectively than,
say, the climate of Manitoba. It is hardly necessary to multiply
examples. But in so far as economic choice is concerned, such differences as these appear in the market in exactly the same form as
do other bases for difference in cost. Thus the superior technology
of a region may be such that it can produce far more goods per
man-hour than a technologically undeveloped country with identical geographic resources. Such differences as these may be equalized in some cases by cultural diffusion. A third type of difference
in cost represents solely the differences in alternatives available
to potential traders. The alternative to cooperation with the trader
in one case may be starvation for him who refuses to trade, while
another person in the same region, or a whole people in a different
place, may be able to turn to another alternative hardly more
costly than the terms offered by the trader. In other words, at one
point failure of trade may mean abandonment of a whole area,
while at another it may simply mean the adoption of alternative
occupations.

Thus to introduce trade involves many kinds of alternatives—
not just consideration of more efficient types of production and
transportation as measured in either energy terms, material terms,
or price considerations. To repeat, the introduction of trade creates
situations in which differences in costs, however originating, operate to change human relationships. Trade, then, can be introduced and continued only so long as it results in such advantage
to those engaged in trading as will permit them economically to
meet the costs arising from the reactions which the introduction
of new goods may produce, whether such costs take the form of
overcoming direct physical resistance, the initiation of new types

of persuasion, the delivery of goods at lower prices, or other steps. All these secondary costs must be met, plus all the costs of production and transportation. Since in a low-energy society all energy derives primarily from the use of plants and animals, which yield limited surpluses, trade initiated between such societies with the consent of the local populace is very limited. On the other hand, with the surpluses possible from stream and sail, such resistance as is based on the surplus derived from plants and animals may be relatively ineffective and trade may be carried on in the face of it. Only such systems as produce some surplus can be brought into the trading area. Likewise only systems that provide sanctions permitting surplus to be taken out of the place of origin can participate. Hence trade arises in systems where the dominant values are such that trading the surplus goods will be more highly approved than devoting them to some other purpose, such as sacrifice to the gods, conspicuous giving, or licentious living. Thus there are three requisites for the establishment of trade between potential trade areas: differences in energy costs between the areas, the existence of exportable surpluses, and the presence of values that are compatible with trade.

The absence of any one of these precludes the use of the ship and the flowing stream for trade. Some of the great river valleys provide all the geographic conditions required. They are so large that they include a wide variety of soil, climate and topography, and mineralization. Consequently they also provide a wide diversity of plants and animals. Often, however, the seeming favorableness of conditions is deceptive. For example, it might seem that those in the fertile regions could obtain furs at the cost of less energy, in the form of food for export, than would have to be expended in growing and processing some fiber with equal protective or decorative value, while those in the colder upper reaches of the valley might gather furs at the cost of less energy than is involved in gathering or raising food. If transportation costs were low enough, this could become the basis of exchange. But since the rivers frequently run *from* these colder regions *to* the warmer and more fertile ones, the use of the stream would provide surplus energy only in the wrong direction. Heavy, bulky grain would have to be moved upstream and light·furs would come down, so that the use of the stream would cause a loss of energy rather than a gain. Thus, the specific nature of goods produced and alternatives for them must be examined before the influence of the geographic factor can be clearly seen.

And even when such geographic conditions are actually favorable, it does not always follow that trade will exist. Those who cannot, by reason of their distance from it, share the benefit of the stream are often antagonistic to those who can; sometimes they have been strong enough to prevent those on the river fringes, who might have used the stream, from developing to the point where they could engage in endeavors not approved by their far more numerous neighbors. Acting alone, such trade-inclined societies were frequently incapable, in the face of the opposition of their hostile neighbors, of developing a culture based on specialization and trade.

In some river valleys the advent of the sailing ship tipped the scales in favor of the trader and against the self-subsistent agricultural community. In general the greater the distance between two areas, particularly in latitude, the greater the difference in productivity as to specific plants and animals. Mineralization and other geographic factors are also likely to be more diverse. On the other hand, all other things being equal, the costs of transportation rise with the distance traveled. Thus costs of trade and of local production can be balanced one against another and a limited trading area stabilized. With the introduction of the sailing ship all other things ceased to be equal for dwellers on those rivers whose mouths would be reached by the ship. With the use of the ship it became possible to greatly increase the distance traversed and thus to increase the geographic and cultural diversity of products obtainable at a given cost in human energy. Now there could be brought from great distances goods which at their place of origin were low in energy costs but which at their point of sale could be produced, if at all, only with a much greater expenditure of energy. For example, wool and furs which are easily produced in cold climates and which can be produced with great difficulty or not at all in warmer regions where they may be highly useful for at least part of the year became available in these more temperate climes. In some areas climate entirely precludes the raising of plants whose use there would save goods otherwise certain to be wasted. Thus the spices that grew in the Indies could be used in Europe to preserve meat. The production of the meat and the waste due to lack of preservatives might add up to the expenditure of more energy than was required to produce and carry to the Indies the goods to be traded and to bring home the spices from their native islands. So the appearance of the ship-borne trader increased the number of alternatives available and altered the order of the energy costs at which goods could be secured. This frequently put a new strain on the old controls through which local reciprocity was secured. For example, one might, though grudgingly, support a spinster sister-in-law or cousin who provided 10 yards of cloth annually in return for her board and lodging, when the alternative was 12 yards in trade from a stranger. But if offered 10 yards of cloth for the equivalent of only 2 or 3 months' food for the spinster, one's choice might be different. This was the kind of decision involved, for example, when residents of villages in India were faced with a choice between maintaining the local spinning caste and having only a little cloth, and destroying the livelihood of that caste by trading for quantities of British calico.

Even where the traditional social controls were strong enough to withstand such considerations, the low-energy producers were frequently unable to stand their ground. As we have shown, energy may be used as an inducement. It must not be forgotten that it also represents potential coercion. The sailing ship made it possible to bring into the valley, in the shape of men and guns, force that did not originate there and was not dependent upon the surpluses produced there. It made it possible to bring from distant lands men who could eat only if they established trade, and who could live better by working for the interest of the trader than by remaining attached to the overpopulated lands from which they came. Added to the forces of the townsmen and such of the valley dwellers as were willing and able to profit from trade, they became a force sufficient to create such realignment of the culture as trade required. Thus economic and political factors worked hand in hand to alter the culture of the self-contained village of the low-energy society. Frequently the religious and moral systems of the trader, which justified what was being done, were likewise introduced, the power of the sword being used, if necessary, to convert the infidel.

To make our analysis clearer before we pass on to another point, perhaps we should recapitulate: The sailing ship produced a field tremendously more extensive than that of any previous converter; it operated on a gradient much more gentle, and its costs were therefore much lower than any previous one. It permitted energy to be concentrated in a manner hitherto impossible and made the use of force over large areas much more effective than any previously existing form. But its use stopped at the shore, except where it could be joined with the use of the flowing stream, which had its own characteristics. Consequently, on land sail accentuated the characteristics growing out of the use of the stream. These included support for exploitative stratification. The upstream portion of the trade at least was initially likely to be in luxuries, since only in downstream towns and cities could sufficient surplus be concentrated to make it possible for energy which might represent the bread of thousands to be exchanged for luxuries, such as furs and spices, perfumes and ornaments, for a few. Only in an urban environment could the value of goods whose original production carried, in addition to their economic meaning, a host of implications be transmuted into a neutral medium, money. In the agricultural areas these goods continued to represent merely part of a relationship that must be treated as a whole. Operations to extend trade until it included some of the necessities of life for those in the hinterland depended upon further changing its culture so as to permit removal of some of what had hitherto been claimed for local use, in return for goods brought in through trade.

The use of the ship was also limited by the volume of goods which the region was capable of delivering to it. Areas not traversed by rivers were often not able to produce goods which were sufficiently valuable to justify their being carried by man or animal over great distances. Such areas remained unexploited during the dominance of sea-borne trade. Only through the use of a river basin could the surplus of the interior of the continents be made available to the trader, and this most often through the medium of a city.

CHANGES WROUGHT BY THE SHIP

The ability of the sea-borne trader to deliver at the point of contact surplus gathered from elsewhere made it impossible for those not near rivers, seas, and oceans to stop the trade of their coastal neighbors except by a continuous effort which itself altered or destroyed their culture. Urban civilization, developed upon the seashore, being in part maintained by power developed by the use of sail, frequently became an incubus from which the interior could not escape. Cities often became parasites which drained the hinterland of much of its surplus. After the invention of gunpowder, the ship itself mounted weapons hardly to be matched by fixed guns except at such points as had few, and easily guarded, approaches. The surplus of a whole river basin, or that part which could be reached from the river, became available to him who controlled the sea. Sometimes he came as pirate, privateer, or representative of a "legitimate" monarch bent on plunder. Sometimes he appeared as tradesman, offering at a high price products cheap in a distant land, in return for the surplus produced by a large population. But always he was limited by the ability of the area in question to produce surplus.

Monopolization of Sea Trade

The limit on the amount to be traded was fixed not only by the cost of transportation between points but by the ability of an area to produce goods to be traded. Hence a great reduction in the prices charged by the trader (with resultant loss of profit) frequently resulted in no commensurate increase in his business. The consequence of increases in the number of traders was therefore largely expressed in decreased profits. Under such circumstances the rewards to the trader for monopolistic control over the seas and monopoly of the gains made from the ship were tremendous, and the penalty for uncontrolled competition was likely to be disaster.

Monopoly had to take two measures to maintain itself: first, to secure the gains to the owners of the ship rather than to all those who participated in her building and operation; second, to limit the permitted number of ships to the optimum. To secure the first condition was relatively easy. During long periods the only areas that produced surpluses adequate to build ships were those in which serfdom or slavery operated. To deliver to a ship a hundred or a thousand men was frequently to rid the countryside of surplus population which, if it had stayed, would have reduced the possible energy surpluses available for trade or consumption by the landowner. The lot of sailors was no better, nor much worse, than that of other men; as they had not shared surpluses produced upon the land, there was no thought that they should do so at sea. Once monarchs became aware of the wealth to be gained from a growing class of merchants, there came into being the maritime counterpart of the conscripters who carried men off to soldier on land. It was only when men on the land had gained the power to demand more than subsistence that it became necessary to share surpluses with them upon the sea.

The system under which all gains derived from the ship belonged to the shipowner did not prevail among the early Greeks, Norsemen, and other freebooters, who were primarily raiders, and hence fighters, rather than merchant seamen. Loot was shared among these fighters so that they would not destroy the group by fighting over it. In general, however, the very process of creating surplus for trade produced a change in the desirable ratio between land and the population living on it. This created agricultural unemployment and idled men, who were than glad to find a place where the need for their muscles guaranteed at least a chance for survival. It was unlikely that the shipowner would find himself unable to recover his costs or would be forced to share his profits because of the bargaining power of his crew.

The problem of securing monopoly or maintaining monopolistic competition as between shipowners was one much more difficult to solve. Through long centuries piracy was at least normal, if not moral. But, as we have seen, a vessel that required oarsmen to manipulate it in battle and fighters to protect it lost much of the surplus it might otherwise have delivered. The Phoenicians kept their nagivation secrets well and circulated such horrendous tales of the dangers of the sea as to frighten off many potential competitors. But the Minoans and their successors, the Greeks, contested this supremacy, at least in their own waters, and made it costly to trade in that area. With them, for a time at least, it was share and share alike among the crew, but as commercial practices grew and merchant capitalism copied from the Phoenician model developed, such sharing was replaced by the concentration of wealth which produced the Periclean age.

It was the Romans, conquering both the Greek and the

Phoenician colonies in Africa, who secured a firm monopoly. Through their control over the sea they developed a system which delivered to Rome the surpluses of the whole Mediterranean world, making possible specialization and division of labor and releasing thousands from the necessity of remaining on the land in order to secure food. As we have seen, they were able to produce a true merchant ship which generated very large surpluses. But as their empire faded they lost control of the Mediterranean and it again became infested with pirates, who plied their trade until well into the nineteenth century, necessitating the arming of the ship and reducing the surplus it could produce.

During the Renaissance the Italian states revived trade under competition and still profited mightily from it. The Portuguese and Spanish, plundering the New World, called upon heaven and a church made new-rich by their exploits to protect trade which their own political and military prowess was unable to monopolize securely.

In the following two centuries the English and the Dutch arose to challenge and defeat the Iberians. Then began the struggle with France which was triumphantly concluded at Trafalgar. For almost a century Britain ruled the seas and largely determined the conditions under which trade upon them could take place. Much of the social organization of the present world, particularly that part which deals with foreign trade, still bears the mark of this period.

Admiral Mahan's *Influence of Sea Power in History*, which became the source of so many policies, was based upon an examination of the role which the navy played in making the position of trading nations dominant. It did not occur to Mahan or to his followers that what he was talking about was a statement not of immutable natural law but merely of a consequence of the use of particular converters and the social organization that grew up with their use. Equally, a good deal of what has passed for economics rests upon the assumption that British experience with high-energy converters sets the only pattern for their efficient use. It will become clear when we examine other high-energy converters that this is not necessarily so.

A general theory of the way in which sail and stream are likely to affect society has now been developed. More specific reference to some historic uses of these energy sources may cast some light on the usefulness of this theory.

SAIL AND STREAM IN ANTIQUITY

It has already been pointed out that the Egyptians built their system primarily on the exploitation of agriculture. Their institutions were such as to make effective use of the surpluses produced by that technique in the Nile Valley, and, in comparison to those generally being produced elsewhere, their surpluses were large. Ships would be useful only if considerable trade was permitted. To turn to trade meant the introduction into Egypt of variables which might upset relationships between groups, individuals, and regions which had proven in the past to be very fruitful. To turn to trade meant the introduction of goods not produced under the sanctions of Egyptian law, religion, and morals. To turn to trade, then, was also to increase the power and prestige of the traders; to encourage men who would reduce objects with artistic, religious, social and moral connotations to a neutral denominator, price; and, more dangerously, to set up a group which might bid for the loyalty and arms of those who found no satisfaction in the existing order of things. A few sailors bringing luxuries for the consumption of the court did not constitute a competitive way of life. But a great number of middlemen might become a danger, and one that need not be tolerated, for the economy of Egypt was by far the most highly productive in the world; no goods were being produced elsewhere cheaply enough to induce or compel the rulers to overthrow the existing system in favor of widespread trade. Hence the use of the ship was rigorously limited.

For the Phoenicians the alternatives were quite different. Their agriculture was much less productive, and they had no long period of isolation, enforced by natural barriers such as those which guarded Egypt, in which to develop a stable system for its exploitation. On the other hand, the Phoenician tradesman early became a satisfactory adjunct to the Egyptian system and as such was able to provide surpluses adequate to overcome the resistance to trade of the agrarian population in his own neighborhood. The limits to Phoenician development were, thus, imposed not by internal political necessity but by inadequacies in basic technology (which held down the surpluses to be carried), by restraints put upon trade by the Egyptians, and by the constant struggle with other East Mediterraneans for possession of the sea. When, in time, dynastic Egyptian imperialism swept away the Phoenician base in the homeland, Phoenicia's colonies became the foundation of her new trade-based economy, and Carthage received the surpluses that had hitherto been used to build up the other Phoenician cities. Finally, of course, all this was destroyed by the power of Rome.

The Greek situation was similar. Many of the Greek towns were, to begin with, little more than pirate camps; their wealth came initially from the sea, and it was with sea-borne power that they came to dominate the small enclaved agricultural areas that constituted their hinterlands. But for that very reason the surpluses to be exploited in the Aegean and in Greek cities were small. From the first they were commercial cities, quite unlike the agriculture-based towns on the Nile, the Tigris, and the Euphrates. If the Egyptians could not take to the sea because their agricultural surpluses were too large, the Greeks could not survive because theirs were too small.

The necessary balance was achieved by the Romans. A period of exploitation by sea was followed by expansion upon the land; surpluses produced upon the land were converted into new fleets, supported a new merchant class, and hence produced a new political balance. Overland trade by the Romans resulted in the spread of the agricultural techniques developed in Egypt and the Fertile Crescent. Thus new landowning groups providing the means and the will to check the power of the merchant came into being. Agricultural specialization in Africa and elsewhere around the periphery of the Mediterranean provided huge surpluses of slaves and food to be used by the successful conquerors. Thus, military, political, and economic balance was maintained.

As each succeeding conquest on the land made possible more extensive trade, it also forced wider use of the ship to render that trade profitable. But though the Romans fully exploited the ship in the Mediterranean, they never made the inventions required for its use on the oceans. The end of the process came when the distance from the Mediterranean and adjoining seas so diminished the surpluses available from the ship as to render the Roman legions weaker than their opponents. Such limits were not reached at once, and the various fortunes of successive rulers led now to overextension followed by withdrawal, now to long periods in which the surpluses were consumed at home in "bread and circuses," in great monuments and other public works, or in civil war. Great roads made less steep the gradient of low-energy converters on the land. Conquest of territory permitted the cavalry and the chariot horses to feed along the way, and the spread of agricultural techniques tremendously increased the surpluses produced in the territory overrun by the legions. But ultimately all these surpluses were exhausted and the limits of empire discovered and made static.

The excesses of the Roman system eventually undermined the basic energy sources upon which Roman power was based. Other areas, particularly those which became modern France, developed increasing power through agriculture. The attempt to hold these areas in the empire weakened Rome still further. As her grip upon the Mediterranean world loosened, opportunity for gain from the ship lessened. The size of the surpluses to be transported was greatly reduced by Rome's long exploitative hold, which had drained the land of its exhaustible resources in soil, minerals, and forest products, and by the deterioration of the population due to the excesses of slavery. On the political side the revival of regional governments meant refusal to trade upon the exploitative terms which Rome had maintained; this refusal was backed up by populations which were attempting to restore in Europe and the Near East locally coherent systems. Trade revived again only after the fear of trade had become less than the desire for luxuries on the part of local rulers. From this trade the medieval city-states built anew a commercial civilization. But they were never able to expand it to the point where it could overcome the power of the feudal landlords on either side of the Mediterranean.

THE SAILING SHIP AND THE COLONIAL SYSTEM

Spain and Portugal then seized upon the opportunity to exploit the oceanic world with new techniques of navigation. The surplus produced upon the Iberian peninsula was, however, never large, and a great portion of it always was diverted to the maintenance of the army and the church, through which the monarchs secured and maintained control. Spain's use of the ship called for conquest, the rapid exploitation of exhaustible surpluses. The bulk of this wealth was consumed by physically nonproductive classes at home. The monarchs could not have freed themselves from these classes had they wished to, for they had always to be prepared to defend themselves against pretenders and their borders against jealous neighbors. The loyalty of the army, however, depended upon its rewards, which consumed surplus as quickly as conquest made it available. Moreover, had any serious attempt been made to expand trade in Spain and Portugal, it would have meant an enlargement, in the home country, of the merchant class. By delivering cheap goods from abroad the merchants, in town, might have vied for favor with the monarch and have undermined the social system upon which the power of the feudal lords rested. But even without the development of trade, Spain and Portugal utilized the ship to secure for themselves formidable empires, the disintegration of which has taken hundreds of years.

The Low Countries, having secured their independence from Spain, utilized the sailing ship to obtain the products which their own hard-won soil produced but sparingly. The ship afforded employment to sons for whom that soil could provide no employment. Like the British, the Belgians and the Dutch tended to engage in trade which was mutually profitable at least to the bargainers, however exploitative it may have been of some of those who initially produced the surpluses traded. Thus in the Low Countries, as in England, the merchant class became important in politics by supplying the means of maintaining the army and navy. However, these states had to defend themselves against their neighbors on the land and were not simultaneously able to provide the means to vie with the British for control of the seas. Thus, Low Country merchants were forced to accept in world trade that position which the British were willing to cede to them.

The story of the French was similar. No sooner did the sailor produce a surplus than the soldier ate it up. French rulers developed overseas trade only to be robbed, through the expenditures of the army, of the navy with which to defend it. The French, no more than the Spanish, landowners were willing to see a rival source of wealth emerge.

It was in England that the sailing ship produced the full

revolution of which it was capable. As an island, England had certain advantages over the Continental powers. Her principal protection was obtained by the use of the sailing ship, itself a surplus-producer, instead of an army. The surplus necessary for defense against invasion was smaller than that required by her neighbors, so that energy could be used in producing more converters without endangering the survival of the country. The armies of the Continental powers were a constant drain upon their surpluses, and in addition the feudal lords deliberately set obstacles to the further expansion of trade. In Britain, on the other hand, surpluses produced by the buccaneers were largely reinvested in new fleets, and the growth of port towns followed. British monarchs, trying to offset the strength of landlords who were competing with them for power, seized upon this new source of wealth and in return extended necessary protection to the traders.

At first luxuries filled the holds, but the expansion of trade required a source of wealth more permanent than the plundering of the buccaneers. A lasting trade depends upon the exchange of goods which can continuingly be produced in large quantities and disposed of in many places—items for which there exists a broad and steady demand. England could meet this requirement because of her natural advantage in the production of wool. A landlord could gain more through the exchange of wool for the products of the East than through the use of his land to produce this or other goods for sale to artisans and other producers in England.

The transition of wool production led to the impoverishment of English food-raising areas. Food came to be supplied from lands abroad more favorable to the growing of grain. The transformation of farm land into grazing land, for the purpose of producing the necessary surplus of wool, forced the peasants off the land into the towns, where they provided manpower to be used in the fabrication of cloth from the wool. Eventually, through the spinning jenny and the water frame, the power of men, women, and children was replaced by that of water.

All these facts are well known. What we want to point out is that as the exploitation of the ship reached its limits in terms of the existing internal economy of England, those who favored change were able to change that economy to make possible further exploitation. More and more Englishmen were thus enabled to multiply their own power a hundredfold upon the sea, while the great mass of other men continued within the same limits as had characterized Egypt under the Pharaohs. England's sons were shipped abroad to create in the near-empty continents of North America and Australia new, specialized versions of low-energy systems, while upon the sea England's navy developed the monopoly by which that specialization was made safe and kept profitable.

During the colonial period of American history, the colonists of the New World were unable to break that monopoly. Some tradesmen did manage to escape from both England and the Continent, bringing with them the techniques by which competing systems could be set up. The abundance of land, the relative shortage of labor, and the break in cultural continuity which accompanied adaptation to the frontier all contributed to the creation in the Northern colonies of an area which was competitive with the economy of the mother country rather than complementary to it. So long, however, as surpluses from the interior of North America had to be delivered at river mouth, to be transported abroad by sailing ship if they were to be profitably used, no active threat to British monopoly in foreign trade could be developed without Britain's consent. This was demonstrated in the War of 1812 and the Napoleonic Wars, when British control of the seas led to defeat of both the colonists and Napoleon.

Britain was the first in modern times to exploit sail to the full, since she was first able to adopt the necessary changes in culture, and her history most clearly illumines the consequences of the use of sail. These can be analyzed in terms of effects on the part of the population that builds and operates the ships and originates the trade and on the part that participates in other ways in the use of sail. Of course, some trade took place between predominantly shipbuilding and trading countries, but trade between such countries was less likely to produce surplus than was trade between one country which engaged in shipbuilding and trading and another which remained predominantly agricultural. Among traders, each attempting to maximize his gain, the nearby resources of a neighbor with similar soil and climate were less likely to offer large differentials in productivity than were distant shores. Nor was the culture of a nearby society apt to be sufficiently different to permit the kind of exploitation possible in distant lands. As minerals became more significant in trade, the early emphasis upon trading at a distance was somewhat reduced because differences in metal production between neighboring countries affected favorably the likelihood of trade between them. However, except for gold and silver, metals were, until after the advent of steam, unlikely to be the basis of extensive trade. Certainly there was far more trade between countries that built and operated ships and those that did not than there was trade based upon differences in the production of metal.

THE SAILING SHIP AND THE MERCANTILISTIC SOCIETY

In the shipbuilding country the adoption of sail, because of the changes it required, gave rise to a certain amount of internal resistance, and it was probable that this resistance would be effectively mobilized. Shipbuilding could be carried on only with the cooperation of the landowners, who provided timber and other necessary materials. Manpower was also under their control, since the food which workers ate came from the land. If the landowners were obstinate, demanding too large a share of the surplus in return for their cooperation, ships could not be built, nor could goods be exchanged except through revision of the existing system of power and property. Adaptation of a society to the fullest use of the ship required a shift in land use, new developments in technology, alteration of the status system, and other disturbances which were expensive; the spread of trade via ship thus required enormous increment in surplus energy.

Sometimes one, sometimes another point of resistance served to check development. Where resistance was encountered, those seeking to expand trade had to divert energy to meet it. The surpluses resulting from the use of the ship were expended here to secure cooperation of landlords, there to bribe legislators, elsewhere to win the acquiescence of the clergy or to provide arms for the military. As a result the adaptation gave the appearance of being a rather slow evolution. The shift in use of land to feed sheep rather than people forced the abandonment of many of the diversified self-contained social units which had come to characterize Britain. The enclosure movement took place only as ship-owners were able to provide a market from which the landowner could gain more in wealth, power, and prestige than from his previous use of land. As an alternative to this means of gaining his cooperation, the shipowner sometimes provided the landowner with the arms and the wealth by which others who also lived on the land could be driven off; surpluses to be traded were thus provided. The dislocation of the people who were removed to make way for sheep produced demoralized bands of peasants, who, denied access to the land by which alone they could claim its product, were often ready to ally themselves with anyone willing to feed them. However, such men had to be bought and kept bought, as more than one merchant class found to its sorrow. This also put claims on the energy supplied by the ship.

Furthermore, the expansion of the use of the ship led to changes in other elements of the culture. Greater wool production permitted the use both in spinning and in weaving of the rotary and reciprocating motions which could be provided by the water wheel. Thus another energy source was tapped. The roles of many persons were changed. With the use of machine spinning and weaving the contribution of the wife, mother, daughter, or spinster relation was reduced, but there was no corresponding change in the distribution of income among families to offset this loss. The customary division of labor was unbalanced. Again, the resulting displacement brought about a reaction designed to restore the old system. The new inventions were conscientiously sabotaged until a new generation came into being, some of whom were scattered on new lands abroad, some appeased by increased goods, and some cowed by power.

Elsewhere the struggle to make trade possible took a somewhat similar course. In summary form we can say that within the economy in which shipbuilding took place, inventions involved in the use of the ship could spread, and adaptation to it could take place, only through dispersal of much of the surplus among the groups found there. The trader, always a marginal man in the older, low-energy cultures, thus gained the means to achieve a higher status through this dispersal of the surplus from the ship which he now controlled. If the clergy occupied a strategic position, the trader could gain its blessing by contributing to the erection of cathedrals and endowment of monasteries, by supporting crusades against the infidel, or by making whatever material contribution might be thought to glorify God or enrich the church. If military men stood in the trader's way, he could supply the necessary sinews of war and gain their support. Because of the newly gained ability of the trader to engage in conspicuous expenditure or display, he could share the once exclusive status of the landlord. The merchant prince, contributing the riches of the Orient to a luxury-loving court, could marry into one of the old families, which were frequently in need of new energy to bolster up the relative decline of agriculture, and thus could lose his former identity, and glory in a new title. If other means failed, the trader might enter into political competition for the loyalty of the masses, whose only means of subsistence had come to be the food which he brought from abroad. The emergence of the trader as a claimant to the apex of the status pyramid was slow, and in many areas it was never fully achieved because of the limited effectiveness, in the area beyond the tidewater, of the technology of sail and its contributing converters. But in all cases where the ship was used there was an increase in the power of the trader.

The shift in political power which accompanied the recognition of this changed status was dependent on many variables. It was secured in some places by the crude force of the ship. In others traders took advantage of the dislocations and dependency which were a consequence of the shifts in land use and in technology that accompanied spreading trade. The speed with which the process took place depended in part also upon the unity and cohesiveness in the area into which trading was being introduced. In some areas it was rapid enough for the old unquestioned bases of power to be threatened. That is to say, political power was no longer conceded by divine right of birth or other hereditary device; it had to be demonstrated by the ability to command such force as could overcome the power of new claimants. It had to hold the loyalty of those whom it commanded despite the enticements offered by those who controlled other sources of wealth and power. Sometimes the struggle led to dictatorship by the trader. In other places, as in England, the result was that system of compromise and competitive bidding for the support of groups and individuals which characterizes democracy. Among her neighbors the exploitation of sail was never so complete, nor the necessity to placate new groups commanding new sources of energy so great, as in England, but all countries which made use of sail faced consequences resembling in kind, if not in degree, those that developed in England.

Some of these differences in development were related to differences in natural resources and similar factors beyond the control of man. However, some were the result of the specific policies adopted to preserve the gains of the ship-borne trader. He was interested in maintaining the existing sphere of trade or expanding it. Acts which would result in replacing trade by producing goods locally reduced the opportunity for profit, and, what was often more important, it reduced the power and influence of the trader relative to other groups in the country. So the trader prevented wherever he could those changes which would wipe out the advantage of overseas trade. For example, the spread of technology from England to the colonies reduced such advantage as was based on superior British techniques. Consequently the trader joined with conservatives in the colonies to prevent the development of local industry. Another danger he constantly confronted was the breakdown of the code which permitted him to gain a "fair" return. So he attempted to set out "spheres of influence" in which each trader would monopolize control over shipping.

On the other hand, such improved techniques as permitted the mother country to increase its superiority over other areas were welcome. The trader who, in so far as technical change was concerned, welcomed innovation at home resisted it abroad. There it was often easier for him to make concessions to a small ruling group, thus gaining their support in the battle against the reactions which trade produced among the larger part of the populace, than it was to accede to the kind of competition which, had it been permitted to work unhampered, would have forced him to accept only a very small return. The trader, "progressive" and "liberal" at home, joined forces with the "conservative" and the "exploiter" abroad.

The ambivalence of attitude necessary to support the system contributed to its being defensible only in pragmatic terms, and by a philosophy which was extremely vulnerable to any criticism based on rational consistency. All the arguments used to justify behavior at home had to be reversed as they applied to the "natives" who made up the distant members of the exchange system. They might be denied status as human beings because they were infidels or were considered to be members of an inferior race not entitled to share the good things of life on account of their having been born different. They might be classified as immature or backward, a people eventually to be blessed, but not now. Voluntary activity induced by the mutual advantage of specialization and trade was praised at home, while for a foreign area coercion which destroyed the economic system, or some component of it, was justified by the assumption that what was good for the "mother country" must also be good for all those with whom she traded.

Organized social thought in defense of the system took the name of *mercantilism*. Trade was urged as a necessity for the maintenance of the power of the state, and the power of the state was to be used to further trade. The negative consequence of trade, in terms of its destructive effects on existing cultures, was minimized. It was urged that, in the long run, trade was bound to bring gold and silver, permit widening of the area of exchange within the country, and encourage specialization and division of labor, which in turn would result in increased wealth. Trade was to be pushed, with the aid of the power of the state, into those areas which yielded the largest surpluses. There was to be no competition among the exploiters of the ship. Rather, the granting of exclusive privileges of trade was to serve as a guarantee that all the surplus would be retained somewhere in the system of the exploiting country, more particularly in the hands of traders and their friends.

Of marked significance was the change in attitude toward the taking of interest. In low-energy society, borrowing was often a sign of need rather than an indication of the seizing of opportunity. The borrower sought usually to meet a current obligation he could not otherwise pay off. It might be the price of the services of the medicine man, or the demands of a priest. It might be the cost of a wedding or a funeral. It might be the price of seed in a time of disaster when the required seed could not be put aside from existing stores. Seldom did it mean that the borrower, by borrowing, would get to be better off than he was when he borrowed the money. Loans made to buy land, for example, usually had attached to them interest rates approximating the economic rent of the land, or, in places where land was extremely scarce, even something more than the economic rent, since the purchase of land would permit the use of otherwise unemployable labor. Thus, while the moneylender was a necessary adjunct to many low-energy societies he was a harbinger of evil, a symbol of disaster, vilified but tolerated.

In the transition from low to high energy brought about by the use of the ship, the moneylender's services became more and more useful and less and less odious. Since the ship made it possible for hitherto untapped energy to be used, its use permitted great gains in physical productivity, and those who contributed to shipbuilding came to expect to share in those gains. Also, there was always the chance of disaster, and the gain from one voyage had to serve as a kind of insurance against loss in a subsequent one. The small surpluses which characterized even large units using low-energy converters frequently made the aggregation of the surpluses necessary to build a ship a matter for cooperation. Usually it was only by combining the resources of several landlords or merchants that a ship could be built. This necessitated the invention of a social means to the accumulation of converters, and a moral and legal jusification for the financing of such an organization. The church was required to make exceptions to its ban on the taking of interest when done in this form, and the role of the moneylender became a respected one. Laws protecting the shareholder against the trader also began to develop. This kind of financing was the forerunner of the modern corporation, whose subsequent expansion we shall note.

It was the ship, then, that made important, and brought about approval for, the widespread use of money and of exchange based on price and the taking of interest. It was with the sailing ship that a few small nations of western Europe developed control over the trade of the world and gained such power as to subordinate many times their own numbers to the political and economic ends they sought. Certainly the ship was no "sufficient" cause to explain all that happened where it came into use, but certainly also there is no reasonable way to explain how such power could have been attained without the use of the energy of sail. It is only now, as the world built on the control which sail permitted is evolving into new power patterns, that we can discern some of the reasons both for the rise and for the fall of Western dominance.

CHAPTER 5

Steam: Key to the Industrial Revolution

As timber for the building of ships became scarce in England, shipbuilders were forced to turn to iron for hulls; the increasing use of machinery also required iron. But the use of charcoal for the melting furnaces led to further thinning of the timber stands, resulting in erosion and, with it, resistance from the landlords. So the iron makers turned to coke, which is made from coal. This use of coke for smelting, added to the use of coal for space heating in the growing towns, meant deepening the shafts in coal mines, and it was to pump water from the mines that the steam engine was brought into use. For a considerable time no further major use of steam was contemplated. The subsequent extension of the use of steam to the railroads made steam an integral part of the system which existed primarily for the purpose of bringing goods to shipside for trade. Steam converters took the place of men and horses in operating pumps in the mines; they slowly replaced horses for pulling cars on the railways; here and there they replaced the windmill and the water wheel in grist and textile mills. But the old general social structure long persisted —on land maintained primarily by low-energy systems, and on the sea by the sailing ships which transported surpluses for exchange.

THE STEAMSHIP

Placing steam winches aboard to raise the sails and anchor and to load and unload cargo, made it possible to reduce the size of the crew of the sailing ship and thereby to increase the surplus energy per man to be gained from the sails. Time spent in port for loading and unloading was likewise reduced by the use of steam-powered hoists. Such engines eventually became auxiliary sources of ship propulsion and finally replaced sails. The shift from sail to steam as the dominant source of surplus was slow and undramatic, and its significance was neither noted nor evaluated by those who were actually bringing it about. But steam is not necessarily used to best advantage in a system built to exploit sail. This was not immediately manifest because the energy available to the leading maritime powers of the West was so great compared to that available to the low-energy societies in the rest of the world. There are, however, significant differences between conversion of energy by sail and stream and conversion by steam, and these became increasingly evident.

The steam engine, like the organic converters, depends upon an exhaustible supply of energy. Unlike the sailing ship, whose use of the wind does not diminish the supply, the steam engine must obtain its fuel at fixed points, where it is available only in specific amounts. It must obtain this fuel at the cost of some of the energy gained. Its use thus follows the centripetal pattern exhibited by the plant. That is to say, as you move away from the source, energy is consumed. To conserve energy you must utilize it near the source. The gradient in the field is somewhat less steep than that of systems using men or animals for transportation, but the field is nevertheless limited. Moreover, the gradient of the steam-driven ship is much steeper than that of the sailing ship.

The sailing ship was most effective in the areas where the trade winds blow, but it could operate well, though with somewhat lower efficiency, elsewhere. The highways of sail and the location of the ports serving sailing ships were based upon these facts. But the efficient use of the steam engine depends in part upon the location of fuel sources, which are not found at sea. The forests near rivers and seacoasts would yield fuel for only a short time, and transporting wood from a distance would greatly reduce net surpluses. Only such fuels as coal and oil provided a supply of energy adequate for long-distance ocean travel. But coal is seldom found at tidewater, and those areas where agriculture supported large populations engaged in sail-borne trade were frequently far from sources of coal. Thus, to be useful, coal had to be transported, at the cost of part of the surplus available at the mine, to the populations concentrated by sail and low-energy converters. The geographic distribution of population set by sail was not that which was destined to grow up around steam, though many old sites were maintained because trade patterns developed under sail were continued under steam.

Ecological and Other Effects

Other differences between the patterns of effective use of steam and sail are to be found in the characteristics of the converters. One of the problems of the designer of a steam engine is to transfer the maximum proportion of the heat obtained from burning coal or other fuel to the water in the boiler. This is done by exposing as large an area of the boiler as feasible to the flames. Once the steam is generated in the boiler, however, the aim is to confine all the heat possible, so that it can be released usefully in driving a piston or turbine impeller. Other things being equal, up to a point the larger the steam engine the more efficient it will be, that is, the more nearly it will satisfy these two physical requirements. It is thus desirable to make the steam unit as large as practicable and to assemble at one point tasks requiring the work of which the engine is capable. This means the concentration of machines which use large amounts of energy and also of operators to control the machines.

The congestion in the immediate vicinity of the large engine producing great power was accentuated by the means of transmission of power available when the first steam engines were built. The cams, shafts, belts, and gears that were necessary produced a steep gradient. The inefficiency of the early types of engine also meant that a large portion of the fuel was wasted in combustion. Centers of production near the mine mouth offered great economic advantage over those at more distant points. To lessen the losses incurred in the conveying of fuel to engines located at a distance from the mines, a means of transportation using the surplus derivable from coal was needed.

THE LOCOMOTIVE

This was most quickly manifest in England, for even though coal lay at tidewater, the food and minerals required for shipbuilding and trade were often not procurable by ship. As the steam engine was substituted for men and horses in working pumps and winches, so it came to be substituted for them in hauling shipbuilding materials and cargo. This source of power achieved mobility in the form of the locomotive, a converter with characteristics quite unlike those of the stationary engine. The locomotive is capable of delivering great power while on the rails but is helpless and delivers no power off them. Its field is ribbonlike, as is that of the flowing stream. Unlike the stream, however, it can deliver surplus energy both in going to and in coming from the source of potential energy. It is not marked by the necessary contrast in size and weight of shipment that differentiates the downstream from the upstream journey. Thus the locomotive uses part of the energy expended in its journey away from the source to carry fuel for the return trip. Further, energy in the form of food can move in one direction, offsetting energy in the form of coal moving in the other. Populations could be relocated to make use of sites near the coal mines while remaining dependent upon the food produced in more distant areas where surpluses from food could be produced more efficiently. Though relocation of population to make the most efficient use of the new source of energy, without diminishing the surplus food available, became possible, it was still necessary for sufficient men to be available in the food-raising regions to fulfill the needs there during periods when labor was in greatest demand.

Use of the locomotive was affected by another characteristic: there is a distinct interval in space between the points at which its energy can be made useful. It will be recalled that, by the law of inertia, it takes more energy to move a body at rest or to alter the velocity of a body than it does to maintain speed once gained, for once a body is in uniform unilinear motion it will continue to remain so with only the force necessary to overcome friction. This fact, while true for all converters, was accentuated in the case of the railroad.

To start or to stop a wheelbarrow or a horse-drawn wagon does not require an amount of energy that will significantly alter the cost of the operations in which they are likely to be used. It does take a lot of energy to bring a ship into port or to get it under way, but this amount is relatively small compared to the amount of energy used by the ship in a voyage. Steam engines are comparatively large and heavy for the amount of power they produce. To start, accelerate, decelerate, and stop a train requires a great deal of energy, and if variations in velocity are frequent, energy costs of operation mount swiftly. This was particularly true in the early days, when iron and steel were comparatively weak and unreliable and when designers were ignorant of how to calculate strength, stress, and strain. Also, in those days fuel and water were used comparatively wastefully and had to be carried in large quantities. Increasing the size of the engine to improve its efficiency meant greater weight not only of the engine and its fuel and water but also of the lengthened train it was enabled to pull. Longer trains imposed a greater strain on each car because of the increased weight of those behind it. As a result the weight of the draft gear was increased, and this too added weight disproportionate to the carrying capacity of the car. Inertia thus became a more significant factor. If efficiency was to be secured, stops must be as infrequent as possible. The efficiency of the engine increased with the length of the intervals between the stops necessary for fuel, water, and repair, and the use of the train was most economical in the vicinity of such stops. Since intermediate stops added to the costs of operation, they were abandoned as rapidly as feasible.

Ecological Consequences

The lengthening of intervals between stopping points set up a new pattern of location for regions using railroads, differing from the pattern set up, for example, by stage coaches or, particularly, the pattern set up in old agricultral areas, where the distance between villages was determined by the efficient use of the land in terms of population density. In China, for instance, villages tended to appear wherever the services which they rendered were equal to the energy costs spent in getting to them. Fertile areas permitted increased concentration of population. This in turn permitted such services as those of the priest, medicine man, midwife, or butcher to be supported by a smaller area than was possible where the surplus energy gained from crops was less and the population consequently more scattered. The location of towns in areas where population pressed less closely on the energy available might be determined by other factors, such as the requirement for protection, the common use of a cathedral, the use of common wells or water holes, etc.

With the advent of the steam railroad, transportation between towns 50 miles apart became less expensive, provided they were both on the railroad, than transportation between towns 10 miles apart of which one was not on the right of way. Service specialists located on a railroad might draw clients from a distance of a 100 miles who could not have afforded to come 30 miles by another mode of transportation involving low-energy converters. Consequently, railroad division points, where change of engine and crew and car inspection were required, were convenient locations for towns, and these served a much larger population than had hitherto been possible. We shall have occasion to look more closely at these effects later.

The steam engine was perhaps more significant for the surpluses of energy it made available than for any other aspect of its operation. We must recall that apart from the sailing ship there was, before the advent of steam, no important source of mechanical energy other than those dependent upon the use of plants as a primary source of energy. The sailing ship itself was a supplier of surplus useful only for the transport of the product of surpluses generated by plants. There were definite limits on the mechanical energy available in any low-energy society, for mechanical energy was largely a direct function of population, and population was in turn a function of the effective use of agriculture.

Wood and Coal as Fuel

The introduction of the steam engine permitted conversion of heat energy directly into mechanical energy. It could use as fuel almost anything that would burn and therefore could convert the waste products of food raisers, or the products of land otherwise almost useless, into mechanical energy. In many cases wood was used as fuel. The average annual yield from trees in terms of mechanical energy is *less* than the average yield of most crops. A soft, quick-growing tree such as the Wisconsin aspen will produce about 2 tons of wood per year per acre, and Florida pine will yield about 3 tons. Such yields compare favorably with some crops, unfavorably with others. They are, for example, greater than that of tame hay, which on the average in the United States yields 1½ tons per year per acre of material that when burned releases less energy per pound than does wood. On the other hand, a year's crop of 100 bushels per acre of Iowa corn, including stalks, husks, cobs, and grain, will yield about 20 million Calories as compared with 8 million Calories for the complete heat product per year per acre of Wisconsin aspen. So a wood-burning locomotive such as the early ones which operated at less than 2 per cent efficiency could not replace a hay- and corn-eating horse of 20 per cent efficiency in any area where corn and hay could be raised. This is true even if we take into account only the direct operating costs of the locomotive and disregard the much higher fixed costs which its use entails.

Trees grow in many areas where food crops will not, and where there is rain enough they will largely replace the grass which might have served to feed livestock; in these areas the heat energy of burned trees supplies mechanical energy not otherwise available. However, in the great river valleys, where low-energy society was able to support a considerable population, the heat available from trees was useful in cooking food and in smelting and forging metals. There, since trees were scarce and were used for other purposes, they would not be available as a fuel supply for the locomotive. Only where an abundance of such items as minerals made high-cost transportation feasible could a wood-fueled railroad be built and maintained. There the energy costs of the railroad would be low compared to the energy saved by the low costs of utilizing a rich source; further, the locomotive would be used so infrequently that the trees along the right of way could regain from the sun the energy dissipated by the railroad. In other areas the necessary rate of fuel consumption would quickly exhaust all the economically available wood. After that happened another fuel would be required for continued operation of the railway. In most places, then, locomotives burn coal or oil.

It will be recalled that the steam engine came into use in coal-burning areas. It was from the surplus produced by mining coal that the steam engine gained its first advantage. Coal and the other fuels which consist of remains of ancient plant and animal life offer an entirely different set of limits from the sources of energy that make use of the recurring presence of the sun. Instead of limits determined by the annual rate of conversion of sunlight into plant life, we have limits which depend on the total supply deposited in a particular place. The availability of this deposit is dependent upon man's ability to devise means of getting it out of the ground. The possible rate of return in the form of surplus thus is represented by a series in which part of the energy gained in mining is immediately enlisted to reduce the number of men and animals needed in the mine. Though early mining methods were very inefficient by present-day standards, a comparison of the surpluses produced even then by mining with those obtained by use of the organic converters may be enlightening.

The Surplus Provided by Coal

At first the English miner hacked the coal out with a pick and it was carried by man or animal to the mine entry. A man could mine 500 or 600 pounds a day, depending upon the thickness and purity of the coal in the seam being mined and its distance from the mine entrance. The heat value of coal varies considerably from field to field and even from vein to vein, but good bituminous, which produces about 3,500 Calories per pound, will serve as an illustration. A coal miner who consumes in his own body about 3,500 Calories a day will, if he mines 500 pounds of coal, produce coal with a heat value 500 times the heat value of the food which he consumed while mining it. At 20 per cent efficiency he expends about 1 horsepower-hour of mechanical energy to get the coal. Now, if the coal he mines is burned in a steam engine of even 1 per cent efficiency it will yield about 27 horsepower-hours of mechanical energy. The surplus of mechanical energy gained would thus be 26 horsepower-hours, or the equivalent of 26 man-days per man-day. A coal miner, who consumed about $\frac{1}{5}$ as much food as a horse, could thus deliver through the steam engine about 4 times the mechanical energy which the average horse in Watt's day was found to deliver. Little wonder that the iron horse began to replace his organic forebear!

This was, however, only the beginning. With no change in the amount of coal delivered by the miner per day, the mechanical-energy surplus delivered could be greatly increased by raising the efficiency of the steam engine. At 2 per cent the surplus would be increased to 53 man-days per man-day. Raising the efficiency to 4 per cent would more than double that. And there remained the possibility of using the cheap mechanical energy made available by the steam engine to replace men and horses in the mine. Progress in this direction in the old sites has been hampered by the character of the veins, by resistances in the social organization, by faulty taxing policies, and by other factors. In the original coal mining regions the surplus is thus far below the level that is technologically possible.

More favorable conditions existed in areas such as the United States. These permitted continuous increases in the surplus delivered per miner. Sources of coal were more abundant, which made it difficult to bring coal production into a system of "monopolistic competition" such as frequently characterized the use of the ship. Many of the policies which were firmly rooted in English mining practice could not be transplanted to the American scene. Thus, technological advances could be initially installed here, whereas in the English mines they had to fight to supplant still usable, if less efficient, devices. Moreover, the competition of oil and natural gas became a threat which tended to reduce inefficiency in the coal mines of the United States. All these factors are reflected in the present high rates of production in mines in this country.

The average production of coal per miner in the United States is more than 7.3 tons a day. If put through a modern steam electric generating plant, this coal will yield about 19,500 horsepower-hours. Even if burned in an average locomotive, which is only $\frac{1}{5}$ as efficient, it will yield about 3,900 horsepower-hours. Of course this is not all surplus. Considerable energy is represented by the machines used in the mines, and such operations as cutting, loading, propping, etc., also use much energy. For example, in 1949 about 7 kilowatt-hours of energy were used in the mine for every ton of coal mined. Even so, coal mining in the United States is regarded as being technologically backward compared with other industries. Some advanced machines now in use deliver to the conveyors 100 tons per day, and electronically controlled mining machines are now in limited use which will eliminate the need of miners as such. New methods of using unmined coal, such as controlled burning, promise to give rise to competition between old and new sources of coal. The use of the gas turbine permits gas from controlled-burning mines to be converted into electricity at the mine mouth without the use of large quantities of water.

This will make it possible to use hitherto inaccessible or unused sources. Efficient mechanical shovels permit heavy overlay to be removed, exposing coal which would otherwise have to be mined by shaft and tunnel, thus yielding a smaller surplus. All things considered, the present rate of production in the United States is to be regarded as at a point rather far from the limits on surplus energy from coal which will eventually be reached.

BRITISH AND EUROPEAN RAILROAD USAGE

It will be recalled that in the early days of the steam engine the daily surplus of mechanical energy produced by one coal miner was about 25 horsepower-hours. It will also be recalled that the sailing ship was delivering more surplus than that in the form of transportation in the days of the Pharaohs in Egypt. The English ship was delivering about 250 horsepower-hours a day for each crewman when coal came into general use. So, even when only its fuel costs were involved, the locomotive could not directly compete as a form of transportation anywhere that competition between ship and rail was possible, as in coastwise traffic. Since its track and fixed structure represented added cost, the steam railroad was relatively inefficient in comparison with the ship. Thus, railroads were built primarily to supplement the functioning of the stream in bringing goods to the ship. They fanned out from port cities to serve trade. This pattern of use of the steam engine fitted in well with British thinking and practice. However, it was often not economical in the use of energy, for coal was sometimes transported from the mine to a distant coastal city, there to drive machines which could just as well have been located nearer the mines. This use of fuel to transport fuel was not of great import in the islands and peninsulas of Western Europe, where the coal in use was relatively near water. But it would have been extremely wasteful in the interior of the continents. Here British practices were not applicable.

During the period when it was happening, the British never completely understood how British coal had come to replace British wool and other organic products as a major source of the differential advantage they had over most other areas of the world. They measured their position in terms of price alone, and price indicated merely that Britain could continue to deliver goods in distant places at prices lower than the cost of producing them locally or lower than those of others offering to sell the same product. Thus, the shift from a cost differential based on organic converters to one based on coal and water power went almost unnoticed. Once the English were militarily and politically secure within the Empire, by which time they had lost the power to coerce many of their suppliers and buyers outside it, the shift to the doctrine of free trade was made. Now the insistence was that the market alone was an adequate guide, and that price should reign. Since British productivity was very high compared with that of most other places on earth, and since Britain was the source of most investment capital, the consequence was, where free trade was adopted, an enlargement of those industries in Britain which could benefit from the use of coal, and a diminution of agriculture and other industries in which coal could play no part. Therefore, the system built up around sail continued to increase British power throughout the nineteenth century, and it seemed neither necessary nor profitable for any group to raise the question whether the new uses to which Germany and the United States were putting their steam power might not turn out to be more effective in producing a viable social, economic, and political structure. "Economics" was largely based on British experience, and economics of this sort held that the American and German systems were "unsound" and bound "in the long run" to fail.

"Price" versus Productive Efficiency

During the nineteenth century the auxiliary steam engines on the sailing ships gradually became efficient enough to replace sail. The roundabout trade routes based upon the use of the wind came into competition with those that made increasingly effective use of steam to bring cargo to ports which could, with the aid of the railroad, tap resources previously unavailable. This altered the significance of various ports and trade routes. But fundamentally the British attitude that "trade" rather than physical productivity is the true test of efficiency for a society remained dominant.

As previously indicated, "low" price represents many things. Sometimes low price represents a geographic fact such as availability of sought-for natural resources. Sometimes it represents technological advantage. And sometimes it represents the ability of the trader to force necessitous men to cooperate in return for no more than subsistence pay. More productive men, located where there are more opportunities for employment, may refuse to cooperate for this low return. The mounting standard of living in the United States made many goods more costly to the foreign trader here than, for instance, in China, even though the physical productivity of the American worker made it possible for the goods to be produced more cheaply here. The American worker was able to claim part of his higher productivity in higher wages; accordingly, American prices were higher despite the fact that American physical costs were lower than the Chinese prices. Being guided by considerations of price, the British found themselves building up a system which, since it was incapable of differentiating between the reasons for differences in costs, sometimes made them dependent upon areas in which it would be profitable to trade only while a very low standard of living existed for the residents. They thus enlarged their investment in areas where they could trade only so long as no alternative to British rule existed for the native population. These areas were often politically less secure, militarily less defensible, and actually physically less productive than other areas, in which production might have taken place if all the consequences of the trading pattern had been examined. Some of the theory of foreign trade today is but a restatement of the axioms which lost Britain her dominant world position. The theory was, however, built into British culture and helped to mold British use of the steam engine.

The pattern of railway use developed by the British was followed with modifications elsewhere. That is, the railroad was thought of as being supplementary to sea- and river-born trade. Occasionally military policy dictated that a railroad be built with a strategic objective in mind, replacing either a river or an ocean as a primary means of transportation. Thus in the middle of the nineteenth century the Germans built a railroad to their own ports from their centers of production and, by favorable rates and tariffs, cut off a good deal of the German traffic which had sustained Antwerp, almost ruining that city as a port. The Austrian Sudbahn similarly diverted traffic from the foreign-held ports at the mouth of the Danube to Austrian-controlled Trieste on the Adriatic.

USE OF THE RAILROAD IN AMERICA

It was in the United States that steam had a chance to show the outlines of a pattern of civilization based on large surpluses from sources other than food and sail. The early coastal settlements and the plantation South, being part and parcel of the English system, developed few railroads, and such as there were served British trade. But with the westward movement a new kind of civilization began to emerge. The American "age of steel" was an outgrowth of the use of cheap transportation, furnished by steam, on the Great Lakes, the canals, and the Ohio River, plus the development of railroads. This transportation system permitted the products of the plains to be used to support an industrial population growing up around the coal of Pennsylvania and eastern Ohio. American cities grew in the interior, beyond the reach of the British cruiser and the control of London banks. The railroad subsequently provided the means by which the industrial North overcame the power of the agricultural South; Northern victory could not have been achieved without the use of steam. The railroad helped to populate the plains in spite of the resistance of the Indians, and it brought together minerals which never could have been assembled in the days of sailing ships and caravans. While the locations of some early American cities were determined by the same factors that produced the commercial cities of Europe in the days of sail, and the pattern which they exhibit today clearly shows that influence, cities like Columbus, Dayton, Indianapolis, and Iowa City were located during the development of steam power and in turn show its influence.

Many subsidiary settlements also show the effects of rail transportation. We have spoken of the division points that occur along all rail lines. Here trains must be stopped for service; here they are broken up when it is necessary to take cars out for repair. There are also points of interchange between railroads, where the trains are broken up and individual cars are rerouted. An industry located at one of these stations can be serviced by the railroad much more cheaply than one located at an intermediate point. This is especially true wtih regard to delivery of less-than-carload lots. Usually the railroads built a network of spur-line tracks beside which factories were located so that fuel and other heavy materials did not have to be transported by team-drawn wagons. Factories using less fuel and lighter materials moved into the next zone of sites away from the siding to minimize their own hauling costs, and residences were interspersed as near as possible to the factories in order to minimize the time and energy spent walking to work or the cost of horse-drawn passenger transportation. The retail and hotel district occupied a sector between the passenger station and the remoter residence districts, from which the more fortunate could come by carriage over boulevards or by horse-car.

Although its great weight in proportion to its power made the steam locomotive a very poor means of short-haul mass transportation as compared with the horsecar, a trainload of people could frequently be delivered 10 or 15 miles away from a central city at lower cost than they could travel by horse for 2 or 3 miles. The commuter type of "bedroom community" was a natural outgrowth of this fact. The influence of electricity and of the internal-combustion engine set in to modify this pattern before a complete adaptation to steam could be manifest.

Prototype of the High-energy Society

From this point on, the American rather than the British pattern must be taken as the prototype of high-energy society. The use of rail, as compared with sail or steamship, offered England few of the advantages it afforded in the United States. A social organization set up to exploit sail and trade could not be fully effective in making use of steam. Hence the new pattern has been most fully worked out in the United States, though areas in other parts of the world have also made some progress along the same line.

Steam power had numerous shortcomings. The greatest of these, as has been indicated was the ratio of the weight of the engine to its power. We have seen how this drawback operated in connection with the railroad. In addition to the problems created by inertia, great weight necessitated the use of a very expensive type of track, which, in turn, meant that the railroad could be used effectively only within or between areas of relatively great population density, since only by frequent use could the great costs of fixed structure be economically recovered. But the fact that its weight precluded frequent stopping made the steam train inefficient to serve the needs of a dense population for local transport of either materials or passengers. It was the weight factor, further, that prevented the use of steam in agriculture: the steam tractor was so heavy that it packed the soil, it bogged down in many fields which could be hoed or plowed. The steam tractor could not be used economically on the small diversified farms; these represented the most efficient use of land when tilled by men and horses. The handicaps of steam power could be overcome only by great advances in design and in metallurgy which would permit the use of very high temperatures and pressures without the drawback of great weight. Failing that, steam engines must be complemented by another converter with fewer disadvantages. Both of these developments have taken place, but not in a fixed order so that "stages" can be worked out to show how one gave rise to or replaced another. Moreover, they were accompanied by the use of new sources of surplus energy, which also had a place in determining what occurred.

PETROLEUM

Finding a substitute for steam required a source of energy other than raw coal. Like coal, petroleum was known and had occasional use long before it became a major source of power. An oil well was dug on the island of Sante in the Ionian Sea in the year 400 B.C.; oil from it was distilled to make fuel for lamps.[1] As early as A.D. 100 the Burmese were drilling for oil, and it was also mined at other sites scattered over the world. Petroleum came into wide use first in the United States as a source of light. The explosive distillates which make up gasoline were a nuisance by-product until the invention of the internal-combustion engine brought them into demand and made them a chief objective of the industry. Although natural gas has been known about as long as petroleum—the Chinese dug wells for it as deep as 3,000 feet a thousand years before the birth of Christ—its discovery today is for the most part incidental to exploration for oil.

The development, refining, and transportaion of gas are frequently associated with the production of oil, so that in attempting to calculate the surplus produced we must consider oil and gas together. Natural gas is used more widely in the United States than in any other country in the world; it is an important source of energy here, but it must be regarded as a somewhat short-lived bonanza rather than a base for long-continued development.[2]

In the case of petroleum and gas mining the calculation of the surplus energy derived is more difficult than in the case of coal. Coal companies usually sell the raw coal at the tipple, and in available statistics coal-mine employees are not usually grouped with coal refiners or processors. But since oil is generally sold by the oil companies in some stage of refinement, oil and gas employees are as likely to be engaged in processing or refining as in well drilling or pumping, and so, in reports, workers in all the processes are lumped together. Moreover, there is considerably greater outlay for exploration and discovery before workable sources of oil are located than is the case with coal, since coal reserves are already well explored. Drilling is expensive, and the holes that are drilled are more likely to turn out to be dry than productive. Then there is more cost entailed in processing oil than in putting coal into usable form for delivery to the consumer.

It is thus difficult to make an over-all calculation of the costs which should be included in making an accurate estimate of the surplus energy available from petroleum. To make an extremely rough comparison between this and other fuels, we have (1) divided the total energy produced by coal mines in the United States in 1950 by the number of workers listed by the U. S. Bureau of Labor Statistics as being employed in the coal mining industry for that year; (2) divided the total energy produced in the form of oil and gas by the number of employees so listed. The ratio of heat energy produced per man employed in gas and oil to that produced per coal miner in 1950 was roughly 4⅔ to 1. Put in another way: for every kilowatt-hour of heat produced by the coal miner in a day an oil or gas worker produced 4⅔ kilowatt-hours. The ratio is not changed much when we subtract the energy used in producing these products from the total produced. About 0.2 per cent of the heat energy of bituminous coal mined is consumed in mining operations, and about 0.1 per cent is consumed in the case of anthracite. On the other hand, 3.3 per cent of the oil and natural gas produced is used to mine oil and gas.[3] It is evident that the surplus energy produced by each worker in the petroleum industry in the United States today is much greater than that produced by the coal miner. Since the surplus of the coal miner is very large, and that of the oil and gas worker is even larger, it is clear that the energy costs of producing energy in the form of coal, gas, and oil in the United States have become so low that even cutting them in half would not seriously alter the surplus available.

Social Effects of Oil

At first glance it would appear inevitable that, with its much greater surplus, oil would replace coal—would act as a magnet drawing off population and industry from the old energy-producing areas. This has been to a degree the case, and certain specialized industries, such as those producing petrochemicals, have been built up in the regions where oil and gas are abundant. However, a number of factors mitigate against any wholesale reorientation of industry away from coal and toward petroleum and gas. The first is that the reserves of petroleum in any specific area are known to be relatively small as compared with the known reserves of coal in the major coal-producing areas of the world.[4] In a number of cases, oil fields have been pumped out and abandoned even before the short-lived structures built up to serve oil-well employees had outlived their usefulness. Much of the effort of the petroleum producers has been directed toward making it possible for oil fields to be exploited rapidly so as to reduce taxes and other overhead costs which are fairly independent of the volume of oil produced. This has, of course, been controlled in some areas by proration or other legal device. But there are some very large fields which are being exploited as rapidly as possible. Such instances would seem to indicate that oil is a short-term energy source when considered as a base on which to erect the structure of a civilization.

Second, and very important, while petroleum is at the moment a cheaper fuel (energywise) than coal, it cannot be used as efficiently as coal in smelting iron. While coke can be made from petroleum, it does not have the structure necessary for blast-furnace use; and, being a residue from the production of the distillates and lubricating oils, it is not produced in the quantities which would be necessary if it was to be used in smelting. Thus steel-producing centers will probably continue to be located on the basis of the energy costs of bringing coal and iron together and transporting their product to market.[5] Steel centers, in turn, give rise to a host of associated industries. Being located near steel mills is very advantageous for many industries, particularly those which produce large quantities of scrap, since this proximity reduces to a minimum the cost of transportation of the scrap.

In a sense the influence of oil regions in forming a basis for the growth of population and the relocation of industry is negated by the fact that oil can be so cheaply transported. This fact and the fact that oil is so widely used as a fuel for internal-combustion engines, which are widely used in automotive equipment, have resulted in a pattern of very scattered and widely dispersed use. Petroleum products are much more likely to be shipped far from their source than is coal.

To sum up, in consequence of these three factors—difficulty of substituting other fuels for coal in steelmaking, relatively small deposits of oil in any one region as compared with coal, and low cost of transportation of oil—petroleum is less likely to affect the distribution of population (that is, to cause the kind of relocation that resulted from the adoption of sail or coal) than the great surpluses it produces would at first seem to indicate.

It appears, then, that a relatively great but short-lived source of surplus energy contributes to the emergence of new techniques and alters some of the patterns developed by other converters but does not lead to a permanent shift in the location of power, speaking either spatially or in terms of the power position of a class or nation.

What we have said about oil is even more applicable to gas. At the moment it is so cheap and so easily transported that it is being used in large quantities at the very mouth of coal mines, But the reserves are likely to be exhausted much more quickly than those of coal. The lines which today carry natural gas from Texas through Ohio and Pennsylvania to New York and New England may, before many decades have passed, be delivering both to Texas and to the East the product of the gasification of Ohio and Pennsylvania coal.

The prospect of reducing the energy costs of producing coal is, as noted above, very favorable. Machines and processes have already been developed which can greatly increase the per capita output of coal in many mines. The present low cost of gas and oil tends to prevent their widespread adoption, but the increased wages in the coal mines and the growing loss of business to competing fuels are bringing closer the day when wholesale adoption of new techniques will be undertaken. Then the cost of mining coal should fall far below what it now is. On the other hand, in the major oil-producing areas there is no promise of a similar revolution in technique that will compensate for the growing costs of development and the increasing depth at which oil is to be found. Exploration and development have been greatest near industrial states, and new reserves are therefore likely to be found at increasing distances from heavily populated areas. This will add another cost element to the competition between fuels. There is thus no present prospect of decrease in the costs of securing oil to compensate for the probable increase in surplus from the mining and processing of coal. As a matter of fact, many of the advances in petroleum chemistry are capable of contributing greatly to the efficiency with which coal is used. For example, instead of depending upon distant sources for the hydrocarbons from which petrochemicals are now made, it is probable that states like England, France, and Germany, which are apparently deficient in petroleum, will seek and find a source of these materials in their coal. So the centripetal pull of the great coal beds of the world will probably continue to exert a major influence, and the character of fields generated by coal-burning converters—though somewhat distorted by the use of other fuels—will probably remain basic in the shaping of society for some time to come.

NUCLEAR FUEL

This statement may be challenged by the proponents of nuclear energy for peacetime use. The size of the surplus to be gained from nuclear fuel for such use is at the moment indeterminable. It seems probable that many times as much energy was expended in building the equipment and assembling and processing the materials necessary to produce the first atom bomb than has been made available from the fissionable materials out of which it was made. The present annual expenditure of power in refining ores containing fissionable elements is also enormous, and while it is true that a pound of uranium will under favorable circumstances yield the equivalent of 1,500 tons of coal, figures are not yet available to show that it does not require more energy to make the product of a pound of uranium available for peacetime use than it does to make available its energy equivalent in the form of coal, gas, or oil. In any event, as we have already indicated, the energy costs of producing energy from present fuels are now very low,.and a new low-cost source would be most significant in serving specialized purposes which the other more abundant and easily available sources of energy are less well able to serve. One study [6] making use of such figures as have been released for research purposes indicated that atomic power would be most likely to compete successfully in industries using large quantities of heat as such rather than in those using electricity or mechanical power. It might also serve areas requiring large amounts of power which lie far from coal, oil, gas, or hydro power and are poorly served by railroads or navigable waterways. The general conclusion of this study was, however, that it was likely to work no major revolution in areas now well supplied with other power sources. Moreover, since the original investment is large, research is costly, and production requires large numbers of trained technicians, instruments, and other adjuncts to high-energy societies, only already industrialized areas are at present equipped to make use of atomic power.

ELECTRICITY

Electricity is a form of energy in increasingly widespread use. In most cases however it is derived from the sources of energy already discussed. Very small amounts of electricity are secured from the use of batteries. It has been known for over a century that certain chemical reactions are accompanied by energy changes that can be measured by the same instruments that gauge electrical potential and current from static generators. These chemical changes would represent a significant new source of energy for man's direct use if they could be converted cheaply in great quantities. So far this has not seemed feasible; moreover, the potential of such conversion is apparently small as compared with the energy regularly coming from the sun or that to be found in such cheap sources as coal. The direct conversion of the energy of the sun into electrical current, in amounts and with characteristics that permit its cheap and ready use, is another alternative which has been the subject of speculation and research. It is possible that such a development will make even more efficient use of the sun than does photosynthesis by plants. In fact there is some evidence that silicon-strip batteries may be practical to replace conventional ones for use in places difficult to get to, for example, in airplane beacons located on high mountain tops. But for the present at least, the overwhelming proportion of usable electricity is created by a generator attached to a source of mechanical energy. This energy may be derived from any of the fuels or any of the converters of mechanical energy which we have mentioned. Electricity usually represents not a new source of mechanical power but mechanical power converted into another form.

CHARACTERISTICS OF ELECTRICITY

The mechanical power delivered by a motor never equals the mechanical power that went into the generator supplying the current to drive it. Since conversion thus involves some loss, the use of electricity reduces, rather than increases, available mechanical energy. Why then make the conversion into electricity? The answer is to be found in the characteristics of electricity. In the first place, it can be divided or combined with little loss. Also, it can be converted into heat, light, and sound, into X ray, infrared, ultraviolet, radio, radar, and television, and waves of various other frequencies and amplitudes, and into mechanical power. This is a convenience where many forms of energy conversion are likely to be used at the same site. Furthermore, it can be transported easily, quickly, silently, and comparatively cheaply. The gradient in the field is extremely gentle and the limits of the field are very wide as contrasted with mechanical transmission. Therefore, while the conversion from mechanical to electrical form actually lessens the surplus available, the energy losses are in most cases more than offset by other gains. The chief exception is in the use of electricity for space heating; for this use the advantages of electric heating over heating by gas or oil are not sufficient to offset the loss in conversion from heat through mechanical energy to electricity and back again into heat.

It is difficult to discover exactly what portion of the mechanical energy which would otherwise be available is lost through conversion into electricity. The steam engines which are used to drive generators were developed for just that purpose. They might have altogether different characteristics, and perhaps be much less efficient, if they had been designed for use with mechanical transmission rather than for being attached to generators. For example, the best of the reciprocating steam locomotives never delivered in the form of tractive effort at the draw-bar as much as 10 per cent of the heat energy that was contained in the coal placed in the firebox. On the other hand, the average efficiency of the steam electric plants in the United States in 1950 was about 16.3 per cent, and the most efficient delivered better than 20 per cent.[7] In the case of the steam engine the characteristics developed for conversion of its energy into electricity, by increasing the surplus to be derived over that obtainable from engines not using electrical transmission, actually offset to some degree the losses incurred in conversion.

Electrification of Transport

Electrification of railroads was in fact embarked upon to take advantage of the facts of which we have just spoken. Making the boilers and the steam engine stationary and paring down the driving mechanism carried on the tracks to a simple motor greatly reduced the weight-to-power ratio which handicapped the steam locomotive, and made it possible to exploit the efficiency of the turbine. This permitted lighter equipment and lighter track, and the accompanying decrease in inertia made frequent stops less costly. By the use of electricity the steam engine could be made large enough to be efficient, and the power it produced could be distributed among a number of motors. In place of one long train a number of shorter ones could be run, with no accompanying decrease in efficiency of the steam engine in use.

The trolley car, which similarly made use of electricity, replaced the horsecar and filled in some of the interstices left between the infrequent stops required by the use of the steam train. The development of the interurban train (heavier than the trolley but much lighter than the steam train) to serve outlying regions permitted the specialization of services which none of the small areas served could support alone. However, this kind of transportation was feasible only for passenger traffic, which, since passengers can in most cases get on and off by themselves, operates with short stops. To handle any considerable amount of freight, stops must be made longer, and this interferes with the frequency of service demanded of passenger vehicles. In addition, carrying any considerable amount of freight necessitates an increase in the size of the crew. The streetcar was specialized primarily to carry passengers, but some of the streetcar tracks were used in early morning hours to deliver small amounts of freight, particularly the supplies needed to operate the street railway.

Peculiarly enough, a situation thus arose in which it was possible to handle the transportation of humans more cheaply than that of materials. The consequences were that while it was still necessary for the factory to be near rail facilities, where the cost of team haulage could be kept at a minimum or dispensed with, workers could move away from the areas around the factories and avoid such penalties of congestion as overcrowding, insufficient light and contaminated air, lack of play space, etc. Residence areas began to extend outward along the trolley and interurban lines. The trolley car could be stopped at very short intervals, so that walking from a stop to any point between stops became a trifling matter. Compact rows of residences formed a continuous line along the rails and back from them for short distances. Either by running parallel lines in a checkerboard fashion or by zigzagging along diagonals drawn outward from the retail centers, it was possible to fill in cheaply all the space between the periphery and the center of the city. Interurban trains produced a distribution of population which exhibited a pattern like a number of strings of beads radiating from a central point, the rails serving as the thread and the communities centered around the suburban railway station being the "beads." This is a pattern still discernible around cities like Indianapolis whose growth was largely based on steam.

The use of electricity for other purposes than transportation developed a little more slowly. The structure of the city, as well as traditional business practices and architectural design, were based on the pattern in which congestion due to the use of the old type of converters had been capitalized upon.

The electric generators in use at first did not offer any great incentive for the adoption of another pattern. Electricity is commonly produced by revolving a specially wound coil of wire in a magnetic field, or the reverse. The electricity generated by the spinning armature has to be delivered to a fixed conductor through which it can be delivered to the user. Some device for efficiently transferring current from a rotating to a fixed point is necessary, and a system of commutators and brushes at the generator accomplishes this purpose. Now, if voltages are very high, the resistance at the point where the commutators and the brushes are in contact will create arcs which waste current and are also likely to destroy the commutator. Thus current must be initially produced at relatively low voltages. But the cost of transmission is much higher at low voltages than at high voltages. The first generators produced low-voltage direct current, which cannot easily be transformed into high voltages. This is not particularly significant if the current is to be delivered over a short distance, but, since the weight of the conductor varies directly as the square of the distance current is transmitted, it becomes immensely significant if any great distance is involved. Consequently, as current is conducted away from the generator the energy costs of building lines, and the losses suffered through conduction, eat into the surpluses until it becomes cheaper to build another generating plant at some point nearer to that at which the current is to be used than to transmit the power to that point.

Generators, other than those used for trolley and interurban lines, were first used to supply illumination. The quantity of current used for this purpose by any one customer was small. Hence, in order to recover transmission costs, the number of customers in the area of service had to be high, even to use a small plant. Frequently a user of power such as a factory, hotel, or hospital could buy or make all its current from one of these small plants more cheaply than it could buy current from a central station. Therefore, while the gradient in the field of the direct-current low-voltage generator was much less steep than that of mechanical transmission, it was still too steep to permit a power plant to serve any large area efficiently. Thus no great demand for power could be concentrated at any one point. The direct-current generator, which limited the demand on the steam engine, kept it small and thus, since the efficiency of the steam engine increases with its size, often constricted its efficiency far more than did the actual limitations inherent in the then known materials and designs.

The introduction of the alternating-current generator changed this situation and made the generation of electricity much more effective.

High-voltage Transmission

Alternating current can be transformed from low to very high voltages, and vice versa, without much energy loss. Hence it is possible to generate current at a low voltage, "step it up" to a high voltage for transmission, and "step it down" at the point needed. The reason this is desirable is that the required weight of the conductor varies *inversely* as the square of the voltage. Consequently, with high voltage, current can be conducted on a small line which would be burned up if the same amount of power was put through it at a lower voltage. The problems of handling and transmitting high-voltage current were solved in quick succession. As a result there has been a rather rapid increase in the voltage at which current is transmitted. At present the maximum is around 330,000 volts. The entire power surplus of Hoover Dam, for example, is conducted to Los Angeles by cables not much thicker than a man's thumb. While such very high voltages were not immediately obtainable, even the first alternating-current stations could be built much larger than their forebears. The limit on the size of the steam turbines used to generate current was lifted, and engineers began to investigate the possibilities of new designs, new materials, and new methods to take advantage of large size, higher steam temperatures, and higher pressures. The result was a rapid decrease in the slope of the gradient in the field, with a great consequent widening of the limits to the area served by a plant.

Thus as the length of the line which could efficiently carry a given amount of power increased, the area to be served by one generator increased even more rapidly. This is of course due to the fact that lines can be strung in all directions from the power plant, the potential field being a circle, which increases in area as the square of the radius. There was a corresponding increase in the ability to serve less congested areas, or to reduce the advantages to be gained by congestion. It is now a matter of relative indifference in terms of energy costs whether a motor is located 50 yards from a boiler or 5 miles. The difference in cost of lighting for two houses, both on a high-tension line and, respectively, 1 and 3 miles from the generator, is frequently not as great as the difference in cost for two houses 500 yards apart but connected by low-voltage current. Differences in power costs between plants nearer to and farther from power stations were greatly reduced, and in many cases the costs of transmitting power to a new plant at some distance from the power station were less than the costs arising from congestion in the old location.

It is still true that the cost of generating current and delivering it at a great distance is higher than the cost of delivering a comparable quantity of energy in the form of oil and gas by pipeline or of oil and coal by rail or barge. A point is reached at which it is cheaper to locate additional steam-electric plants where they will have to be connected to their fuel sources by rail, pipeline, or barge than it is to generate more current from a central station and deliver it. Within the radius so determined the exact location of large consumers of power is frequently in energy terms a matter almost of indifference. In the case of small users, however, the cost of stringing and servicing lines represents a rather large part of the continuing cost of delivering current, and such users are most economically located near the lines connecting the generating plants with each other or with large users of power.

Connecting several power plants in a grid makes it possible to deliver power equally cheaply to consumers of equal amounts of energy in areas of equally great demand. Just as the streetcar, by charging a fixed fare in an entire zone, made it almost a matter of indifference whether one rode 5 blocks or 15, and hence tended to equalize residence rentals within each fare zone, so the effect of the grid has been to make differences in energy costs negligible within large areas and thus to equalize the land charges related to power costs within these areas. The areas of equalized costs produce a pattern altogether different from those previously existing, and their effect has only recently begun to be felt. But they have not affected costs related to the handling of freight other than fuel, so long as that freight has had to be brought by team from rail terminals. This pointed to a redistribution of industry: industries using light materials might be transferred away from those congested sites where industries handling heavy masses had to be located. Selective migration of industry occurred as the light industries moved to sites which were less congested, nearer their markets, or nearer the residences of their labor forces.

HYDROELECTRIC POWER

The effect of the invention of the alternating-current generator on the use of water power was analogous to its effect on the use of the steam engine. As we have pointed out, power generated by water suffered from exactly the same limitations as characterized the use of other devices based upon mechanical transmission. But in addition it suffered from the fact that the areas in which there is sufficient fall to make it possible to handle the volume of water necessary to generate much current are the very areas which are unable to support a dense population based on agriculture or trade. Consequently, the introduction of a means of cheaply transmitting water-generated electric power a great distance frequently made the energy of rivers available at points where the river would otherwise have had no economic value. The modern hydroelectric turbine has exceeded 90 per cent efficiency in converting the potential energy of the water at the top of the dam into electricity. Since the energy of falling water is cost-free, hydroelectric power delivers great surpluses. However, the surplus can often be secured only by building very expensive dams, flumes, penstocks, and other works in addition to turbines and generators. The life of these works is limited by the fact that areas in which there is rapid fall of water are also likely to be areas of great erosion; the filling up of the dams with silt makes them useless for water-storage purposes. Hence investment in them has to be quickly amortized. When these costs are added, the hydroelectric plant is sometimes no more efficient in delivering surplus than the steam electric plant. For example, the Huntley plant at Buffalo produces power more cheaply by steam than Niagara Falls does by hydroelectricity. Thus hydroelectricity can be considered one more source of surplus, an alternative to the power from coal, oil, or gas, with the same general implications. In special circumstances it may pay to take materials for processing to the hydro plant, rather than to deliver the power to areas more convenient for other purposes. The building of aluminum plants in Alaska is an example. For one region hydro power may be by far the best source of surplus, for another it may be a very poor source.

Electricity helped to remove some of the limitations of the steam engine. It made power delivered to fixed sites relatively cheap. It changed the potential of the railroad, modifying the limits imposed by the nature of steam locomotives. But the means of power it provided, though mobile, was fixed either to a railroad track or to a central power plant through the medium of transmis sion lines.

Steam and electricity hardly changed the character of most of the problems of the food raiser, though they did permit the creation of agricultural specialists by providing a cheap means of transportation of the product. Most of the early increase in production per man in United States agriculture resulted from the use of the horse. With land abundant and population limited, horses, which could deliver energy at a very high rate in the short planting or harvesting seasons, came into their most effective use. But compared to the potential which might be secured by utilizing coal or oil as fuel they were extremely inefficient. Thus, experiments directed toward producing a replacement for the horse, both in the fields and in the cities, were stimulated by the prospect of very high returns.

THE INTERNAL COMBUSTION ENGINE

Such a replacement must be efficient in fairly small sizes, weigh relatively little per unit of power produced, and be flexible. What was called for was the invention of an engine that would change the nature of the application of heat. As we have seen, the problem of the steam engineer was to preserve the heat generated in the form of steam in every way possible. But the internal-combustion engine generates heat within the cylinder in which motion is produced by the explosion which drives the piston. Unless the temperature of the heat generated is immediately reduced, the next charge of gas entering the cylinder will be prematurely exploded. Consequently, the larger the area available to dissipate the heat in proportion to the volume of gas to be exploded, the higher the initial temperature of that explosion can be. The engineers accomplished this increase in area-to-volume ratio by decreasing the size of the cylinders. To get more power they multiplied the number of cylinders. The problem now became one of getting rid of the heat being conducted through the cylinder walls. In a large internal-combustion engine much of the energy produced is spent cooling the engine; a small engine, which can directly radiate heat to the atmosphere, does not suffer from this disadvantage. In a small engine, then, a greater proportion of the energy released by the explosion can be used to create mechanical energy than in a larger one. The small internal-combustion engine satisfies many of the needs for mobile power which the steam engine was unable to fulfill. Moreover, the internal-combustion engine burns gasoline, which pound for pound is about 1½ times as powerful as coal. Since gasoline is burned in a more efficient engine, the margin of its superiority to coal as a source of energy becomes even greater. For the same reason the amount of fuel carried can be reduced. Water is used only for cooling, if at all, and much smaller amounts of water need be carried than with steam.

The Diesel

As the gasoline engine was being developed, engineers were also experimenting in an effort to produce an engine which would burn powdered coal, and the first diesels were designed with this in view. In diesels, fuel is injected into the cylinder at the top of the piston's stroke. The fuel is there ignited by the compression-heated air and the heat remaining from previous explosions. Since the fuel is not injected until the moment of explosion, the diesel can be operated at much higher temperatures than the spark-ignited engine. This makes it a more efficient converter.

The ash produced by burning coal quickly ground away the metal of the cylinders and pistons of the early diesel. As a result, coal-burning diesels were not perfected. However, the fractions of petroleum left after gasoline had been distilled off provided a cheap fuel without ash. Since these oils were by-products of gasoline, they could be sold cheaply. Further, in many countries fuel used on the highways is in a different tax category from other fuels, and diesel fuel, being untaxed, was cheaper to use than gasoline. The combined effect of high efficiency and low-cost fuel led to the introduction of the diesel where great weight, necessitated by the high temperature and pressures at which it works, was not a handicap. In the locomotive, for example, a certain amount of weight is necessary to give the engine traction with which to start the train and to increase the friction between wheels and rail when the brakes are applied to stop it. The diesel operates at rates up to about 35 per cent efficiency; this rate is higher than that of any but the most modern steam plants and is far in excess of the 7 per cent efficiency characteristic of the best reciprocating steam locomotives. The average efficiency of the diesels in use on American railroads in 1950 was about 23 per cent,[8] while that of the average steam locomotive was about 4 per cent. The diesel has taken over many of the jobs previously performed by electricity, steam, and spark-ignition engines.

Recently the effort to make direct use of coal in a prime mover has been revived. Through the use of an ash collector placed between the point of combustion and the point of application, the burning gases can be delivered free of abrasives to a turbine blade. The present experimental gas-fired turbine offers an efficiency of about 25 per cent, lower than that of diesels fired with petroleum products but higher than that of diesels fired with oil derived from coal. In coal-producing regions the gas turbine seems to offer another means to avoid many of the inefficiencies and drawbacks of the coal-burning steam locomotive.

Social Effects

With the diesel and the spark-ignition engine, small mobile power units can be used to bring power to places far removed from fixed power sources. They can be taken into field and forest, into mines, and on board small boats. The advantages once gained from concentration of power users are thus greatly reduced. Moreover, the energy costs of the congestion that arises from using automobiles and trucks in the cities built around streams, railroads, and trolley cars mount much more rapidly than any energy gains that might come from so using automotive units there. With a network of roads and highways and a grid of power lines, industry can be taken away from centers of congestion. It is now much cheaper to bring power and materials to residence areas, or to empty spaces in which such residence areas with their associated services can be built up, than to redesign and rebuild the central city in order to make it an efficient means to use modern converters. The story of the movement from the central city is well documented.[9] The pattern that emerges shows the influence of the automobile, the pipeline, and the power grid in modifying the size and the shape of the zones of equalized cost which radiate from highways, railroads, rivers, and harbors, and in distributing population, industry, and trade within them. Again the influence of fixed physical structures and, perhaps even more powerful, that of social structure, which gives certain groups far more weight than others in determining the location and nature of trade and industry, has the effect of distorting or delaying the appearance of a system designed to take full advantage of the new sources and new converters. But where new cities are growing up and new industries are choosing sites, the pattern is more clear and the influence of the new sources of energy is apparent.

Just as the social and economic structure reflecting the efficient use of sail proved to be a poor environment for the exploitation of steam, so that produced by steam and its forerunners is demonstrated to be poorly adapted for the exploitation of the power grid, diesel, automobile, tractor, and truck. The manner in which all these new energy sources have affected and are likely to affect the shape of things to come will be our concern in the rest of this book.

CHAPTER 6

The Historical Circumstances

A number of explanations of social change which have been formulated put the greatest if not the exclusive emphasis upon the material conditions of life. Others regard ideas as being all-important and things and events as merely the manifestation of ideas. We do not consider either the full fruition of an idea or the complete dominance of a material condition to be inevitable. Patterns of interaction between the configurations that follow one another in time reveal both continuity and change. Which elements will persist and which will be modified at any particular place in a particular period depends upon the specific patterns that exist there and on the elements that are simultaneously or consecutively introduced into the situation. The problems that confront the investigator who attempts to predict social change are very great, and no attempt will be made here to provide a general explanation of all such change. Yet it is possible to show something of how given patterns are likely to respond to the introduction of certain new elements, and this we hope here to do.

THE ASSUMPTION THAT PROGRESS IS INEVITABLE

To a great many people in the West it matters not what the existing situation elsewhere may be, for eventually, they presume, the superiority of Western culture will become manifest and be accepted all over the world. For some of them the adoption of such ideas as are represented by free enterprise, Christianity, and democracy will necessarily produce all the conditions which today characterize the West. For others the acceptance of Western science, technology, and "know-how" is presumed to provide the key. The fact that, in addition to all these factors, certain peculiar geographic and demographic conditions surrounded the transition which took place here is not regarded as imposing a serious objection to the proposition that certain elements of Western civilization, particularly of the industrialized part of it, provide a model for the future development of the rest of the world.

The particular institutional development that took place in the United States at least made possible, if it was not positively required for, the emergence of high-energy technology. This does not prove that in another area, given other geographic, demographic, and cultural conditions, these institutional arrangements will provide the necessary conditions for the transition. American ideas, institutions, and values undoubtedly permitted high-energy technology to emerge here, and probably enhanced the likelihood that it would, but there is no certainty that it would have happened had the American continent been as densely peopled as was, say, India when the Western invasion took place. Thus the proposition that by adopting American ideology and technology any people can assure their industrial future is tenable only if it can be proved that not all the factors that operated here are necessary to the emergence of high-energy technology.

An examination of the facts surrounding a specific transition from a low- to a high-energy system may enable us to discover which of the accompanying conditions were essential factors, required wherever the transition is made, and which were incidental to the setting in which this particular transition was made. If all the conditions which existed in the United States, for example, must be reproduced where high-energy technology is to be developed, then it is obvious that many places cannot develop it, for many of the factors surrounding our transition to high-energy technology were such that they can never be reproduced. On the other hand, it may appear after careful analysis that, given the conditions that prevail in many low-energy societies today, the transition can only be made if measures are adopted and social structures utilized altogether different from those which were successful in the United States, Great Britain, or Germany.

The Role of Choice in History

We need, then, to be very careful in analyzing what has happened in the areas which have already advanced along the continuum from low to high energy, to distinguish between events made necessary by the social system used, those made necessary by the technology used, and those made necessary by geographic and demographic facts. There have been, as we have seen, numerous instances in the past when a society equipped with some of the means necessary for progress toward high-energy technology began the transition only to be pulled back by the limiting effect of the absence of one or more of the other necessary conditions. While those who believe in the inevitability of progress will not be deterred from claiming that these abortive attempts do nothing to weaken their thesis, we take the position that the evidence can as well be used to deny as to support the inevitability of transition from low- to high-energy society.

Here we assume that both material phenomena and human choice are involved in any social situation. Unless human choice matters in determining what will happen, the ability to weigh the consequences of past events will in no way affect the course of future events, and no scientific effort is justified. Assuming, then, that human choice matters in determining what is to be, such choice must itself become to a degree predictable if scientific investigation is to have any meaning or worth other than the aesthetic values it provides. If the vagaries of choice are such that the antecedents of choice remain unknown, science can no more affect the future than mythology can.

It is necessary, then, to postulate that the general tendency of men making choices is to act with sufficient rationality to assure that the orders of choices that they make from time to time do not completely contradict one another.[1] In fact it can be shown that a fairly consistent ordering of choices does take place in every known society. Through the use of scientific means it is possible to predict such ordering with much greater accuracy, for example, than it can be predicted by deductions from propositions about human nature in general. It is also possible to anticipate to some degree the way in which changes in the orderings of choices will take place when given changes are introduced among a people who share a given set of values.

Granting that, as a result of the conditions imposed on the developing personality, a given ordering of choices does commonly take place in a society, so that this is regularly chosen before that and after something else, it is also true that only rarely is an individual, let alone a large aggregation, encountered who is able to satisfy in action all his desires. In the world of fantasy a man's every wish can be fulfilled, but in the real world only those wishes can be achieved which the wisher has the power to achieve. Limits on his power force him to choose which of his values shall lie below the level of choice for action and which shall actually be realized. Of the limited possible courses of action, those are chosen which can be attained with least sacrifice of other values. The cost of anything, then, can be said to be equal to the values otherwise attainable which must be sacrificed to secure it.[2] Thus all kinds of values, material and nonmaterial, economic, aesthetic, political, moral, and religious, must be placed by the individual in a hierarchy which has some persistence in time. That a value holds a place in the hierarchy is revealed by the decision to pursue it rather than to retain or to attempt to secure alternative values. The hierarchies of individuals may differ widely yet reveal a consistency reflecting common experience. This derives from the fact that the values considered to be very significant in any culture are carefully taught to all individuals. The pattern of a social structure is, then, at once a cause and a result of human choice.

The Role of Energy Costs in History

The great significance of a change in the cost of energy arises from the fact that energy is a part of the cost of achieving all values. It takes energy even to dream. Now, as we have seen, the values that must be sacrificed to secure a given amount of energy may be enormously greater if one source of fuel or one converter rather than another is used. Shifts in energy source are, however, of varying significance, for the cost of obtaining the necessary energy may represent a large part of the cost of one good and only a small part of the cost of another. Thus when there are changes in energy costs, the costs of achieving various ends change, not equally for all, but differently. There is then a new sorting out and ordering of values by individuals and groups which is quite uncharacteristic of situations where costs have varied only slightly over a long time and can be considered to be "fixed." In such situations "normal" values represent a statistical distribution around these fixed costs. However, when costs begin to vary greatly, the "norm" in this sense is lost. It is a necessary consequence of our premises that when those sharing common values are confronted with similar changes in the costs of securing those values there will be a similar change and a new normal order of choice. Thus the expectancies of repeated choice which we call social structure will undergo change, and the new norms will be derived from experience with changed costs. When, or whether, stability sufficient to permit the rise of norms with anything like the high predictive value of those in the old system will appear is currently a matter for speculation. But in fact new expectancies with a fairly high degree of predictive value do appear, and it will be our business to examine these.

What must not be forgotten is that since the more significant values of all men are not the same, we can predict the outcome of introducing specific changes in the energy available to men in different places and at different times only if we know the patterns of choice that existed before the changes took place.

Assuming that men contemplating change are interested in securing that change at the least cost of other values, some of the factors affecting the choice between changing and not changing will arise from the resistance of those who do not share the anticipations of those proposing change. Not all changes reward all men equally, nor do all require the same sacrifice of all men. The degree of resistance to be encountered will have to be foreseen if one is to anticipate what the consequences of change will be. If the costs of such resistance are large, they may either putatively or actually exceed the gains to be secured by change. Other alternatives, involving other costs, may then be contemplated. Thus, when an invention is made which promises a decrease in the energy costs involved in securing a particular end, it frequently turns out that its use for this particular end is resisted and other, unforeseen uses become the medium through which the new technique is introduced into the culture. An example is the submarine: designed for commerce, it became a war vessel. There may also be a number of individuals and groups seeking to utilize the new means in different ways and/or to secure different ends. Then there is frequently a random or experimental movement which, failing to find a successful outlet, is aborted. So the Greeks abandoned the use of the steam engine (which was known to them).

At other times energy made available by a new invention is channeled into a force great enough to displace custom-sanctioned means. So, for example, the automobile replaced the horse.

The early gains from an invention or new application of energy may be largely dissipated in overcoming the factors that arise in reaction to its appearance. If the rate of gain in energy is lower than the rate of increase in energy costs stemming from this reaction, there will be regression toward the previous point of stability. Frequently in the clashes between men seeking to promote and those seeking to avoid change there is destruction of converters, of effective organization, and of other factors governing the size of the flow of energy so great that regression passes beyond the previous point of stability and there is likely to be a return to the simpler and more stable sun-plant-man system. But if the peak of reaction is safely reached and passed, new channels are created and new patterns of choice arise. A society grows, then, by a tentative process. An existing system directs the flow of energy to the performance of particular function. As the existing structure succeeds in performing function, part of the flow of energy is fed back to reinforce the structure through which it is converted. However, if more energy is required to operate a structure than can be returned from the function performed by it, the structure becomes less capable of directing further flow. An elaborate organization which was able to direct the flow of energy when one set of converters was used may prove quite incapable of channeling the flow from others. So new structures must emerge or the flow of energy will diminish.

Interdependence of Choice and Energy Costs

On the other hand, if a social structure is successful in functioning under changed conditions it also gives direction to the new flow of energy, with more or less permanent effects. A slight initial push early in the development of a social structure that subsequently succeeds in converting a large amount of energy gives direction to that much greater force, which in turn continues to magnify the effects of the initial influence. Thus, even though the initial direction was a result of the choice of an alternative no more capable potentially than many others of efficiently serving the converter in question, the nature of the uses to which surplus energy was put by reason of the social structure within which it was introduced may continue to govern that use simply because it *was* the early choice.

We can today, thanks to the work of physical scientists and technicians, discover the energy gains and the energy costs of introducing particular converters in so far as the physical aspects are concerned. We cannot, however, set up any general theory which at once takes into account these costs and the other costs that were involved when the transition was made. For present judgments are made in terms of current costs, whereas judgments made in the past had to be based upon costs in the past.

There are many points at which a different choice might have "changed the course of history." It is interesting to speculate about how the world would look today if the Greeks had been able to extend the use of the steam engine, if the Romans had developed techniques of navigation permitting them to expand into the oceanic world, if Napoleon had used the surplus of France for conquering the Ruhr and building a network of railways instead of sending his legions to Russia and to Egypt, if the Germans had earlier appreciated the possibilities of land-based power and had not attempted to rival England's control of the sea, if the Japanese seafarers had, in the early seventeenth century, been able to overcome the power of Japan's feudal lords and expand trade. But any scientific hypothesis must be tested by the examination of empirical evidence, and we have no such evidence, no historical facts, to examine. So the hypothesis must remain in the realm of speculation. It *was* England that first made the transition to a high-energy system, it was English coal and English waterfalls that provided the surplus, it was English economic and political power that overcame the resistance of hundreds of little low-energy societies. Until very recently it was English institutions, explained by English political and economic theory, that came to dominate all those areas of the world outside Europe where the use of high-energy converters reached any spectacular level. We know that these techniques and institutions and ideas, combined with the geographic and demographic situation that then existed, did lead to the transition. We can presume that they would again produce similar results under similar circumstances. But we also know that neither ideas nor techniques nor demographic factors nor geographic factors are now what they were then. The course of history has been given direction, but while its present direction is a consequent of what then was, it is also a configuration that *now is*, and it is in *this* form that it will affect the future. Only with these things in mind can we profitably examine the past to understand the future. We shall look, then, at the evidence to see if we can discern some general but definite prerequisites for the transition.

One of the propositions on which the theory of the inevitability of technological progress rests is the idea that practically all the gains made by substituting high-energy converters for organic ones can be used to accumulate more such converters, capable of converting more energy, to be diverted into still more converters. This series is represented in capitalist economics by compound interest. In the light of what we have just said it is clear that only that portion of the surplus energy secured can be diverted to increase the number of converters which is not required to overcome the costs arising out of the changes necessary to secure the increase. If these costs mount faster than surplus, regression is more likely than progress. Analysis of past transitions may show some of the conditions under which it has been possible to make surplus available in quantities sufficient to meet these costs and still to provide for more new converters.

THE POPULATION FACTOR

The crucial area for analysis centers in the relationships between food raisers and other members of society. Arrangements must continue to be such that food for all will be produced, even for those who produce no food. The *minimum* requirement for energy in the form of *food* is a function of the *size of the population*. This must be met before the need for any other form of energy can be met. In a sense this statement is tautological: obviously those with power enough *can* deny access to food, or the means to produce food, to those weaker than they, but the inevitable consequence of the denial is a reduction in population to the point where the minimum requirements for food *are* met.

This necessity to supply the population with food greatly affects the way in which, as well as the probability that, the transition to high-energy society will be made. The continuous and frequently increasing demand for food may require that practices be adopted quite other than those which could be adopted if there were a choice between increasing the supply of food and increasing the supply of other fuel.

Western history shows that a large food-raising population *can* be made to switch to the use of high-energy converters if an economic and political system can be set up which brings this population into effective control over the products of a large area of sparsely settled arable land. Germany, France, and England and their near neighbors adopted high-energy converters while receiving large supplies of food from Eastern Europe, the Americas, Australia, and New Zealand to supplement that produced at home. These areas were occupied in pre-Columbian times by people with an agricultural technique which left vast areas uninhabited and populated the inhabited regions only thinly. Russia is making and has made use of Siberia and other sparsely settled land in the U.S.S.R. Japan started her revolution with a population limited by feudalism; through Western trading practices she gained access to food from the surplus-producing regions of the Americas and Asia, and by conquest she gained control over thinly populated areas in Manchuria and Oceania. Even so, the growth of population outstripped Japan's increased capacity to find people willing and able to supply food to her people. Since there are no longer available the empty continents of pre-Columbian days, the method of expansion and conquest can no longer be considered to be a method of transition to high-energy society. Alternatively then, if such a transition is to be made, some other means of creating the necessary relations between food raisers and operators and manufacturers of high-energy converters must be found.

One thing we must know, however, is the relative productivity of the systems. For a number of reasons it is difficult to discover exactly how the productivity of food raisers was and is being affected by high-energy technology, even in areas in which such technology has had widespread effects. Two of these reasons are outstanding. In the first place, other changes in farm practices, not directly related to the use of high-energy converters, have had much to do with changes in that productivity. While such practices of scientific agriculture as rotation, fertilization, insect control, and the application of plant and animal genetics may originally have depended upon the appearance somewhere of a high-energy society, many of the practices can be adopted on farms without the simultaneous use of increased power. When these practices are introduced together with power agriculture, it is difficult to discover how much of the gain in productivity can be assigned to each factor and what conditions are necessary to produce each type of gain. Equally hindering to the researcher is the fact that the overwhelming bulk of published data is in terms of monetary units. This is legitimate, since the immediate decisions affecting production are preponderantly made in terms of some common denominator of values, and money measures a great many of these factors. But for the longer run, where energy probably is more significant than for the short run, monetary terms are not so satisfactory as measures in terms of energy itself. The best that can be done here is to attempt to overcome this very real handicap by making use of such data as are available in appropriate terms.

However reported, the fact is that the ratio of population to possible food production is a highly significant fact for consideration in explaining the transition from low- to high-energy society. A limit to the *maximum* population in an integrated area such as that occupied by a nation, is set by the total of the food it is possible to make available in that area, divided by the average level of food consumption to which the population can adapt. The *minimum* number of food raisers needed to secure that amount of food is set by the "peak load" which is required in the bottleneck operations connected with planting, cultivating, and harvesting the crop. It is possible by the use of migratory labor to make the population available during particular times greater than that which is continuously resident and continuously employed in farming. Alternatively, it is possible to find in the food-growing area regular employment from which workers will be excused during the busiest periods. Both these alternatives require a kind of social mobility difficult, for reasons we shall discuss later, to maintain, but since they are possibilities they should be kept in mind throughout the subsequent discussion.

In American Agriculture

Peak-load operations may come, as in the cultivation of wet rice (particularly in two-crop country, where the harvest of the wheat and the planting of the rice crowd each other), at planting time. In some cases, as in fruit and vegetable raising, the peak load may come at harvest time. In the temperate zone, where the growing season is limited, the greatest demand for labor for a great many field crops is likely to come in connection with the preparation of the seedbed. Certainly this is the case in the farm areas of North America, where land is abundant. Here the horse, which could increase the area of seedbed that could be prepared in the time available, more than earned his keep. The use of the horse made possible a net increase in the *total* food produced per capita of farm population and also an increase in the *surplus energy* produced per capita. With the advent of the iron plow, capable, when drawn by a team of horses or oxen, of ripping open the thick turf which had defied the efforts of the food-raising Indians to cultivate the land it covered, the great fertile plans of the Mississippi Valley became available as a new food source for the world. The use of the horse relieved the bottleneck at plowing time. But if plowing could now be done by horses, harvesting was still a hand operation. The scythe and cradle proved to be inadequate to the task so put on them; it was the horse-drawn reaper that gave the answer to the problem of getting the standing grain off the land before it should shatter and lose grain from the heads or the straw should collapse and make harvesting so time-consuming as to cause great losses.

Now the bottleneck appeared in connection with separating the chaff and straw from the grain. The old method of storing the sheaves, to be threshed out by the flail or trodden by livestock and winnowed by the breeze, would not suffice to handle the product of the binder. Two approaches to this problem were made. The first was the use of the steam engine to drive a stationary threshing machine; the second was the horse-drawn combined reaper and thresher. Between them they solved the problem to the extent that plowing again became the factor limiting production. The steam engine was inherently not capable of providing a way out of this impasse; because of its great ratio of weight to power it often could not negotiate fields which were not too wet to be plowed by horses. As a consequence, in the United States the size of the family farm began to be stabilized at the level set by the use of horses in plowing.

During the First World War there was a tremendous increase in the demand for food necessitated by the enormous use of man-power. The shortage of manpower on the farms in turn made factors which would increase the yield obtainable with a small number of men very valuable. The development of the tractor was thus greatly facilitated. The tractor was originally regarded merely as a substitute for the plow horse, and tools which would make its power available for operations other than plowing were slow to be invented. However, as the potentialities of the tractor were realized, new tools were developed which permitted it to be used for cultivating, planting, weeding, fertilizing, sawing, spray-ing, elevating, combining, hay baling and chopping, picking corn, cotton, potatoes, and sugar beets, and other farm operations. The tractor raised the productivity of the man on the farm to new heights. It is hard to say what the eventual limit may prove to be, but the Middle Western farmer who frequently is able to produce 7,500 bushels of corn in a growing season has produced a total of food far beyond the wildest dreams of the hoe-culture farmer.

There is a tendency, in view of the successive removal of limits on the size of the crop which one family can grow, to conceive of the series as being an endless progression of larger and more in-genious machines, replacing more and more men and giving rise to larger and larger surpluses. It was precisely this kind of think-ing that led to the creation of the enormous state farms which were set up in Russia. Considering the disastrous failure of these farms, and many similar experiences in the Americas, it behooves us to examine the process more carefully, in order to see where the limits on the use of machines in agriculture lie. We need to know the degree to which these limits are set by the nature of plants, climate and topography, technology and transportation, as well as social and psychological barriers. We need also to know the cost at which these limits can be reached. The use of energy in agriculture is an alternative to the use of that energy elsewhere; thus agriculture competes for energy with other industries.

The Frontier

What is technically and socially possible, then, may be so un-economical that it will rarely if ever be done. It is clear that if men are to be relieved of food raising each farmer must produce more food. To increase the amount of food raised per farmer the amount raised per acre must be increased or more acres must be cultivated by each farmer, or both. The American answer was to be largely in the form of increased acreage, though both methods have been used. In the days of Thomas Jefferson the size of the American family farm was about 20 acres. With the use of the horse-drawn iron plow the area that could be cultivated by a family increased to 40 or more acres. This meant in the older, already settled areas, halving the number of persons directly de-pendent upon farming. Along the Eastern seaboard, particularly in the Northeast, commercial and industrial pursuits making use of the energy of water and sail provided employment for the pop-ulations so displaced. In many areas in New England it was the pull of such occupations rather than the threat of failure or star-vation that depopulated the farms. Farther west the adjustment was greatly facilitated by the enormous amount of cheap land available. A farmer in the older and more settled areas, confronted with the fact that he could not locally buy enough land upon which to settle his sons, could frequently sell his land for enough money to buy a farm for each of them at the frontier as big as or bigger than that which he originally owned. In 1862 the Home-stead Act provided 160 acres of free land for each adult member of a family. This was at the time far more than could be cultivated by a single family. In most places the land varied in fertility and in other factors that affected its capacity to bear crops. Conse-quently only the land most suitable for crops was cultivated; the rest was set aside for pasture, wood lot, or wasteland.

Sometimes the number of farmers moving west to these larger farms was not great enough to reduce farm population sufficiently. That is to say, the lower unit price of food which resulted from the increased production on the larger areas made it necessary, in order to maintain a farm, to sell more food than could be raised on the smaller farms. The consequence was a series of farm fail-ures, mortgage foreclosures, and tax sales which produced emigration and permitted these farms to be integrated into larger farm units. Some small farm areas included too little land fitted for commercial agriculture to permit this kind of aggregation. There a succession of poorer tenants mined the soil and used up fixed structures such as fences, sheds, barns, and houses until the land fell into complete disuse, became part of a pure subsistence system, or was incorporated into a larger unit in which it could be used for pasture, wood lot, or recreation. Such areas as these never contributed to the food surpluses necessary to feed the industrial populations. Hence they cannot help us to understand how similar areas elsewhere in the world might contribute to the transition to a high-energy system.

While the westward movement was taking place in this country, food surpluses being produced in the New World were transported to industrial and commercial areas some of which were located in Europe. This facilitated industrialization there, for it supplied means whereby the population required for industrialization could be fed without being kept on farms. As we have seen, at that time the converters in use in manufacturing required concentration of workers in a very small area. Such congested populations could not have been fed from the small food surpluses produced by small farms using low-energy converters.

Effects of Immigration

At the same time, means to increased productivity in both the New World and the Old came from the rapid exploitation of non-renewable "crops" in the colonies. Forest products, including naval stores, furs, and buffalo hides, were gathered much faster than they would be reproduced. Similarly, the soil was rapidly exhausted by the failure to fertilize or rotate crops and by the mining of the readily available minerals. These practices provided the means to build towns and cities, roads, schools and churches, factories and machines which in their turn could be made useful long after the land upon which they were originally produced had ceased to produce anything of value. The supply was further increased by the very extensive outpouring of energy from the coal mines in England, and later Germany, delivered to the United States in the form of machines and tools and supplemented by skilled workers with the knowledge necessary to operate and reproduce them. Thompson estimates that in the nineteenth century alone more than 60 million people emigrated from Europe. These immigrant populations have frequently been looked upon as unskilled manpower, capable of adding only the energy of their muscles to the building up of the frontier. The truth is that they were transplanted operatives of a high-energy society; they had not only the skills and knowledge necessary to build and operate high-energy converters but also the attitudes and economic values which that system had developed in Europe. To sustain and enlarge the system built up around sail, and the concept that trade was an adequate means of making effective use of resources, the British poured out energy like water, and with the flow of goods went millions of Britons, bound to preserve much of the culture developed at home. To this flow, of course, there was ultimately added the tide of energy from the coal mines, oil and gas wells, and waterfalls of the United States.

We may gain further insight into the nature of the process by which the transition to high-energy society was achieved in the West by considering the effects these conditions and processes had on food raisers in Europe itself.

Industrialization of Britain and West Europe

We have already in part discussed the effect this movement had upon the British, for it took place under the dominance of sail. Social organization which permitted surplus energy to be traded and which called for the creation of specialized patterns abroad supplementary to those at home was well adapted to the spread, if not to the ultimate maintenance and development, of the use of steam. Coal at tidewater gave England a great advantage which was shared by no other naval and trading power. The rise of the industrialist led to the formation of a new political alliance. The trader and the industrialist became powerful enough to overthrow the landed aristocracy. British constitutional history shows the shifting institutions through which this alliance was made manifest. A study of marriages into the aristocracy by rising industrialists and the creation of new titles of nobility shows one of the means by which the social consolidation was effected. Legislation such as the repeal of the corn laws reveals how the doctrines of mercantilism were effectively replaced by the new liberal theories of the Manchester school. In place of the previous belief that controlled trade could be made to foster the kinds of exchanges which would bring wealth to the nation, the idea was developed that trade should be carried on with anyone with whom traders found it profitable to trade. The code protecting agricultural England was ruthlessly destroyed,[3] and the British farmer was forced to compete, for the products of British mines and factories, with people across the sea who were, by climate, topography, technology, and land-to-population ratio, better fitted than he to produce food. The advantages which Britain originally held—her control of the sea, the political structure of empire built with the surplus of sail, the early techniques of power manufacture, the abundance of coal at tidewater, the culture which permitted rapid conversion of energy surpluses into new converters —all these facilitated the abandonment of protection for agriculture, to the accompaniment of a tremendous accretion of new wealth and a rising standard of living. It was only as these initial advantages disappeared that Britain began to question the wisdom of the laissez-faire system as developed by Adam Smith and the classical economists and sanctioned by the achievements of Victorian England.

Even so, it was only because millions of her subjects migrated that Britain was able so rapidly to change her technology to one dependent upon food grown elsewhere. Emigration contributed to the solution of the problem in two ways. First, it transplanted people already familiar with British culture, hence willing to operate on new land in cooperation with the mother country; secondly, it removed from British politics large numbers of unemployed who probably would have resisted the change which drove them off the land. Had the conservatives been able to call, for the support of their reactionary policies, upon a newly enfranchised electorate which included those myriads who went abroad, the story of Britain might indeed have been different. As it turned out, the great majority of those who supplied British food got a vote, if at all, in some other political unit than that which controlled British policy.

We have earlier pointed out how the British took advantage of their peculiar situation to produce the conditions necessary for the increasing use of the sailing ship. As we then indicated, their original gains came primarily from taking advantage of cheap transportation and the regional specialization of production which this made possible. The development of law and morality supporting trade was accomplished simultaneously with the development of democratic government. It resulted in a social situation within England in which the surpluses of trade were spread in such a manner as to create and sustain the culture necessary to continue and expand that trade. But the monopolistic character of trade based upon sail also tended to reserve to countries with naval power the surpluses gained from trade. The share of surplus accruing to the other party to the deal usually was enough for only a few. Thus at home the Englishman's concepts of "human nature," "property rights," and other ideas necessary to the operation of foreign trade were functional, in the sense that British social organization tended to create and preserve them, and they in turn rationalized the system. Abroad, however, democratic ideas frequently had the opposite effect. The very migration of Englishmen trained in traditional British "rights" led them as colonists to resist the system as it operated abroad. Wherever these rights of Englishmen existed primarily as a consequence of the military power which England was able to deliver through use of her navy, they disappeared as soon as that power was weakened. The "mature" colony thus gained materially through seizure of the surplus which had been produced by converters largely built with British tools and the energy of British sail and British coal mines. The international respect for the private property of foreigners which often arose through and was maintained by British power and the transfer of people bearing British institutions to sparsely populated lands thus initially supported, and then undermined, the illusions so carefully nurtured by the Manchester liberals.

For the Continental countries the problem was much more difficult, though seemingly it should have been easier. Germany, having converted directly from feudalism to industrialism, had the advantage that her old system facilitated centralization of much of the new surplus in the hands of a few, who could more easily be induced to accept change than could the mass of peasants. Moreover, the Germans were able to profit from British experiments in creating the technology required for the efficient use of coal. Thus they were spared both the costs of unsuccessful physical arrangements and, sometimes more important, the costs of creating social structure which did not work. They could use the great flow of energy from the Ruhr to change social structure and values which had developed in rural Germany under the conditions prevailing in low-energy societies. They had the physical means to entice men from the pursuit of values through the old ways to the pursuit of the same values through new means, or to the pursuit of new values which high-energy technology could secure for them more easily. Even here, however, the transition was not easily made, and peaceable means had to be supplemented by "blood and iron." People in the old Catholic areas of Germany such as Bavaria strongly resisted, exacting concession after concession before changing their way of life. Even under Hitler these areas made continued industrialization of agriculture difficult, if not impossible. It was the surpluses produced in the United States, in areas controlled by the British, such as Canada, Australia, and New Zealand, and in those making use of feudal landholding, such as Argentina and Eastern Europe, that supplied the largest part of the increased food upon which Germany's new industrial populations fed. In France, just as a new technology emerged which might have rationalized the previously centralized control over large holdings and the resultant surpluses, the Revolution distributed the control over those surpluses among the peasants. As a consequence mechanization was very difficult, and even today the greatest block to the use of high-energy technology in France is probably the resistance of the peasant-proprietor on his small holdings. All of Western Europe shares, in some degree, the problems of Germany and France.

Let us recapitulate. The modern use of high-energy converters developed, originally, in England. Two hundred years of operation under sail, the then most effective converter, wrought many changes in a culture previously adapted to low-energy converters. The new system resulted in the widespread migration of Englishmen, relieving the land of some of its burden of overpopulation. The same movement carried British institutions into new areas, where further migration from original colonies could relieve the overpopulation which had been created by the spread of mechanized agriculture. The British property system also permitted the transfer to these new lands of enormous quantities of goods produced by English mines and machines. Thus, while title and "legal" control remained in the hands of British owners, the new converters and machine-made durable goods actually were frequently located in the agrarian countries, often replacing or more than replacing the nonrenewable assets destroyed by the invasion of industry. The development of local control over the income from these assets, whether through nationalization involving outright seizure, confiscatory taxation, increased demands by organized local labor, or otherwise, was in most of these areas simply a matter of time and opportunity.

The development of these new lands abroad enabled all the states of Western Europe to use the English-developed pattern of transition to some extent. But even this enormous migration did not enable Europe itself to adopt the necessary changes in farm size. Yates [4] finds that today, even in Denmark, a leader in European agriculture, there are more than 6 active agricultural workers for every 100 acres of farm land; in Italy and in southeastern Europe there are more than 15 such workers. This is accentuated by the fact that in actual operations of cultivation small holdings are cut up into many pieces much smaller than is indicated by totaling the property owned by one family. This makes farming with the American type of power machinery impossible. The average number of male agricultural workers in the United States and Canada is only 1.56 per 100 acres [5]—and this is decreasing. In contrast the world average for industrial countries is 5, while in Middle American and Caribbean regions 100 acres must afford employment to 20 men.

THE PROSPECTS FOR ASIA

When we turn to Asia, we find that the situation is of course much worse. In Bengal [6] the average net cultivated area per head of agricultural population is less than an acre, and 46 per cent of the farming families had less than 2 acres each. In Yünnan [7] about 100 families (500 to 600 people) share 150 acres of land. In Indo-China there are about 50 and in India about 24.

In the United States the average farm in 1950 comprised more than 215 acres. Small farms are difficult to maintain on a paying basis. In Ohio, at the present moment, a farm of 100 acres of average land is too small to maintain a family on any other basis than raising specialized products with unusual value, such as tobacco, or those requiring a large amount of labor as compared with that required to raise corn or wheat.

Contrasting the per capita area required for the kind of mechanization used in the United States with that available to the world's farmers, it is obvious that international migration has ceased to offer a means whereby the size of the average farm can be greatly increased.

Internal migration from farm to nonfarm regions might provide a means to solve the difficulty. But to make this possible it would be necessary to provide jobs for the migrants under such conditions that they would return to the farmer enough goods and services to compensate him for increasing his production sufficiently to feed them. To reduce the number of farmers to the point where high-energy converters could be used on the farms would take an immense amount of employment in nonfarm production.[8] It is estimated that to put Indian agricultural labor on 10-acre farms equipped with a pair of oxen would produce a surplus of 15.5 million farm workers. To put them on 25-acre farms would require 30 million new jobs in 10 years if in the meantime there was no charge in the survival rate. Obviously 25-acre farms can make little use of the kinds of machines which advantageously use the power of high-energy converters. On the other hand, the volume of new nonfarm employment required for even this change in man-per-acre ratio is enormous. It would require an immense increase in the available converters to give industrial employment to 30 million workers. This is about half the total number of workers currently gainfully employed in the United States. We shall examine a little later the energy costs of efficiently employing men in industry; for the moment it will suffice to say that no one has yet come forward with any reasonable proposal by which India or China could supply enough energy to provide the converters necessary to employ those rendered unemployed by farm mechanization or even by the restriction of the number of farmers to that required for hoe-culture farming at its point of maximum return.

Internal migration has, of course, been part of the answer in both Europe and America. In Europe those who left the farm for the city were forced to compete with each other for job opportunities which would enable them to secure food. They worked for little more than the cost of subsistence. The goods they produced with the aid of the energy of coal and falling water were exchanged for goods produced abroad with the expenditure of much less energy. But the increased productivity of the European workers, high in energy cost but low in price, could be exchanged abroad for much more food than the workers consumed. This food was used to induce otherwise unemployed men to produce more machines, which could in turn use more coal and/or water power to produce more goods for exchange for more food.

In Western Europe the rising power of the industrialists, both worker and employer, forced farmers to submit to competition with cheap food from abroad.[9] The consequence was a fall in the price of food, a decline in agricultural prosperity, and new waves of migration, both internal and international. In Eastern Europe, on the other hand, the hold of the landlord was not broken. With the support of the peasantry, tariffs and other restrictions were used to stop industrialization. But the landlord, faced with the necessity of buying abroad the industrial goods he could not produce at home—particularly the weapons necessary to defend his system—was also faced in the export market with falling prices for the food he had to sell in order to buy these industrial goods. He thus made greater demands on the peasantry. At the same time the population of Eastern Europe was increasing. The result was great disparity between the increased population and the decreased income. As a consequence Eastern Europe today, in demographic terms, resembles Asia more and more closely. Wholesale displacement of farm population appears to be less and less probable. In the crowded areas the price of farm land is greater than the capitalized rent, for since the limit on productivity is set by the amount of land available to him, and since his labor can be applied in no other way, the peasant often not only pays the landowner rent but also shares with him part of the increment resulting from his own labor.[10] The creation of large units suitable for machine agriculture results in greater agricultural unemployment and even more pressure on the remaining land and still greater increases in the price of land. Landlords can consequently secure tenants so easily that rents may run to 60 or 70 per cent of the crop. Such a reward is, in many areas, far in excess of what could

be secured by investment in farm machinery and the resultant industrialization of agriculture. Moreover, it is "natural" in the sense
that no elaborate social structure, with its attendant costs, is
needed to keep it in operation. On the other hand, a system that
involves the shipping of food away from a locality while a part of
the local population starves requires constant bolstering up
through a continuous supply of energy from other sources. Those
who occupy more than enough land to feed themselves must be
protected from those who have less land than they can cultivate
and less than enough to support families of the size that it is there
considered moral to beget and rear. If for any length of time that
outside supply of energy is not forthcoming, in the form either of
goods to induce or force to coerce, the land is likely to be broken
up into smaller family-size holdings which it is later very difficult
to combine. This is what has happened in France, Mexico, Poland,
and many other areas, including both Communist China and portions of the U.S.S.R.

Forced Collectivization of the Land

A good many schemes which would induce farm populations
voluntarily to abandon these small holdings have been attempted.
None seems to have been very successful. Only outright seizure of
the land, with no, or very limited, compensation to the owners,
seems to offer a solution. In most areas of the world such seizure
would be possible of course only with a complete revolution in
ideas about the sanctity of property.

It will be recalled that in the United States and in the British,
French, Dutch, Spanish, and Portuguese colonies the land was
originally claimed by Westerners in huge tracts. This revolution
took place during the period of European conquest, when the
property rights of the local population were pretty much honored
in the breach. Such seizure is not now favored by the Western
states. It is, however, the method proposed today by the Communists. But wholesale confiscation and forced migration have not
as yet resulted, save in a few areas of the U.S.S.R., in a ratio of
land to population which would permit efficient use of most of the
techniques possible with high-energy converters. All the known
means of persuasion, plus the invention of new means of coercion,
have been necessary to induce the Russian peasant to abandon his

land and the techniques around which his old social system was built. In the meantime two developments have been taking place which make the problem for the Communists even more difficult. The first is an immense increase in the Russian population resulting from the use of preventive medicine, the abolition of both abortion and free knowledge of contraception, and a policy of public approval of high birth rates. The second factor is the addition of satellites to the Russian orbit. A population of more than 600 million people who are now largely dependent on low-energy techniques is added to the Russian sphere. If these people are to make the transition to a higher-energy base they must do so with the aid of the surpluses from their hoe culture, from the small industrial base left to them from an earlier day, or from the increased output from Russian factories and mines.

To complicate matters for the Communists there is a great drain on the Russian system to provide the rapidly obsolescing weapons believed to be necessary to hold the "gains" of the revolution against the feared onslaught of the non-Communist world and also to intimidate those who, within the system, might otherwise revolt. The combination of these factors reduces the probability that the Communist effort will succeed, at least in the whole of the greatly expanded area over which it presently is attempting to operate. On the other hand, the Russians are greatly aided in their effort by the fact that their old culture permitted a large part of the surplus produced in an area to be used at the discretion of a very small minority, which might, if it thought best, remove all of that surplus from the local community. This is in sharp contrast with the social system of China, where feudalism was abolished about two thousand years ago and where claims on most surplus have long been in the hands of families largely physically resident in the local community, who consumed the greater part of it there. So the problem of transition for China is even greater than that faced by Russia.

COMMUNISM VERSUS CAPITALISM

At the moment, then, only two general approaches to the problem of transition are offered. One accepts the British system under which private property holders, induced by the hope of profit, compete with one another in an effort to create the kind of agricultural unit which will make high-energy technology efficient. In this struggle the principle of the sacred rights of property acts to prevent such interference by government as might otherwise arise from the efforts of those who regard the actions of property owners as being intolerable. The Communist view is that efforts to create efficient land units by a minority controlling government are legitimate and desirable. If our analysis is correct, neither approach seems to offer great hope of success. The problem of transition is frequently glossed over or disregarded by proponents of capitalism as well as of communism. By both schools it is assumed that industrial agriculture is so productive that it will eventually be practiced by all the peoples of the world. We do not here subscribe to that position. Some of the reasons have already been given; in the analysis which follows we shall adduce further evidence.

CHAPTER 7

The Industrialization of Agriculture

As we have seen, it is difficult to separate gains in agriculture made through the application of energy from oil, coal, gas, and falling water from gains secured through the application of other means of increasing efficiency. However, if we are to predict the future of mechanized agriculture, such an analysis must be attempted.

In a market economy, where labor has the alternative of working in the fields or in the factories, it may be cheaper in monetary terms to replace men with machines than the reverse. This is the situation in the United States and other large areas of the West. Because we are accustomed to these conditions we tend to translate money costs into physical costs and to assume that when money costs are lower energy costs must also be lower. This is not necessarily so, since great amounts of energy from nonfood sources may be equated in monetary terms with small amounts of energy in the form of food. Actually, as a little reflection will show, *the energy costs of the operations involved in mechanized food raising are higher than those incurred in hand cultivation.* For clarity the reasons for this are tabulated below.

1. More energy is required because the work is done more quickly. It will be recalled that the energy required to do a job varies not only with the mass and the distance involved but also with the time consumed. The amount of energy is not directly proportional to the increase in speed; rather it varies as the square of the velocity. Thus, decreases in time are purchased at greater and greater penalties in the form of the amount of energy used.

2. The tools which permit the great increase in the power used must themselves be larger, heavier, and more complex than the

134

hand tools which they replace. Therefore, they take more energy for their production, maintenance, and repair.

3. The greater area per production unit involved requires that more energy be used in getting to and from the work site, and in transporting the product to the place where it will be consumed.

4. In most cases the productivity of land varies within the areas cultivated. In utilizing the larger and more powerful machines which permit increased speed, much of the selectivity possible in hand cultivation is sacrificed. The result is decreased yield for a given expenditure of energy.

5. In many areas where a shift to larger farms is to be made, there are already fixed assets in the form of farmhouses and barns, roads, fences, and hedges which become useless in relation to the larger unit. There may also be assets such as churches, shrines, and government facilities, and commercial enterprises such as stores and artisans' shops, as well as the residences of their operators, which become useless as the decline in population density reduces the number of people they can serve below the point necessary to maintain them. Thus, in addition to the operational costs of the new system there are initial physical losses to be compensated for, or the resistance of their owners to sustaining their loss otherwise to be overcome.

6. There is the previously noted fact that human sentiment and habit create inertia. To overcome this requires the expenditure of energy.[1]

7. Finally, of course, there is the problem of finding employment at favorable terms for the population no longer locally useful because it has been replaced by the use of other converters. This may be the problem most difficult of all to solve.

HOE VERSUS PLOW

Before going further let us examine some concrete illustrations of what we have been discussing in the abstract. Fortunately there is a recent study [2] showing something of the relative costs of hoe and plow culture in terms that can be converted into energy units. Oscar Lewis compared the two systems in Tepoztlán, a village in Mexico, and gives specific figures drawn from a sample that is probably representative of many other areas. He shows that cultivating corn by hoe takes more than 3 times as many man-days as does plow cultivation. The figures average out at about 50 days for the plow and 165 days for the hoe, for each hectare cultivated. The proportion of those days in which oxen are used in plow areas as compared with those in which men work without oxen is not given; from the description of the work, however, it is clear that the oxen are used a good deal of the time. If we rate a team of oxen at 1½ horsepower and assume that of the 50 days spent in plow-culture farming there are 30 days in which the team is used 10 hours a day, we get a total of 450 horsepower-hours for the oxen and 50 (figuring the man at ¹⁄₁₀ horsepower, or 1 horsepower-hour per day) for the men used, or a grand total of 500 horsepower-hours to produce a hectare of corn with the plow as compared with 165 horsepower-hours for hoe culture.

Oxen are about as efficient as men in converting plants to mechanical energy, so to produce fuel for a team of oxen rated at 15 horsepower-hours per day takes land on which plant food yields 15 times as much energy as is required for a man. This is not to say that it will take 15 times as much crop land, for the ox will eat food grown on land which will not grow food crops; moreover, it eats no energy-wasting animal products and does not require any land for the raising of fiber for clothes, as would a man. Nevertheless, the costs are real, and some of the land used for ox feed must be subtracted from that which could otherwise be used by the hoe-culture farmer for raising food. If land were available in sufficient quantities and the growing season were short, this loss could be compensated for by the increased crop made possible by the increase in the area which could be cultivated by the use of the ox. However, in Tepoztlán the growing and planting seasons are long, and land is not abundant. There are many other areas now using hoe culture where the same situation exists.

It is sometimes argued that the loss in energy occasioned by the use of the ox or horse may be offset by the greater fertility arising from the deeper tilth possible with the plow. Actually, it is more and more apparent that in most places it is the first few inches of topsoil that carries the highest fertility; deep plowing thus decreases rather than increases yield. In the case under study Lewis[3] found that "a comparison of the yields of the two types of agriculture reveals that hoe culture yields are equal to the best yields in plow culture and are generally about twice as high as the average yields of plow culture." This is primarily due to the facts that the hoe farmer can select soil of greater fertility and that he can raise a type of corn which cannot be raised with the plow. Curwen [4] has shown that the change in the character of the shape of the field which is required when the plow is introduced is an old phenomenon. With the hoe the field tends to be circular and otherwise to follow contour lines that reveal or have resulted in soil fertility. In horse plowing, since the mass put in motion is considerable, the effects of momentum induce the farmer to plow in more or less straight lines, thus cultivating both the more and the less fertile soil—and incidentally encouraging erosion. In the area which Lewis studied, the plow farmer has taken over most of the land which can be put under the plow, leaving to the hoe farmer only the fringes and the areas where rocks, thin soil, and other factors make plowing impracticable. The necessity of spreading his efforts over a large area have the effect of requiring the hoe farmer to spend a great deal of time and energy going to the work site and returning to the village. Thus hoe farming as it is now practiced is less productive on the average than it could be if the whole village were engaged in it. If hoe farming at its greatest possible efficiency could be compared with plow farming as it is now practiced, the general disparity in energy costs between the two systems could be shown to be even greater than the estimate just given.

Rising population in Tepoztlán has forced more and more of the hoe farmers to go back to the methods which characterized the country in an earlier period, when the forest was cleared by burning and two crops were taken from the soil so made available. But it takes land so long to recover its fertility, once it has been so cropped, that this offers no permanent solution. In the meantime the mounting pressure on the hoe-culture farmer induces him to offer higher and higher rents for the use of more convenient land. At the moment the plow farmer is attached, through the export of his surplus, to urban areas which will supply him products in amounts sufficient to overcome his relative inefficiency in producing surplus energy. But plow culture, which limits the size of the local population, is under constant and increasing pressure, and the resultant mounting rents make it probable that in time the owner of what is now plow land will get greater rewards from renting it to hoe farmers than from using draft animals to produce surplus to sell to those in urban areas.

In Yünnan [5] before the Second World War owners of as little as 5 to 10 acres of land no longer thought of working, since they were able to secure labor for a small fraction of the total return from their land. It is easy to see why under such conditions tension between landowner and farm labor mounts, and why the peasantry is easily induced to join a movement for redistribution of the land, however wasteful by Western standards the hoe culture made necessary by this reduction of the size of individual holdings of land appears to be. At the same time we can anticipate that mounting costs of food in urban areas will result in support for political measures which will assure that the hoe farmer will be kept from preempting the urban food supply.

HORSE VERSUS TRACTOR

Comparing hoe culture with mechanized agriculture is even more difficult than comparing it with plow culture using draft animals because many of the factors in machine agriculture are not of local origin and no accounting exists to show just what their energy costs are. Such costs are usually known only in monetary terms and are therefore not directly usable. Moreover, the fact that the tractor does not require feed, and hence does not involve a reduction in crop land, removes one source of resistance to the introduction of tractor farming. Despite these complications, the same striking disparity is apparent. Available research limits our choice of illustration and makes it difficult to know how good a sample we are presenting, but *these are merely illustrations;* the principles involved are not dependent for their verification upon them, but upon abundant research in the field of physics and agrobiology.

Rice Production: Japan and the United States

The Japanese wet-rice farmers probably produce more than any other large class of hoe-culture people. The average return is about 50 bushels per acre. Cultivation and harvest take about 90 man-days per acre, or 90 horsepower-hours. Compare these figures with those of a study made in Arkansas in 1947, where wet-rice farming also yielded about 50 bushels per acre.[6] It is carefully done and represents an adequate sample for the area concerned. To raise 50 bushels of rice in Arkansas took 14.1 man-hours, 4.3 tractor-hours, 1.3 truck-hours, and 434 kilowatt-hours of electricity for pumping. In addition fertilizer containing 32 pounds of available nitrogen was put on the land. The tractors used 3.6 gallons of distillate and 0.05 gallons of gasoline per hour. The truck is figured at 1 gallon of gasoline per hour.

Since we shall be alluding to figures of this kind again, we give in detail the method of conversion into horsepower-hours. Distillate (No. 4 grade) yields 56.96 horsepower-hours heat energy per gallon. Motor-grade gasoline is figured at 48.83 horsepower-hours heat energy per gallon. We set up the computation this way:

Tractor 4.3 hr at 3.6 gal distillate and 0.5 gal gasoline per hr

$$56.96 \times 3.6 \ = \ 205.6 \text{ hp-hr per hr distillate}$$
$$48.83 \times 0.05 = \ \ \ \ 2.4 \text{ hp-hr per hr gasoline}$$
$$= \ \ 208 \ \ \text{ hp-hr per hr fuel for tractor}$$
$$4.3 \text{ hr used} = \ 894.4 \text{ hp-hr heat value of fuel used by tractor}$$

For the truck . . . . 1.3 hr at 1 gal gasoline per hr
$$1.3 \times 48.8 \text{ hp-hr} = 63.44 \text{ hp-hr heat value}$$

Converted at 20 per cent efficiency this gives

For the tractor	178.88 hp-hr
For the truck	12.69 hp-hr
Farm operators 14.1 hr at 0.1 hp per hr	1.41 hp-hr
Pumping 434 kwhr electricity at 1.34 hp-hr per kwhr . . .	581.56 hp-hr
Fertilizer * 32 lb available nitrogen at 1 hp-hr per lb . . .	32.00 hp-hr
Total	806.54 hp-hr

* This figure was taken from U.S. Power Commission Bulletin, "Power Requirements of the Electro-chemical, Electro-metallurgical and Allied Industries," 1938. It is possible that there have since been marked reductions in cost in this field.

Comparison shows that the operating-energy costs alone ran about 9 to 1 against machine agriculture. Japanese average production was 5,663 horsepower-hours per acre heat value, or, at 20 per cent, 1,132.6 horsepower-hours mechanical energy. Subtracting 90 horsepower-hours for the 90 man-days used in cultivation, the surplus was 1,042.6 horsepower-hours mechanical energy. Taking the Arkansas product at the same figure, subtracting the costs only of the energy actually used in operation and making no allowance for repairs and amortization of the machines, the surplus is only 326.06 horsepower-hours per acre. On the other hand, the Japanese surplus was 1.25 horsepower-hours per man-hour, while the American surplus was 23.1 horsepower-hours per man-hour.

The Japanese have utilized a great proportion of the means which modern technology provides to increase their physical productivity, while continuing to use hand labor. Their use of organic fertilizers and their methods of seed and plant selection, cultivation, and harvesting bring their productivity per acre up to that in the United States. Thus it is possible, at least in rice farming, to secure as much total energy, or feed as many people, from an acre with hand labor as is secured in the United States from an acre tilled with machines. From the Japanese point of view, to use in agriculture a large amount of energy which could otherwise be applied in industry, thus creating unemployment among erstwhile farm workers, who must as a consequence either starve or eat without producing, would not seem to be an efficient use of available energy.

From the American point of view—or considered strictly from the angle of producing surplus energy—the 23 horsepower-hours per man-hour of surplus energy to be gained by expending energy on the production of rice when compared with about 1,500 horsepower-hours per man-hour of surplus from the coal miner, and more from other sources, leads to the conclusion that the rice-producing operation represents an unwise choice. Of course, before any firm figure is used, the relative costs of the converters required to produce and maintain the tools used by both coal miner and rice grower must also be computed.

The case of rice was chosen because figures were available, and not because it is representative. Japanese rice production is very high as contrasted for example with that of India, where in 1932 only 14 bushels were raised per acre, though the yield in Japan is about ⅕ less than in Italy, which produces relatively small quantites. On the other hand, rice production in the United States in

1950 averaged 49.11 bushels per acre. Thus the comparison of American and Japanese production of rice is at least not unfair.

Other Comparisons

A more representative example is available in connection with wheat. Buck [7] found that in China in 1933 it took 26 man-days to produce an acre of wheat, with the average production 16 bushels per acre. A study made in Idaho, where, on irrigated land, average production was around 30 bushels per acre (more than double the United States average in 1949 of 14.1 bushels) showed an expenditure of about 45 horsepower-hours per acre. In this case, while the energy expended per bushel in the United States was almost the same as in China, the expenditure per acre in the United States was 19 horsepower-hours greater than in China, not taking into account the energy needed to compensate for the implements used or the costs of the irrigation system, which are in Idaho largely reflected in the price of land rather than, as in Arkansas, in pumping costs. On 30 bushels per acre of wheat, at the expense of 45 horsepower-hours, the surplus per acre yields 891.33 horsepower-hours. Assuming 12 man-hours per acre, the surplus produced in the United States is around 75 horsepower-hours per man-hour, or considerably more than that gained from pump-irrigated rice in Arkansas. However, on the national average of around 15 bushels the surplus is only 34.43 horsepower-hours per man-hour, assuming that costs in Idaho are typical.

Let us compare the costs in terms of corn, which is very widely used in the United States for livestock feed. A comparison of the energy costs of United States corn with those of corn raised in a Mexican village is enlightening. Average production of corn in the United States for 1949 was 37 bushels per acre. This is the equivalent of about 1,500 pounds of shelled corn. Lewis [8] reports that in Tepoztlán the average production using the plow is "9.6 *cargas* of shelled corn a hectare," or 1,181 pounds of shelled corn per acre. In accordance with his estimate that hoe culture produces much more than plow culture, running up to twice the average of plow land, we can assume for purposes of comparison an average production of about 1,500 pounds of shelled corn. On the other hand, the average cost of Tepoztlán corn, previously shown to be 66.8 horsepower-hours per acre, is to be contrasted with 158 horsepower-hours spent directly in Arkansas to produce only 25 bushels, or 1,000 pounds, of shelled corn. When we recall that hoe culture in Tepoztlán included clearing the land as well as planting and harvesting the crop, the contrast is the more startling.

Another type of comparison, from a study of Indiana farms, may be enlightening.[9] It was found that to produce an acre of corn required 8.8 hours of tractor time. At the rate of 3.5 gallons of gasoline per hour the fuel cost is about 31 gallons. Ayres and Scarlott estimate that an average acre of corn yields about 89 gallons of alcohol, which has a heat value about ⅘ that of gasoline, so that the corn would be equivalent to 71.2 gallons of gasoline. Deducting the energy costs, we have a yield of the equivalent of only 40 gallons of gasoline per man per 8.8 hour day from corn, which yields the highest energy of all the widely grown field crops in the United States.

WHERE THE HOE IS INDISPENSABLE

In every case these illustrations show hoe culture producing more surplus energy per acre than mechanized methods. It would, of course, have been possible to cite less efficient low-energy societies. The comparisons used indicate that it is *possible* for hoe culture to produce more food from a given land area, and more surplus energy, than mechanized farming. As a matter of fact, hoe culture can more effectively make use of such scientific practices as plant and seed selection, hybridization, thinning and pruning, soil selection, the selective application of fertilizer and insecticides than can machine cultivation. Thus once the techniques are developed, more food and more energy can be produced from a unit of land *without* machines than *with* them. Other changes in culturally sanctioned practices that currently limit productivity, such as overgrazing (with resultant erosion) and the burning of manures for fuel, might also be made without adopting the use of machines. A direct supply of fuel for heating, for example, might increase the use of manures for fertilizer. The difficulties of modifying any or all of the social factors involved here might be very great, and it is not affirmed that they could in all cases be successfully overcome. Nevertheless these are real alternatives, which, if adopted, could result in an increase in the standard of living and/or survival in rural areas. It is more likely that such practices would be willingly accepted by rural people than the introduction of methods that would mean forced migration for some of them and continuous limitation of opportunity to use land for their own and their families' subsistence. Moreover, these practices are very likely to be introduced under the auspices of the same humane movements that work to reduce infant and maternal mortality and the death rate from disease and otherwise to promote population growth—in the very areas in which, with machine cultivation, the population would be locally less employable. With the size of the population base that exists in Asia and Eastern Europe and much of Oceania and Middle America, it is probable that, as in Japan, the introduction of more scientific agriculture will result in increased agricultural productivity but will also be accompanied by changes which increase population by such numbers as to make the continuation of intensive hand methods an absolute necessity if starvation for many people is to be avoided.

It appears that, if the objective is to secure support of the largest possible population, hand methods of intensive cultivation provide the answer. If a higher material standard of living is sought, it can be secured only by limiting population to the number that can be fed by methods that use high-energy converters to release men from the land. It must be kept clearly in mind that securing the largest possible population and securing a higher material standard of living are mutually exclusive objectives.

Another method of increasing the supply of food, where land is relatively abundant and *labor* is the bottleneck at certain periods has already been mentioned: the temporary use of migratory labor during these periods and its supplemental employment elsewhere. The difficulty encountered here, in a society completely or primarily dependent on low-energy converters, is that the energy increase available to this mobile part of the population can be no greater than the increase in productivity which results from its use in bottleneck operations. The increase is, except under unusual conditions, necessarily small, and the costs of transportation, the maintenance of dual living facilities, and/or costs of transporting and maintaining migratory families usually militate against any considerable use of migratory workers.

Some special relations between high-energy societies which

provide seasonal employment for the labor surplus of overpopulated agricultural regions do, of course, help these regions at once
to deal with their problem of overpopulation and to supply the
demand for food in the urban areas to which they are attached.
But this is merely another example of the way in which a high-
energy system can be supplemental to a low-energy one. It offers
no solution to the problems of the low-energy area taken as a self-
contained unit.

Where those engaged in agriculture are permitted to operate in
the same economic and political system as those using high-energy
converters, with the population having the free choice of entering
industry or staying on the farm, and prices reflect the monetary
consequences of the choice, urban bids for food will be weighed
against demands for food and other goods by those in the farming
areas, who may choose either to remain and produce food or to
leave and enter urban employment, there to produce agricultural
machinery to replace them in supplying food. In a completely
agricultural area, where people have no opportunity to migrate
to high-energy-producing regions and no choice of using the
products of such regions save through exchange of food or goods
made with the aid of men and/or other plant-consuming converters, the purchase of agricultural machinery and the fuel to
run it leads to a different kind of judgment about the use of men
versus the use of machines.

The Primacy of Food as an Energy Source

Food is of course different from other energy sources, since it
can be substituted for other forms of energy, which will not, in
turn, replace it. Since life itself is dependent upon food, its *value*
to the consumer may be so high that it will be exchanged for any
amount of other energy available to him who seeks it. Where food
is scarce enough, it may command services at a price equal to all
the energy made available by a man consuming that food and
producing another fuel, even though the other fuel so produced
yields a hundred times the energy of the food consumed. For example, the coal miner might, as he apparently does in Russia,
have to turn over all the coal he mined in a day for little more
than the food he and his family eat in a day, even though the heat
value of the coal he mined might be a thousand times that of the

food he and his family consumed. The coal miner is not able, in the Russian system, to bargain directly with those who have food for sale. Between him and them stand not only the authority of government but also all those who must cooperate to make and to manage the converters by which coal is transformed into the goods sought by the farmer. All these must share in this energy, and judgment as to the validity of their claims on it must take into account technological, geographical, and social conditions.

What the industrialist demands from the farm is not the maximum energy he can secure, or necessarily any labor force; it is food itself, in sufficient amounts to maintain the industrial population and assure its growth. However, once this specific need is met, food, along with other goods and services, is sought at the least sacrifice of the values prevailing in the industrial society. It may be a matter of indifference whether the goods bought are produced with the energy of food put through a man or another animal or with that of coal, oil, or falling water put through a machine. The hoe-culture farmer faces different alternatives: he must use his food-fueled body either directly to produce what he wants or to produce food for exchange for other goods. In either case what he offers is a low-energy product. Those who control the use of land may consider substituting in the productive process the inputs of low-cost fuel for labor which must be fed with high-cost food. If his social system permits, the landowner may choose to exchange a day's supply of food for only a fraction of the energy made available by a coal miner in a day rather than a day's work from a laborer willing to work for him on the farm at subsistence but able only to deliver through his work the product of a hundredth of the energy that could be secured through employing the coal miner. Thus, apart from claims which can be made through kinship or other means of social identification, manpower produced in low-energy systems may be denied all claim to even a rising productivity.

Increasingly, modern men are for some purposes considered to be merely an alternative to machines, which can be run on the cheap surpluses of coal, oil, gas, and falling water. In comparison, food is a high-cost fuel to be put through an expensive converter. A man with converters which will use cheap energy can displace many men whose fuel costs make them unemployable in an economy that disregards claims not based on rational calculation of inputs in terms of outputs. If a population with equal access to both sorts of fuels and converters was allowed to increase so that it pressed on the available food supply, and food was offered in a free market, the food raiser could command all the other energy produced by the society in compensation for his cooperation in providing food. Such situations rarely, if ever, exist. There is a great deal of evidence showing how population is limited in primitive society. Similar evidence exists for early civilizations. It is likewise true that until recently most food was consumed by its producers directly and entered the market in only limited amounts.

In feudal times in the West population was limited by the fact that productivity was a function of organic converters, The worker's share was a fixed fraction of that productivity; it did not increase as his family increased. As a consequence, population could increase during years of plenty, but weaker individuals were bound to die off in the years of scarcity. The feudal lord sought the maximum surplus; increased labor beyond a given point yielded less than the food consumed by that labor. Those landlords too "humane" to recognize this fact were frequently conquered by those who restricted the number of laborers, raised horses, which produced greater surplus, and overran their weaker neighbors. The feudal lord was usually the only man who controlled food in excess of his needs; he was in control of more political and military power than those who might otherwise have forced him to disgorge that food on their own terms. He commanded the loyalty of those whom he protected and owned the land on which their horses fed. Since with low-energy techniques the greater portion of the population must be attached to the land, he was able to subordinate other men and their values to those which he favored. The balance between population and resources was kept at a point above subsistence, and the food raiser did not have to enter a free market.

We have seen how the hold of the feudal lord was broken in England. He has undergone a similar fate in some other parts of the world. Today industrialists command tremendously greater quantities of energy for military purposes than do farmers. Consequently land can be made, by fire and sword if necessary, to serve the values of industrial populations. Those in industrial areas now have the means both to coerce and to persuade land-owners to use land "wastefully" in terms of the maximum population it might feed, while denying people in low-energy areas access to the land on which they might maintain a larger population. For his part, the farmer with control over sufficient land and access to industrial workers may also secure more of his own values at the cost of less sacrifice of those values by producing "food-wasting" beef, poultry, and dairy products than by producing what he needs through cooperation with those who are willing to work for bread but can offer only their bodies to serve as converters. The industrial worker with 20 or 30 horsepower-hours a day of energy may, even though he demands beef in return, produce enough to deliver his product at less cost to the farmer than his low-energy counterpart. Thus the farmer, by attaching himself to the high-energy system, may reduce the efficiency of the land used—in terms of the numbers obtaining food from it—while increasing the supply of other goods which that food will provide for him.

The same situation prevails among those employing men for any other purpose. They may choose to employ workers who are able to demand a wage which offers to each of them much more goods than could be demanded by low-energy producers but who produce so much more in an hour or a day that the cost of their services is less than the alternative of employing hand labor. For example, in the United States the coal miner currently uses in the mine about 1 kilowatt-hour of energy derived from food daily. He is paid an average of about $18 for that energy. He daily mines about 7.3 tons of coal, each pound of which can produce about 1 kilowatt-hour of mechanical energy. So, even at $18 a day, the energy derived from food fed to the miner costs only a little more than 0.12 cent per kilowatt-hour. On the other hand, a man living on rice must, at 20 per cent efficiency, eat 2.35 pounds of rice in order to deliver daily 1 kilowatt-hour of energy; with rice at 20 cents a pound that kilowatt-hour of mechanical energy must cost at least 47 cents. The Japanese rice grower produces about 10 kilowatt-hours surplus per day. Thus, with rice at 20 cents a pound, the energy he makes available costs about 4.7 cents, or almost 40 times the cost of the energy obtained from the American coal miner, even though the miner gets 38 times as much as the rice-fed laborer *must* have merely to feed himself.

ENERGY COSTS OF INDUSTRIAL FARMING

What is gained by using high-energy converters on the farm is not more total food, or more product per unit of energy expended, or more surplus energy. *It is a reduction in the time which must be spent by human beings in producing food.* Many units of energy from fuel may have to be expended for every unit of energy from food saved by this substitution. Because the time cost of securing that energy from coal, oil, or falling water is much less than that required to secure it from food, the farmer with more land than he can cultivate by himself seeks to substitute inputs of this time-cheap energy for inputs of more time-costly manpower. On the other hand, what is sought by the *urban worker is food itself,* and he will sacrifice whatever portion of the energy available to him is necessary to secure it. The release of manpower by the use of high-energy converters in farming has the effect, in areas where the population has previously been climactic for a hoe or plow culture, of releasing men —or creating agricultural unemployment. But that is seldom the objective: it is the inevitable result of this process of substitution.

We may now be able to see a little more clearly the factors that lead men to decide whether or not to increase the number and capacity of high-energy converters in agriculture. The key is to be found in the relation between the cost of time and the cost of energy. When the cost of the time used is greater than the cost of the energy from sources other than manpower required to replace it, machines replace men. When the cost of the time is less than the cost of the energy required to replace it, men will not be replaced. There are thus two sets of factors operating, each of which can be represented by a mathematical series. One series represents the rate of population growth, which determines both the maximum supply of labor and the minimum demand for food. The other stands for the rate of accumulation of other converters. This sets limits on the mechanical energy available from sources other than manpower. The ratio between them is a critical factor in the course of industrialization.

A given rate of population growth provides a certain number of bodies which are potential converters. Social arrangements may determine what proportion of those persons who *might* be used in production will be so used, and these vary tremendously from place to place and time to time.[10] Social arrangements may also dictate how the mouths shall be fed, that is, whether all shall eat bread before anyone eats cake, or whether the demand of some for steak is to be fulfilled before all the children are provided with milk. But these arrangements *must* supply a minimum diet if the population is to be maintained, and they *cannot* use more man-power than the total to be obtained from the population using that food. If England, for example, is to maintain its population at 45 million, it must supply food for that many people, even if to supply that food (whether by importing it or by raising it in England) means the sacrifice of ten times as much energy from coal as can be secured from the food. In turn, the proportion of the population required to secure British food—whether through direct production of that food on British farms or through the provision of the energy required either to trade for food or to produce it by the aid of such devices as hothouses, which increase its energy cost—limits the number of those in England who can produce other forms of energy and the products obtainable through their use. If the population grows, the problems increase accordingly.

The other series, the rate of accumulation of nonhuman con-verters, represents the means whereby energy from other sources can be made available to replace food-using men or provide them with the products they could not obtain through human effort alone. The limiting factor here is the rate at which converters other than men can be produced. As has been shown, the low cost of producing surplus energy from coal, oil, gas, and falling water makes man a relatively expensive converter using an expen-sive fuel. The calculation of opportunity costs will thus favor a continuous increase in the use of machines wherever they can successfully replace men. Here the choice lies between using energy to make converters which will increase the capacity to use cheap surplus energy and using energy to increase the production of food so that men can be released from agriculture. Frequently the latter course merely renders useless a portion of the man-power, whose demands for food require diversion of cheap fuel to produce relatively expensive food. If population can be limited, the increased number of high-energy converters can be used to increase the supply of surplus energy and of additional high-energy converters at a rate which results in a mounting per capita output of those goods which can be produced by machines. As a consequence the costs of reproducing high-energy converters fall, and their greater use causes the disparity between their costs and those of hand labor to increase even faster. Thus by limiting population growth and migration and accelerating the rate of accumulation of converters a society gains the means to increase material well-being. Hence if the series which represents the rate of accumulation of converters accelerates more rapidly than population, the society is likely to move in the direction of high energy. If the reverse is the case, movement in the direction of low energy is to be expected.

In determining whether to use converters to increase the supply of food or of other goods, those who control surplus energy may calculate the results of both courses. Investment in agricultural machinery competes with investment in machinery for industry. If converters are likely to be equally effective in the two fields, the bidding is as apt to result in expanded mechanization of agriculture as of industry. However, if agriculture has any inherent characteristic that necessarily limits the effectiveness with which high-energy converters can be used, a differential rate of entry into the two fields is, to the degree that purely economic considerations govern, to be expected. We need, then, to see whether the energy inputs required to secure in agriculture a given reduction in costs are in fact likely to be equal to or greater than similar inputs in industry. The significance of the difference will vary as energy costs represent a greater or smaller fraction of all the costs to be considered.

In many factory operations, increased productivity follows directly from an increase in the energy used. This is not so in many farming operations. The energy converted by the plant is a function of the characteristics of that plant, the nutrients and water obtained from the soil, and the sunshine falling upon it. None of these factors is directly related to the speed with which the crop is put into or taken off the ground, the activities which are primarily affected by the use of high-energy converters. Only to the limited degree that some seed will get into the ground earlier and some be harvested later than if the work was done by hand does machine tillage necessarily affect the yield. Since the cost of the increased speed goes up as the square of the velocity, increasing the speed of agricultural operations through the use of machinery will ultimately bring the cost of that energy up to a point where it is equal to that of using hand methods to get the same result. But long before any such point is reached, the claims of other uses of energy will be likely to intervene, because there is a special handicap in the use of farm machinery. Few farm machines can be used for anything like the number of hours in a year that factory machines are commonly used. The tractor is being used more and more in the field, but it is in competition with self-propelled tools and also with more flexible electric power in stationary operations. The average use of tractors in the United States is still only about 600 hours a year, as compared with the 2,000 hours common for industrial machinery. The plow can seldom be used more than 20 to 30 days a year, and the cultivator less than that. A pickup hay baler will not often be used more than 50 hours a year, a silage cutter and elevator no more often. Even an all-purpose combine would hardly be used more than 300 hours a year, a corn picker not more than about 200.

In a capitalist economy, to get all the implements he needs the farmer has to bid against industry for the use of the machine tools and energy which are required to build his machinery. If instead of buying them he hires custom work, he pays a rental reflecting this fact, or loses as much in crops while waiting for machines (which are not available to everybody who needs them at once) as he would by buying or by paying enough rental to assure against such losses. On the other hand, in a "socialist" society someone must make the decision to use machine tools and energy to produce farm machinery or other machinery, and, if he is rational, must similarly calculate the advantage or disadvantage of investing energy in agricultural machines with a very limited usefulness as against machines with more extensive usefulness.

Thus, food suppliers seeking the cooperation of industrialists are at a disadvantage except during periods when food is scarce among industrial populations. Only then are they likely to be able to increase mechanized production. At other times the price of food is usually not high enough to provide profit margins equal to those secured by businessmen supplying demands for goods other than food. Not only is the cost of food necessarily higher than an equivalent amount of fuel; the differential cost of the converters used also mounts. In the earliest steps toward industrialization, or in areas entirely dependent upon the sale of low-energy products to secure high-energy converters, it may be possible to raise a child to the point where he becomes employable at a cost less than that of obtaining his mechanical equivalent. In the high-energy society a machine which will deliver energy equivalent to that of a fully grown man can frequently be secured for less than the fee of the obstetrician who delivers a baby. The energy devoted to bringing a man to maturity will, if put directly into operation by way of the coal mine, yield converters with far greater capacity than a man to do those tasks in which machines can be substituted for men. This would militate against unlimited expansion of investment in agriculture even if it were not true, as is the case, that the subsequent fuel and maintenance costs of machines are only a tithe of the costs of maintaining men.

DISTRIBUTION OF ENERGY SURPLUSES

It should be clear from the foregoing that a number of factors operate at present to induce industrial populations generally to claim surplus energy for themselves as against farm populations. This is true for the population generally, but it may not be true for those who wish to invest surplus in a distant market, where monetary costs are lower than in industrial areas. Whether or not, as the class interpretation of history would have it, this differential was the factor that motivated English capitalists to invest abroad, England did export a large portion of the goods which her industrial system was able to put out. The great majority of those in England who were in a position to direct the flow of energy believed in the virtues of trade. While it is true that the trader was forced to make some concession to landlords and to the state and otherwise to disperse part of his surplus at home, he was by modern standards quite free to disperse most of it abroad if he wished to do so. With a fundamental belief that "in the long run" he would get back all that he put in, and more, he traded goods for promises, many of which it turned out were never kept. Sometimes the energy which went into the goods returned to England, as compensation for that expended to produce what was exported from England, was negligible.

Today in England and elsewhere the trader occupies a less strategic position than he formerly did. Many of those in the economic and political system which uses many high-energy converters develop claims on what is produced, whether or not they are directly responsible as such for the increased productivity. If the market apparatus leaves them "underprivileged," they are likely to turn to institutions which recognize their claims. Doctors and other professionals gauge the worth of their services by the income of their clients, so that an increased claim by workers or businessmen translates itself into an increased claim by professionals. Similarly, government and business bureaucrats, teachers, postmen, and distributors may, while continuing to perform exactly the same physical operations that they formerly engaged in, organize to preserve their status position vis-à-vis the industrial worker or owner. Nor do farmers willingly see their share of the national product reduced.

As a consequence, industrial owners and traders have no such freedom as that enjoyed by merchants and industrialists in nineteenth-century Britain. National governments claim a very large part of the surplus, either for military undertakings and public works or for welfare purposes. After taxes, before the owner of converters gets his hands on the surplus produced with them, he has to contend with organized labor and management and with those who distribute the product. Moreover, he is limited by nationalistic efforts of other areas to preserve their own markets, their natural resources, or their way of living. Only within these limits is he free to choose whether or not to make an investment abroad, and whether there to invest in agriculture or other enterprises. Because, as we have seen, for reasons inherent in the nature of agriculture, physical productivity is likely to be higher in industry, investment in agriculture is not likely to prove attractive.

We must realize that most of the time, and for most products, the choice, to trade or not to trade, to invest or not to invest, is largely a unilateral one. That is to say, those in the higher-energy areas have the choice of using the products of low-energy areas or of producing these products, or substitutes for them, at home. People using high-energy technology and able to choose between producing goods to be exchanged with low-energy areas and using their own surplus energy to produce, at the cost of more energy but less time, those goods they might obtain through exchange with low-energy society, will presumably make the decision in terms of their own values. They will not be deterred by the evil consequences to those whom they may never have seen, and in whom they frequently have no interest, from pursuing a policy which maximizes their own values. Thus, where a substitute for the product of low-energy society can be produced in a high-energy society, the latter will probably choose to produce it even at the cost of energy greater than that which could be exchanged for that good.

Political Considerations

Many factors operate in favor of this choice. One of the most significant is the opportunity it affords to employ those displaced in industrial society by technological change and, particularly, to remove from the land the population no longer needed in the farm areas of the high-energy society. This effort toward full employment is an important aspect of continuing technological change in high-energy society.[10] Another important factor is the mounting cost of securing and maintaining in low-energy society conditions favorable to the growth of trade. We have shown why low-energy societies are likely to resist change. Local resistance organized into nationalist movements and equipped with fairly cheap but lethal weapons wielded by superabundant manpower makes foreign trade expensive in many of the old colonial regions today as compared with the days when an expeditionary force landed from a cruiser could be depended upon to keep large areas in check. The cost of holding the empires developed under sail may make trade unprofitable now. Such costs might in large part be eliminated by reducing dependence upon low-energy areas. This can be accomplished by subsidization of chemical and metallurgical research, the development of new plants, and the increased use of synthetic fertilization and other means to increase agricultural production. Industrial populations find it increasingly easier and less costly to devote energy to research which will make it possible for them to produce what they need within the area they politically control than to depend upon the natural products of areas outside that control. Nowadays the universities of the United States and Germany, for example, specialize in developing scientists who can deliver the kinds of facts which make this substitution possible, rather than in training men in the knowledge needed by the diplomat or the colonial administrator. Investment goes into synthetic dyes, rubber, and fiber. Investigation is made into alloys or processes of concentration or beneficiation of ores. Cheap materials-handling and earth-moving equipment make it possible to use low-grade ores economically as well as to invest energy within the boundaries of a political and economic system. Such usages are replacing that system of exploration and conquest or political domination over foreign lands which was once thought to be necessary for prosperity.

RESTRAINTS ON THE DIFFUSION OF INDUSTRIAL AGRICULTURE

Britain's experience with "maturing" colonies and with the rise of nationalism in her "backward" areas makes it clear that increasing the energy available through foreign investment frequently has the effect of implementing ever more strongly the nationalistic feeling that arises in reaction to the disruption occasioned by the introduction of new techniques (or the products of new techniques) which upset accepted relationships. In such cases the autarchy which develops cuts out the possibility of getting any return from foreign investment and discourages further investment. This leads industrial states to stockpile specific goods through what amounts to barter rather than to encourage free trade and foreign investment. Certainly Japan's experience in China, Manchuria, and Korea—as well as British experience there and in India and Iran—demonstrates the fact that the reaction which sets in when trade and investment are undertaken may be much more costly than was calculated when that trade was originally contemplated. Such costs, while no part of those calculated by the trader or investor, are real and must be borne by the system in which he functions; other groups in the system who share the costs may choose to continue to pay them or may turn to any other available alternative.

Those who foresee a rapid expansion of industrial converters all over the world overlook many instructive examples. An outstanding one is the experience of the British in Ireland. In spite of tremendous effort, backed by overwhelming might, the British were finally forced to abandon the idea that the cultivation of large estates in Ireland could be made to yield large agricultural surpluses for Britain. In the United States even a Civil War costing four hundred thousand lives, forty billions of dollars, and untold misery failed immediately to create a new energy base for the South. Until quite recently, alongside the greatest concentration of industrial converters in the world, Southerners preserved a culture basically little different in energy terms from that of Egypt under the Pharaohs. The refusal of the French peasant, given a unified piece of land after the First World War, to keep it intact so that machinery could effectively be used is another case in point. Western theory has too long neglected the implications of this type of reaction to trade-induced change.

We have given too little consideration to the way in which trade disrupted Eastern culture. In China, for example, the introduction of cotton and silk from industrial countries had the effect of reducing productivity among those peasants who had hitherto used sheep to convert the grass of the cemetery and silkworms to convert the mulberry leaves that grew along the canals into fiber which frequently not only clothed them but also created surplus with which to pay taxes and to buy necessary articles from the towns. Cheap cotton, wool, and rayon from the West destroyed their market. With this source of income gone, many peasants lost their ability to hold on to their land. As Fei and Chiang [12] put it, "It seems that the main cause of the concentration of landownership in the hands of town-dwellers lies primarily in the decline of rural industry." As a consequence, much of the "liberty" which was bestowed upon the merchant by Western intervention had the effect of producing penury for the peasant. Efforts of the Kuomintang to introduce in China the Japanese methods of breeding silkworms and spinning and reeling silk with the aid of constant-speed electrical motors at central stations were defeated by the fact that these methods, similarly, had the effect of reducing the opportunity for productive activity among peasants who had to live by that activity.

It must constantly be kept in mind that mechanized agriculture *reduces* the number of people that can locally live off the land, so that if it is to be adopted something must constantly intervene in the food-raising area to induce reduction in the local population. Whether that reduction comes about through starvation, migration, infanticide, or birth control is only in part a matter of local choice; it is sometimes wholly determined by outsiders with power to implement their demands. In effect, industrial areas can ordain starvation in rural areas by preventing migration from those areas and at the same time removing surplus food from the land. They may concurrently invoke values which lead to increased survival (for example, decry infanticide and birth control) and take away the means by which that survival is made possible. It is not surprising that in these circumstances there is confusion, cynicism, and social disorganization.

This disorganization has been greatly intensified by the social and economic instability of industrial countries. Recurrent wars have had the effect of producing repeatedly a situation in which for a time the price of food is very high. During these periods mechanized agriculture is likely to be widely extended. Then, when war has ceased, areas which in wartime imported food are confronted with a choice between continuing to import food, and purchasing the products of high-energy technology. When food and human effort begin to compete for employment against fuel and its converters, the real costs of mechanized agriculture begin to show up. It becomes obvious in many cases that the costs of mechanized agriculture are too high to be sustained in the face of competition with the machine in industry or with hoe cultures and their "cheap" labor. Unless some cultural factor is set up to protect food raisers, disaster will follow. As soon as surplus food is available, at which point it must be measured by at least some of its potential users in terms of the energy which its converter, man, will yield in competition with other converters, food will no long command a price which reflects its unique function. The relative inefficiency of agriculture in producing surplus energy forces the price of food to a level which provides the food raiser with little more than his own subsistence, and even then much food becomes a glut on the market. And in the meantime food raisers lose their ability to claim the products which other industries are set up to deliver to them.

PROBLEMS OF AGRICULTURE IN THE HIGH-ENERGY SOCIETY

As we shall point out later, the widespread use of high-energy technology has had the effect of enormously increasing the range of adjustments which are made through the use of the price mechanism. This has been particularly disastrous to agriculture. It is not possible quickly to increase or decrease the factors affecting either the supply of or the demand for food, yet the price of food in industrial societies with a free market fluctuates more wildly than that of any other product. In agriculture taken as a whole, as distinguished from a group of diversified farmers in a favored area, changes in supply cannot quickly be made and consequently price fluctuates with demand. Demand in turn varies with conditions beyond the power of farmers to manipulate them. This is complicated by the fact that a shift in demand from beef or poultry, for example, to cereals has the effect of increasing the supply of cereals in relation to the demand for them. Industrial unemployment thus translates itself into immediate effects in terms of both reduced demand for and increased supply of certain foods. Furthermore, since many industrial workers are members of farm families and return to the farm when unemployed, industrial unemployment also increases the supply of farm labor at a time when it is employable only by increasing the supply of food or by decreasing the use of farm machinery. This also accentuates the instability of the demand for industrial products. It is little wonder that, all over the world, agricultural populations have rebelled against the operations of the pricing system. Schultz [12] points out that "the excess supply of resources in agriculture is primarily labor" and on the other hand that "the movement of labor resources into and out of agriculture has not been consistent with changes in prices. The cause for this paradox is that another economic force has superseded the effects of changes in relative prices. The availability or non-availability of jobs [in industry] has been the dominating force."

The minimum size of the farm which can effectively use large amounts of power is constantly increasing. Moreover, to maintain fertility a good deal of land has to be operated in rotation. This is no particular handicap where the tools are simple and the prime mover cheap, but when special machines are used, such as the hay baler, corn picker, and combine, it means that three complete sets of machines have to be used and that the land area in use each year for any one set must be great enough to justify its use. One study [14] showed that in Kentucky to use a disk harrow at a rate that would return its cost in 1946 prices, for both the machine and crops, required at least 200 acres. Tractor mowers required 100 acres. Hay balers required land yielding 150 tons, the combine 100 acres, the corn picker 75. Thus to use the baler and mower for the hay, the combine for the wheat, and the corn picker for the corn on a three-year rotation program requires for efficient operation 300 acres of land, even with a favorable ratio between food and agricultural machinery prices. On farms smaller than this the farmer is paying the implement maker part of the productivity derived from the land and from his labor. As we have already indicated, farms in the United States in 1950 averaged more than 215 acres; in that year there were more than 780,000 farms of over 260 acres in use.

The combined effects of shifting prices, fluctuating industrial employment, increased size of land unit, and increased capital investment are numerous, and they have revolutionized traditional farm life and farm communities. Fuel consumption and farm power and machinery have nearly doubled, and the proportion of income going for purchased inputs and depreciation has increased by approximately one-fifth since 1930.[15] Traditionally, farm income largely represented payments for services performed on the farm, that is, the income was largely disposable at the will of the owner. Today the farmer acts as collector for a good many men located in other sectors of the economy, over whom he exercises only the control that any other buyer in that market exercises, and on the same terms. The extreme variation in farm income as contrasted both with the stabilization of prices by institutional devices and with the more stable situation of industrial producers throws a great share of the risk upon the farmer. He must pay the suppliers of the goods and services he uses what they are able to get from other buyers, without reference to what he can get for

his own product. The result has been an increasing demand for
some form of insurance against these risks. The operations of the
free market—which bring the farmer great gains during periods of
food scarcity become an impossible burden when the number of
those with access to food is limited while the productivity of industrial workers increases. The reaction, in many parts of the
West is a demand for protection against industrialized agriculture
abroad and "exploitation" by urbanites at home. Traditionally
"liberal" policies are favorable only to the large farmer with
adequate land located where he can rapidly shift production practices to meet changing demand. To do this he must be able to
hire cheap migratory labor, for which he is responsible only a
small part of the year, and be in many other respects quite un-
typical of food raisers in general.

There are also other necessary consequences industrialized agriculture which contravene past policy and make old institutions
less efficient. The increase in the minimum size of the farm means
a reduction in the number of farm owners and a great increase in
the value of holdings. It is no longer a simple matter for a man to
acquire the acreage necessary for efficient production, and it is
almost impossible for him to save enough to supply other farms
for his children. A farmer who is already possessed of large
amounts of land can better afford to pay more for additional land
which will make use of his now only partly employed equipment
than one whose holdings are so small as to make the use of such
equipment prohibitive. The aggregation of large farms in turn
permits increased use of still more specialized equipment, earnings from which can be used to enlarge the production unit still
further. Capital goes to those farms large enough to use it.[16] The
result is a situation in which the farms that are "family-sized" in
the technical sense that they can be farmed by an average family
are tremendously larger than the farms that are family-sized in
the sense that families are likely to be able to accumulate enough
to purchase them, or to operate them once they are purchased,
in the face of competition with large farmers. Moreover, in many
countries the traditional system of inheritance requires division
of the land among the children at the death of their parents. Thus
the aggregation of land into larger units can be maintained after
the death of the owner only by the sale of the farm and the divi-

sion of its proceeds among the children or through some kind of arrangement which separates the function of ownership from that of management.

Demographic and Ecological Repercussions

The increase in the size of the farm has meant a great decrease in the density of the farm population in farming areas. In the United States the development of the railroad, which could cheaply carry the product of large farms to distant urban centers, together with the practices already discussed, led to residence on the farm, a pattern of agricultural living quite unlike that in older countries such as China, where, in the food-raising regions, villages are about as far apart as farm dwellings are in Iowa or Kansas. Here residence on the farm made it very difficult to obtain locally those goods and services which the villages provided in Europe and in Asia. To fill the need the mail-order house and the central market place, which could provide specialized services for a very extensive area, grew up. The decrease in local demand for these services reduced the demand for other services below the point necessary to support them. For example, the use of the mail-order house to supply implements reduced local demand for church services, schools, lodges, fire protection, theaters, doctors, and hospitals as well as stores, by the amount of demand that the machinery builders and agents of the implement manufacturers supplanted by the mail-order house would have created. The same holds, of course, for many other items, such as heating and plumbing, hardware and building supplies, etc.

Thus the reduction in local population had the effect of reducing effective demand for local services by far more than the difference in the number of persons required to till the farms. The outcome was a great reduction in the vitality of the village community in the farm areas and a transfer of functions to larger and more distant centers. Stewart has set forth statistical evidence indicating that the movement in the United States from farms to urban areas, if it continues to follow the present curve, will result in zero farm population. This situation is now approximated in some areas which formerly served subsistence farmers. In certain counties of Wisconsin increasingly populated by subsistence farmers living on scattered patches of fertile land, the costs of maintaining the schools, roads, utilities, welfare, and sanitary services demanded for all their people by the voters of the state mounted very high; to meet this situation the electorate in 1929 voted the complete removal of farmers from these areas and prohibited further farming there.

In some areas of the semiarid West, where farming could be made profitable only by the wholesale use of high-energy converters, the numbers of the needed continuous residents fell very low, and the overhead cost of maintaining families thus became very great. It was not profitable to farm if families were provided with adequate services either directly by the owner or by his paying sufficient wages or higher taxes. For example, where in order to profit it is necessary to operate 5,000 acres of land in a unit, on which machines might be used (for putting in the crop and taking it off) only 20 or 30 days a year, the maintenance of families during the whole year to supply the necessary labor becomes very uneconomical. If families remain on such large units, the bringing together of enough students in one school, or patients in one hospital, supplied with the equipment and trained professionals to provide the service expected, causes the costs per unit of service to mount so high as to be prohibitive except when very high returns can be made from the land. The result of economic choice is the temporary import of machines and men to put in the crop, and their temporary return to harvest it. In the years in which the crop is so small as to make harvesting prohibitively expensive, enough livestock to consume the scanty crop is put on the land to eat whatever has grown. Between times only a caretaker who will keep up the fences and prevent abuse of the land is needed. Frequently here, as in sheep-raising areas in Nevada, this task is assigned to bachelors or childless couples willing to live in almost complete isolation for fairly long periods. Similar land use is seen in Australia and New Zealand, where the use of refrigeration and ships as well as rail has brought about a situation in which the raising of livestock for a distant market brings greater return than subsistence farming. Here, too, the village community has lost many of its functions and a very large part of the population is urban.

We do not anticipate that the great bulk of farms will reach a parallel situation, for, as we have indicated, the mounting costs of mechanized farming are likely at some point to stop the further development of the process except in specialized circumstances such as those noted above. But it is quite probable that the ultimate limits to which it will go have not been reached.

The reduction of the number of those engaged in farming changes greatly the character of the political relations between farmers and other producers. The hold of the landowner in Britain was, as we have seen, finally broken with the repeal of the corn laws. The power of the farm bloc in the American Senate may disappear as suddenly as did the power of the old Tories in the British Parliament. The farm population will under such circumstances be at the mercy of the urban population.

The results of the process of limiting those with access to farm land to the number which will bring the greatest return to the farm owner manifests itself most completely in the sphere of international relations. Here those with only a limited amount of arable land can exert even less pressure to see that that land is used to feed their children than it is possible for them to apply in municipal politics or a local market.

The plains of Argentina, for example, might be made to provide subsistence for millions emigrating from Central and Mediterranean Europe or from Asia, but it is much more likely that these plains will continue primarily to supply meat for Western Europe. The sheep runs of Australia, which could be made to support a larger population of subsistence farmers and herders, are likely to continue, so long as the United States and Britain rule the seas, and seek these products, to provide wool and mutton instead. The probable future of Denmark is to continue to supply meat, milk, and cheese for the populations of industrial workers elsewhere in Western Europe rather than to increase her own population to the point where food must be consumed in the form of plant products. Eighty per cent of the farm area of the United States is used to produce feed for livestock.[17] Only one-ninth of the Calories this feed would yield is made available for human consumption. But with the increased number of industrial workers bidding for meat, milk, poultry, and dairy products, it is not likely that the American Middle West will revert to the earlier pattern of sending abroad large quantities of grain, pork, and lard. On the contrary, it is much more likely that Canadian and Argentine wheat farmers will yield to the demand for high-cost, high-profit products to supply the tables of industrial workers rather than continue to deliver breadstuffs to low-energy areas, or cut up the land so that more local subsistence farmers can use it.

Some Political Implications

The size of the modern state has been increasing. If a state is to be able to actually enforce its edicts, it must have the power to do so. At present many states are actually less powerful, either in influence or in the ability to command force, than some large organizations which function within their borders. The growth of great centers of industrial power dwarfs the power of neighboring states using low-energy techniques. The need for a mass market, as well as other elements which determine the scale of operations, necessitates a very large area of operations. On the other hand, the possibility of creating a common culture which will support and maintain a very large state is limited. It does not appear that the size of the unit necessary for military protection or industrial efficiency is coincident with these limits. At the moment it does not seem that world-wide detailed social organization is necessary for efficient operation of modern technology. Nor does such organization seem possible, given the cultural, geographic, and psychological limits which have combined historically to shape the world as it now is. There seem to be limits on the size of the effective social unit: beyond a certain point organization cannot be made comprehensible enough for succeeding generations to learn to operate it. It thus appears that large units such as the U.S.S.R., the British Commonwealth, and perhaps the United States have reached the point where any technological gains to be derived from an increase in size would be outweighed by the increased costs of creating and maintaining the necessary social, political, and legal controls. Assuming that these organizations are big enough to maintain their military defense, enlargement would weaken rather than strengthen them. Within such units as these it seems apparent that the greatest per capita energy surplus can be secured through limiting the number of food raisers and population to a minimum set by mechanized agriculture and through maximizing production which can be carried on with the aid of energy from other sources. For those regions where the

population-to-land ratio is already so high as to require the continued production of food even if that means "regression" toward
hoe culture, there seems little prospect of relief to be obtained
from the possessors of abundant converters and coal, oil, falling
water, gas, and uranium, save in the acceptance by the great mass
of the industrial people of the world of some universal self-deny-
ing moral and religious code.

CHAPTER 8

Capitalism in Theory and in Fact

It has been indicated that one of the problems faced by those who seek to move along the continuum from low- to high-energy society is that of assuring an adequate food supply. It has also been shown that such movement is greatly influenced by the ratio between the rate of population growth and the rate of increase in available energy. If population increases faster than available energy, physical productivity is likely to decrease unless there is sufficient increase in the efficiency with which energy is used [1] to offset the growth in population. Such increase is rare and in general productivity increases with per capita increase in available energy.[2]

The specific ratio of increase in energy to increase in population which must be reached to effect movement along the continuum toward high-energy technology is different in each particular situation. Cob and others [3] have worked out a formula stated in monetary terms which represents one means of making a calculation of this ratio. We make no attempt to do this in terms of energy, but it is clear that a slight increase in the rate of increment derived from a large stock of converters will outrun a similar or larger rate of increase from a small population base and that the reverse is likewise true.

One of the primary effects of high-energy technology has been to increase longevity and thus increase population. This has of course been accentuated by the application of science and by the existence of values which favor the use of science and technology to reduce the death rate. In consequence the rate of population growth has generally been increased by the introduction of high-energy technology. One of its first effects may then be such an

166

increase in population as will wipe out the advantage initially held by the rate of accumulation of other converters over that of population.

THE CONTROLLED POPULATION

It is widely assumed that as more energy is used this initial increase in the rate of population growth due to the fall in the death rate will be offset by a decline in the birth rate. But no clear explanation of the apparent connection between increase in productivity and decline in reproduction has been generally accepted. Efforts to show that it is strictly a biological phenomenon have failed. Moreover, there has recently been an increase in the birth rate in some of the Western countries. The nature of this increase —particularly the question whether it represents actual enlargement of the size of the completed family—is at the moment a matter of controversy among population experts. In any case, the relation between fertility and increased energy consumption needs further examination.

Much of the evidence gathered from the experience of Northern Europe, North America, and the British Commonwealth shows that the decline in the Western birth rate was related to the way in which the products of increased energy were distributed. That is to say, the decline was sharpest among the households receiving the largest share of the increased output, and least sharp among households receiving the least share. Thus a lowered birth rate would appear to be the specific result of the impact of specific facts upon potential parents rather than a general characteristic of the high-energy society. The most that can be said, even after analyzing the evidence, is that where the per capita production of energy reaches the level reached earlier in areas like Northern Europe and the United States, and is similarly distributed, fertility will probably decline.

In studying Western experience we also see how increases in energy affected the birth rate *before* the rate of per capita increase in energy reached the point where the birth rate began to decline, and this evidence bears upon the future course of industrialization in the present low-energy regions of the world. Under the special conditions prevailing in Northern Europe, North America, and the British Empire and Commonwealth during the last two or three centuries, the rate of increase of the accumulation of converters was even higher than the huge rate of population increase that accompanied it. However, the original ratio of size of population to land and resources in these areas was quite other than the present ratio in many of the industrialized portions of the world. This difference alone makes it doubtful whether per capita production in these regions can ever reach the level it attained in the older high-energy societies before the birth rate there began to decline. The population of the low-energy areas of the world is so great that to reach the level of per capita productivity at which fertility could be expected to decline would require a rate of converter accumulation far in excess of that seen in the early development of the West. Such an increase appears highly improbable. Thus if the rate of growth of population is to decline in low-energy areas it will probably not be because of a decrease in fertility accompanying increased productivity. The enormous size of these populations also implies that unless a very marked decrease in fertility does occur, population growth will outstrip any increase in converters that is likely to occur.

A crucial dilemma for those seeking to industrialize is that while conditions remain unchanged, fertility remains static, and while fertility remains static it is difficult to change conditions to the point where they will affect fertility. Many efforts to change the birth rate by propaganda and persuasion have failed in the past. This may indicate that it will not be easy to effect such change in the future. Up to a point, a considerable increase in energy may serve primarily to induce changes which are themselves inimical to further increases in productivity. This point must be passed before the battle to create more high-energy converters of increased capacity can be said to have been won. In other words, if energy is devoted to increasing the stock of converters when there are other demands for energy which must first be met, the result will be abortive. The conditions that determine what are the "other demands which must first be met" vary with each specific situation in which an effort is being made to accumulate converters. We have already indicated some of the types of factors which enter into every such situation, and it may be well to summarize here the factors that appear to be necessary for the success of an effort toward a high-energy system.

1. Above all, the stock of converters must continually be used to produce the surplus energy required to offset the decline in surplus energy due to farm mechanization.

2. Energy must continue to be supplied to those on mechanized farms to induce them to continue to use the land under their control in that manner. (Since at times continued local use of machinery and the export of food may result in the starvation of the food raisers' neighbors or even members of their own families, this may represent a cost considerably above that required of low-energy food raisers.)

3. If further spread of farm mechanization is to occur, energy must be supplied to induce both adults and children located in low-energy agricultural regions to leave and to sacrifice those goods which cannot be taken along. These assets, both public and private, may be of considerable present worth but will have no future value. Either they must be compensated for or the necessary force to cause their abandonment must be exerted.

4. Cooperation in producing change has often been secured by promises of increased material well-being. To secure cooperation in this way, the system must continue to deliver the promised goods to keep people playing the roles required in the new system. The material cost of inducing change can be kept to a minimum if those who favor change have been induced to pursue it for moral, religious, political, ideological, or other nonmaterial reasons. There is always the possibility, if not the probability, however, that the expectations built up to induce initial change may be such that they require the continued use of all newly available surplus energy merely to maintain stability and prevent regression. Thus further devotion to surplus to increasing the stock of converters becomes impossible.

5. The likelihood that the situation outlined in 4 will occur is increased by the fact that most systems require the cooperation of many who demand increased reward but continue to perform services which contribute nothing new in the way of increased physical productivity. Salesmen and other distributors, business and government bureaucrats, teachers, doctors, lawyers, and other

professional men are frequently induced to enter these fields by status considerations, and they insist upon maintaining superior status as compared with those whom they serve. Thus when workers whose physical productivity has been increased by the use of high-energy converters get a higher reward, an increase must also by supplied to all these others. The relative size of this non-producing group grows as the stock of converters in use grows,[5] and their demands are frequently well organized and effective.

6. The very speed which changed methods permit requires more energy to be used to secure a given end than would be required if the work were done more slowly.

7. The cost of replacement and repair mounts as the stock of converters is increased.

8. The costs of technological unemployment and obsolescence of both men and materials which arise from changes within industry itself must be met. Either compensatory reward or coercion may be used to induce those who must change to do so; both usually require more energy than would have been expended if no change were sought.

9. To all these costs there may be added others because an "outside influence," not previously dealt with here, may seek to prevent further change, since that change would make it impossible for the outsider to rely upon the local populace to continue their previous functions. The efforts of some of the old imperial powers to maintain the status quo in their colonies and the efforts of some religious orders bent on preserving what they consider to be sacred may fall into this category.

The Role of Imperialism

A good deal of emphasis has been placed on this last factor of outside interference by the many who view the age of Western expansion with a jaundiced eye. They decry the "selfishness" of the imperial powers in specializing certain colonial areas in the production of raw materials and "denying" them the opportunity to industrialize. It is certain that this motive characterized some of the colonial powers.[6] It is also true that in many areas, particularly in the British Empire, a good deal of the energy used to keep the colonial system going came from the mother country and that the outgoing energy sometimes exceeded that represented by what was returned to Britain. The costs of the shift to high-energy technology have been grossly underestimated by some anti-imperialist thinkers, and the significance of monetary profits probably has been overstated. These errors of estimate are most likely to occur when, as happened in many cases, the machines and fuels brought into the colonies were real but the profits turned out to be irredeemable promises worth less than the paper they were printed on. The fact that they misjudged the results of their acts does not make the motives of the foreign investers any more or less noble, but it may account for the disappointment of many who "nationalized" their economy, turned control over to the local populace, and discovered that the result hardly bore out their dreams of what "freedom" would bring in the way of material well-being.

We have already shown that progress toward the high-energy society has been slowed, stopped, and reversed many times in the world's history. There is mounting evidence that this is happening today in many parts of the old colonial empires, particularly those of the French, Dutch, Portuguese, and Spanish, where population pressure has made regression toward a hoe culture almost inevitable. This makes the unique character of the British experiment even more significant.

Great emphasis has been laid here on gains in efficiency which result from substituting converters using the energy of coal, oil, and falling water for organic converters. That is because this is central to the thesis we are pursuing. We do not assume, however, that this is the only way by which energy can be conserved, or efficiency increased. Up to a point, the increased energy required by a growing population and/or higher physical productivity can be secured through more rational use of the same energy sources. Tools can be invented and adopted which use the flow of energy from existing converters more effectively to attain the desired ends. The gains to be made through superior organization of work, particularly the specialization of labor, are also impressive. Regional specialization, which takes full advantage of the differential productivity of various areas also permits great gains in productivity. It was in fact from improvement in organization and superior technique that most of the increases in physical productivity among low-energy societies were derived. It was also from these sources that many of the Victorian economists thought all the increased physical productivity which they observed arose.

Perhaps before we attempt to discuss the validity of their position we should restate here certain phases of the theory we are following. It is presumed that the direction and disposition of the flow of surplus energy are subject to human choice. This choice is largely put into action through social structure. In determining whether to divert energy into consumers' goods or into new converters somebody's choice governs. But we cannot know what the choice will be without knowing who it is that is in a position to make that choice, and what are the factors that influence him. To understand how individual choice is implemented we need to know the specific social structure within which the chooser operates and his power to affect the decisions of the groups to which he belongs and, in turn, the power of these groups to control or modify social policy. It is not possible here to outline all the social structures through which transition to high energy has been attempted. Some insight may, however, be gained from a study of the consequences of the fact that it was English social structure explained by English theory that first broke the barriers which had previously prevented widespread use of sail, coal, oil, and falling water as sources of energy.

The critical ratio between energy increase and population increase was first reached by the British. From this fact stem a number of very important other facts. First of all, there is the physical fact that the flow of energy tends to reinforce by feedback the channels that initially directed the flow. Thus Britain increased the strength with which Britons in places of power could reinforce their previous decisions. Of perhaps equal importance was the fact that British success rationalized the theory used by the British in explaining why their system worked. This fact remains, whether the theory actually did "explain" or was such that had it been followed closely in practice it might have wrecked their economy. Because they accompanied one another, the ideas and social organization that grew up with high-energy technology in England thus frequently came to be treated as synonymous with that technology. Those who sought to adopt the techniques also frequently sought, at least initially, to use not only these techniques and the converters developed in Britain but also their system of ideas and institutional patterns as well. In her decline from dominance England has had to reexamine her system, but meanwhile British ideas have gained great strength through their use in the United States, in the British Commonwealth, and elsewhere. Thus today we see Britain turning away from her classical position while that position is being supported by others.

PRICE-MEASURED COST VERSUS ENERGY COST

Something has already been shown of the physical and technical means used by the British in making the transition. We need now perhaps to examine the rationalizations by which they explained that transformation. British economic theory was based on the proposition that fundamentally there were only two types of factors involved in production. One of these was land, the costless gift of God. All the other factors involved in transforming the elements found on or in the land into economic goods and services depended upon human cooperation. The *costs* of production, then, were to be found in the "pain" experienced by those required to perform acts which were not sought by them as ends in themselves. All the goods produced were presumed to be consumable or capable of being made consumable at the will of those who held claims on them. To secure *capital*, or "goods used to further the production of goods," the holder of some claims on these consumable goods must abstain from exercising his claims immediately. This abstinence was itself a pain, similar to that experienced by those who must sacrifice in production the time which might otherwise be spent in the pursuit of immediately desired ends. Interest, which compensated for this pain, was thus justified, even though the goods which the capitalist abstained from consuming had their origin in land and *labor*. Since, as will be recalled, land was a free gift, all the costs of productivity could be reduced to the pain involved in securing human cooperation.

Reduction in costs must come, then, from the more efficient use of men. Adam Smith's famous illustration of the gains to be made by subdivision of labor in pin making was used as an example to explain all the gains deriving from specialization. The "entrepreneur," who made such subdivision possible, must also be rewarded for the pain involved in spending his time on production rather than in direct pursuit of consumable goods. (He also must be paid insurance for the risks taken.) The law of comparative advantage was developed to prove that differentials in the cost of production, based on the productivity of labor, justfy nothing less than a world market, where labor subdivision could be carried out to the nth degree. Thus values measured in the market must not be made subordinate to any other values, lest labor's productivity thereby be reduced.

Now the *minimum* cost of the labor which went into anything could not be less than the labor cost of securing the food necessary for labor's survival. In the long run, then, nothing could be produced for less than the food-energy costs of producing food. The observed tendency of humans was to reproduce until their numbers were such that they must compete for continuously less fertile land and for tools in order to subsist. To avoid starvation, which was conceived to involve more pain than any possible alternative, workers would have to compete until wages just equaled subsistence. This was the origin of the "iron law of wages." It was the differential fertility of land in producing food that established the basis for "rent," which secured the cooperation of the landowner. The system seemed complete, and in areas where food is the only source of mechanical energy it is hard to find a flaw in the reasoning it exhibits.

In the framework of our thesis it is apparent that the failure of this system of thought was due to the fact that it was based almost entirely on man's experience in the low-energy society: it failed to deal adequately with energy derived from sources other than food or with the continuing use of energy merely to produce converters. The productivity which resulted from the use of new energy sources was ascribed to "capital" indiscriminately.

Now in the low-energy system it was true that, apart from land, labor made up the overwhelming proportion of the factors involved in production, and the costs of human cooperation represented practically all its costs. Man was the principal converter of mechanical energy. Hence, converters could be increased in number primarily by increasing the population, which in turn had some claim on the product. On land almost the only way in which surplus mechanical energy could economically be secured was through increase in draft animals. These, as we have seen, had only limited superiority to manpower. Thus the economic thought developed by the British accounted for all but the very specialized and limited use of the wind and the flowing stream.

Instrumental Costs

The error in looking upon tools merely as stored labor was not great. This does not mean that tools and social organization were not considered important in determining the relative efficiency of low-energy systems. It was realized that such relative efficiency could and did at times determine the survival and spread, or the shrinkage and disappearance, of low-energy societies. But by far the greatest part of the costs of tools could be traced back to labor costs. Producers' goods, that is, goods used only as means and not valued as ends in themselves, could not as such represent very large amounts of energy in these situations where the prime mover was small and could itself be reproduced only by organic processes which it was not possible to speed up very much. It is true that tools were decorated, sometimes at great cost. This cost was, however, met by the aesthetic or status satisfactions derived from the decorations. It did not have to be justified by the gain in efficiency with which tools performed their function as means to other ends. Tools, then, were likely to be produced only as they served rather immediately, either as ends or as means, their maker or those who exchanged consumption goods for them. The social relations necessary to assure that they be produced were fairly easily maintained by motivation arising "naturally" out of the situation in which they were produced.

However, when the prime mover is increased in size and power, and hand tools are replaced by power tools, the amount of energy that must be diverted from the flow between producer and ultimate consumer is greatly increased. Then the social conditions necessary to support sufficient diversion become much more difficult to calculate and to maintain. Power tools are not provided in proper quantities by the judgment of people who look upon converters merely as labor stored in the form of goods which can at will be consumed by those whose past abstinence made them available. They represent the *instrumental cost* of making consumables and should not be considered income—ever.

In high-energy systems the converter may be extremely costly; a machine costing 100,000 kilowatt-hours of energy is introduced quite casually into even a small business. To build such a machine in a low-energy society, or to set aside goods produced with low-energy converters which could be exchanged for such a machine, might require the total surplus of a large community over a considerable time. The equivalent of 100,000 kilowatt-hours is about 134,000 man-days of human effort.

There are great differences between the ways in which a society which has reached the critical ratio of population to converters can secure new converters and the methods that must be used by one which has not achieved this ratio. In the low-energy society, diversion of energy from its regular channels may occur in the form of some rich and powerful man selling his jewels and his castles, breaking up his harem or his court, and forgoing any further conspicuous expenditure and display—the flow of energy which previously went into these goods being directed into high-energy converters. But the recurring sources of energy of this type, even in a large and highly exploited domain, yield only relatively small increments of power. These have in the past rarely been sufficient to supply those initiating a program of this kind of diversion with the means to overcome the resistance of those whose positions and way of life it threatened. Usually it was not from the rich and powerful classes that the flow of energy was diverted. Rather, there was a lowering of the plane of living of a large part of the population. Thus in low-energy societies an increase in the accumulation of converters has usually to be preceded by a *fall* in the amount of energy normally claimed for consumption by various groups in the population; particularly is this so when much of the energy diverted must be expended in the coercion or corruption necessary to secure it.

On the other hand, in a society which has passed the critical ratio there results, as a normal part of the operations normally expected from various groups, the formation of "pools" of surplus energy which sometimes cannot be "legitimately" claimed by those following codes based upon the past normal expectations of the society. Here the problem is to channel the new surpluses into new streams, or to enlarge the flow of surplus to some groups or individuals not previously entitled to control it. Such an accumulation of previously unclaimed energy comes into existence only where the stock of converters is sufficient to meet all the costs of change previously mentioned. It must also be great enough to supply energy in amounts sufficient to allow any accompanying growth in population to be offset so that the population may continue its existing way of life. If in order to get these converters the society has raised the standard and plane of living, these new expectations must also be met. The new claims might not only use up all the new surplus, preventing the formation of pools of unclaimed energy, but might actually place greater claims on the system than it is physically capable of meeting even though great increases in physical productivity are being made.

The most effective mobilizer of converters is, of course, a set of values generally shared which, while sanctioning increased physical production, frowns upon widespread increases in consumption. Under a pure system such as this, the transition from low to high energy could be made rather rapidly, provided the necessary demographic and geographic conditions existed. Most of the increased surplus could be immediately converted into more new means of creating surplus, which could immediately again be converted into more means of creating surplus, and so on, up to the limits of the resources of the area in which the social system existed. In practice, of course, no such pure system could exist. For "diversion of energy into surplus-creating converters" represents not only the physical facts denoted but also changing people from what they have been into something else. It means the creation of new groups who will use different techniques, have different experiences, and depend upon different reasons from those they previously used to justify their behavior. Unless some way is found of effecting over-night the transformation of human habit, emotion, memory, intellect, and identification, no system capable of giving full reign to technological progress will ever exist.

Nor is the picture of saving and investing as a pure function of individual wishes an accurate one. In a social sense the production of converters represents a change in way of life for the many people who stop doing the things they have been doing and begin to do other things. They frequently have no other choice. Either they must produce converters for an employer and, in return, be permitted to choose between consuming and saving, or refuse to do so and, being then denied access both to the necessary land and to tools, be also denied the choice between consuming and saving. All societies establish exclusive claims on some of the factors of production. Thus the power of individual choice is alway limited. The choice to save may even be divorced from the opportunity to invest; in many areas the power to determine who can invest is held by those already in control. Their decision to make use of the savings of others, to divert their own present earnings directly into production, or to prevent further investment in their particular field frequently cannot successfully be contraverted. The holding of land by those whose status depends upon holding *idle* land, of patents by those who regard as adequate the present supply of goods of the kind they produce, of union cards by those who feel that labor-displacing machinery has already threatened them—these are merely instances of situations where social structure serves to reflect specifically the values of those in a position to exercise choice, not the values of just anyone who is willing to abstain from present consumption.

Actually, then, the amount of energy diverted into new converters tends to reach and remain at a point [7] at which the claims on energy are about equal to the flow of energy produced, and such a flow is then traditionally justified. Once established, the equilibrium between the claims and the energy which satisfies them is broken only when some factor makes it impossible to keep the system functioning at this level. Growth of population may threaten existing standards of living, or exhaustion of resources may make the flow of energy diminish. A neighboring system, itself out of equilibrium, may upset local stability by withdrawing energy required for defense from its customary channels. Invention, or creation of new converters, is frequently a result of the effort to bolster up the old system by introducing new elements intended to strengthen it. It was thus, for example, that the use of the steam engine was introduced into the world of sail.

SOCIAL ORGANIZATION

Once the potentialities of an invention have been demonstrated, the techniques can be borrowed deliberately and made to serve purposes other than the original one. The effects of these techniques in a new situation may induce changes entirely different from those anticipated by the borrower. The more or less blind process by which England stumbled into the industrial system gave way to purposeful change in the case of Germany and of the United States. But since in both these areas there were conditions differing from those in England, invention of new techniques and organization was made largely through trial and error. Once the necessary formula for the development of high-energy technology here had been discovered, the new pattern was followed by the Japanese and the Russians. But again special conditions in Japan and in Russia gave rise in turn to consequences quite other than those anticipated either by the "capitalists" who introduced new converters to strengthen their own power and position or by the "communists" who did likewise with the thought that they, better than theorists of the West, understood how to make high-energy technology serve to produce Utopia. In all these cases a tremendous number of previously unseen social consequences arose, many of them quite the reverse of what was expected.

The diversion of energy into the creation of high-energy converters involves extensive social change. The cost of this change even in energy terms is a function not only of the physical operations involved; it also relates to the existing technology that can be borrowed, the pre-existing culture, and the intelligence and foresight with which the differences between what was and what must come to be can be reconciled.

Initially, power converters themselves were somewhat inefficient because they were simply adaptations of previously known devices. It was only as a result of wasting great quantities of energy in trial and error that users of the machines overcame inherent defects in mechanical design. Slowly the concept arose that a power tool was a thing in itself [8] and not a mere imitation of its organic forbear. The technician discovered ways to redesign converters so that they wasted less of the energy required to build and operate them. More recently, electronic controls have led to the creation of machines that do a lot of their own "think-ing" and thus have reduced tremendously the cost of operating them. But such machines in their turn require for their creation, maintenance, and development still further alteration in the ideas, habits, and training of human beings. The limiting factor in this process is thus frequently a social and moral rather than a physical or technological one.

The inertial effect produced in a society consists of the physical accretions which make old ways easy to follow, thus the fact that once a stable situation of the type discussed above is reached, children are "automatically" taught by their parents and neigh-bors to undertake to do what the socially sanctioned system re-quires of them. The educational bureaucracy is slowly induced to supplement this teaching. In these circumstances, means and ends merge, for children are taught not only to seek socially approved goals but also to seek them in socially approved ways. Then means become ends in themselves, since deviation from the sanctioned means becomes as much a source of discomfort to the individual as would failure to achieve the ends prescribed. Con-versely, adherence to the established ways of doing things results in the same measures of social approval as would result from the achievement of prescribed ends.

The process of sanctioning means is not, however, uniform, and there are many means which are considered to be morally neutral in so far as a particular society is concerned. It is in these areas of indifference that new means are most likely to get their start. Here a simple cycle of activity in which the relation of means to ends is clear permits the comparison of the efficiency of one set of converters with that of another. The opportunity is provided to demonstrate how well new means can serve old ends, without the concomitant realization that the change in means will probably involve changes in the ends. Once having entered into competition with the ordained means, an efficient converter may make its way further. Much of the gain must of course be diverted to overcome the reaction which sets in to restore the previous equilibrium, and unless a considerable momentum is developed the reaction may accumulate faster than new support, halting the further spread of the new means.

The changes required frequently involve new relations between people in different sites. The new ways may be found to benefit the interacting societies unequally: most of the gains may go to those located in one site. In such cases some of those who make the change are induced to make it by values which are not locally regenerated and which depend for their sanction upon "outside" influences.[9] The justification which they locally offer for these changes may be altogether different from the values which are in fact operative. Thus the present effort by the United States, in the name of a "free" economy, to put capital by government fiat where it would not go in hope of profit makes no sense at all in terms of the professed objective of defending "capitalism," since it operates in a manner directly opposite to that system which it is supposed to be sanctioning. To predict the places, rates, and occasions at which energy will be diverted into converters, we must, then, not only discover the economic causes and costs of the transformation but deal with *all* the factors which determine whether or not it will be made. Such factors may be called political, moral, religious, social, economic, technical, or what not.

The Need for Social Unity

There are a few generalizations which may serve as a guide to the discovery of the factors at work to affect the probability of change. To secure a shift from production of consumers' to production of producers' goods in a feudal, slave, or other oligarchic system which legitimatizes control in the hands of a few over most of the surplus produced requires only that certain small elites be convinced of the desirability of the shift. Of course subsequent consequences may rob them of the ability to direct the flow of surplus, but then new governing groups must be discovered. Or the other hand, where control over surplus is vested by religion morality, and law in the head of each household, or in political or religious leaders who have in the past distributed it as "free" goods in the form of education, public health, or recreation, or in the form of the means to make war, diversion of surplus from these channels into high-energy converters is a much more difficult task.

It will also be true that diversion of people from their customary ways will be difficult in proportion to the degree to which

their existing culture depends upon tradition, ritual, and super-
natural sanctions, as contrasted with "rational," "secular," or "pragmatic" sanctions. Thus the people of urbanized regions will usually
be more easily induced to change on the basis of demonstrable
results than will those in the greater part of the areas now engaged in low-energy production.

Beyond these few generalizations, to go into the general theory
would be a less satisfactory approach to the question of how converters are accumulated than the study of specific instances. In
pursuing the more concrete method, however, we must deal with
theory to the extent of inquiring into the explanation offered by
those who have made the transition to high-energy technology,
either accepting their explanation or demonstrating why that explanation is inadequate to account for what did in fact happen.

THE THEORY OF CAPITALISM

To return, then, to British experience, British theory, as we have
shown, operated on the assumption that in the long run wages
would not permanently be above subsistence. Hence, labor could
not be expected to provide the stock of consumers' goods which
it would have to live on while accumulating converters. The stock
would have to be secured from those who, having such a surplus
available at any time, could be induced to put it at the disposal of
those who wished to consume at any time. Thus British theory
accounted for the diversion of energy into a stock of converters
by dealing with the time preferences of potential consumers. Interest was required, for only by being paid interest could those
in a position to choose between consuming now and allowing their
claims on existing consumers' goods to be exercised by others
engaged in building producers' goods, be induced to delay exercising their claims. On the other hand, the increased productivity
ascribed to capital supplied the means to provide in future an
increased stock of consumers' goods. If during the period between
the original expenditure of capital and the appearance of the increased flow of consumers' goods, time preferences should change,
interest rates would reflect that change and induce either further
investment or increased consumption on the part of those in a
position to choose. Thus the stock of converters would always
reflect time preferences among those with surplus, which in turn

would reflect the values attached by consumers to present goods. This explanation remains today the central core of the theoretical justification for "capitalism," although it has come less and less to represent an adequate account of what happens in so-called "capitalist" countries.

We have not ourselves here used the term "capital." It is frequently used, as was indicated in the summary of classical British theory above, to stand for all economic goods other than land, labor, and management used in production. Thus it represents not only converters of energy but other durable goods such as buildings, roads, bridges, and dams. It is also used to denote a residual factor to which is ascribed all productivity not claimed for land, labor, or the entrepreneur. Many writers use "productivity" to mean increase in values as measured in terms of price, or some other system of evaluation, as distinguished from physical production. Such productivity when claimed to be the product of "capital" thus may represent effective organization, institutional preferences, capitalized potential increment from land, "good will" patents, trademarks, etc. In this book, however, physical productivity is dealt with in terms of the energy costs of goods and services. Physical productivity may be increasing while productivity measured pricewise is decreasing. Physical productivity may appear in the form of military or political power, religious sacrifice, public display, recreation or health measures, or public works rather than in the form of those goods and services which, in some institutionalized markets, are given a pecuniary value and called "economic." The two types of measurement ought not to be confused even though one may be a function of the other. Hence terms such as "capital," which stands for either physically measured or for evaluated production, or for both interchangeably, must here be eschewed.

We return to the rationalization offered by the British for their increased productivity. There was in the traditional British system of thought room for disagreement as to the size of the shares of consumers' goods which could be claimed by the holders of each type of factor in production. A case was made by the socialists for the proposition that labor, since it was the only active element in production and performed the work that went into it, had earned the right to the total product. Labor was required only to thank God for the free gifts of nature in the form of natural resources which it used to make production possible. Landowners in their turn claimed that in endowing men with a propensity to breed until they had to use worse and worse land in production, God had justified the taking of rent, which represented the difference between the best and worst land in use. Through His endowment of man with a sacred right to private property, He had also made legitimate the owner's claim to that difference. A third position which could be logically held was that any increase in production that occurred when capital was introduced into a productive cycle ought to go in its entirety to those who had saved to make that capital investment possible. A fourth justified management's claims. The existence of such disagreements about who in particular had a right to consume what was produced did not belie the proposition that ultimately somebody would be able to enjoy the consumption of all that was produced. Nothing in that system of thought provided justification of the cost of devoting endless energy to the production of converters which would be used endlessly to produce converters. Yet it is clear upon careful examination that in a high-energy system this is a process which must go on. British thought thus failed in a measure to provide a moral basis for much of what had in fact to take place in British society if it was to remain operable.

One *could* assume from the existing evidence that the factors that led to population growth in England were so powerful that nothing short of reduction to a subsistence economy could stop them. Thus because increased productivity by labor *must* be reflected in a constant increase in the population, whose bids for the land and tools needed for survival *must* increase rents and reduce wages to subsistence level, nothing could be done to improve labor's lot. It was assumed that a similar natural law of competition induced entrepreneurs to invest any saving available. But if, as the theory held, interest supplied the motive for saving, there was no natural law inducing anybody to save when the consequence of competition was investment of savings to the point of zero interest. There was instead continuous evidence of continuous collaboration by businessmen to prevent "overinvestment" or "cutthroat competition." Parliament and the courts were called upon to prevent such conspiracy in restraint of trade, even as they sought to prevent similar conspiracy on the part of labor. But this meant that political means were having to be used to produce what was supposed to be "natural" behavior, so powerfully motivated that nothing could interfere with it. It thus became clear that man's economic behavior was not what the theory explaining it would lead us to expect. In fact, justification for the strictures against conspiracy came not from some inherent element of human nature but from the religious and moral precepts found in British culture which held that it was man's duty to produce all the material wealth it was possible for him to produce. Hence any conspiracy which reduced the production of goods and thus denied them to the consumer took from him what it was his "right" to have. This is a fact not generally accepted; even so recent a writer as Veblen ascribed increased production to an instinct which drives man to be productive just as the reproductive instinct impels him to perpetuate and increase the species.

Moral and Religious Factors

Such works as those of Tawney [10] and Weber discuss the significance of the underlying moral and religious system as it relates to economic production. The tremendous part which Protestant ethics played in determining both that "progress" should take place and how it should take place is shown clearly. Their position would make this moral code the cause of the accumulation of converters. For us it would be meaningless to ask which came first, the moral system which engendered conditions necessary for increases in productivity, or the production which led men to propagate a system which would make moral what they were doing. As we have shown, the interrelation between social structure and the flow of energy permits no point to be taken (except arbitrarily for the purpose in hand) as "the beginning."

Assuming, then the fact that the whole of English culture was more or less involved in the transition, what we want to know is: What facts were most clearly and immediately responsible for the accumulation of converters? Whatever else we find, it is quite clear that a large part of the accumulation was *not* the product of abstention. As we have already seen, the accumulation represented in considerable part the gifts of nature from hitherto unexploited continents. Moreover, many of the claims made on the flow of goods in the old country represented the product of land to which title was orginally established by military conquest, handed out to the followers of the conqueror in amounts totally unrelated to any previous abstention on their part. Similarly, a substantial share of the goods which were used to motivate ship-building came from the seizure of products of America and the Orient. Title to them was secured by the British and the Dutch through military power, which enabled them to compel the Spanish and Portuguese to disgorge their loot, much of which was taken from the "natives." Many of these goods were either directed straight to consumption by the sea lords or were used by them to induce others to direct food and labor to the production of more ships. It was only after this process had reached the point where continued expansion depended upon the use of the recurring product of the low-energy systems that decisions of the type traditionally cited as the source of capital began to be very important.

The Business Elite

By this time the power of the trader and the industrialist was so well established that abstention on their part was hardly required to keep the flow going. Thus to locate the source and determine the nature of the choice between using surplus for more converters or using it for more consumption goods we must deal with the values of this small group of businessmen. Weber and Tawney and their followers have placed considerable emphasis upon the religious and moral attitudes which caused business-men to consider themselves to be the elect of God, bound by their stewardship to efficient production. Veblen, and others, emphasized conspicuous expenditure and conspicuous leisure as aims. In company with others we must emphasize also the development of power for power's sake.

Whatever his motive, the businessman depended on having political power sufficient to enable him to continue to force such changes as he thought were required to secure efficient production. To this end he turned over part of the new surplus to the government, which thus was put into a position to determine the future course of some of the surplus produced. This could be used for exploration, conquest, subsidy, and legislation leading to further productivity, to conspicuous consumption by the court, or to widespread diffusion in the form of bread and circuses for the multitude. Which course was chosen is a matter to be discovered in the intimate history of the particular court of the period. In addition to the sources cited above, there were other savings not induced by the taking of interest. Men fearful of disaster and crisis, aging and death, or necessarily interested in accumulating such funds as dowries for their daughters or land for their sons had to save and, far from expecting interest, frequently would have paid somebody to protect their savings. The factors responsible for the actual accumulation of converters in England were many and varied and are hardly to be accounted for by the official theory that interest rates determined savings and investment.

Rent was also a means of accumulating converters. Justification for control over the income from land was derived from the feudal world or from long usage. Royalties from coal mines, for example, represented a windfall to the landowner and had nothing to do with his prescience, his past frugality, or his performance of social function. Like a good many of today's windfalls, it might be attributed to luck, but it was more frequently held to be an evidence of God's intention to reward the elite. Gains from trade were similarly an evidence of "fortune" or of destiny.

During the long reign of sail, then, many of the conditions necessary to further expansion of converters became imbedded in British culture and sanctioned by custom, law, and religious belief. Only a few of these conditions were recognized for what they were by those seeking to understand and explain the British economy. So when their explanation was used as a guide in efforts made elsewhere to accumulate converters, the results were seldom as expected.

Accumulation through Exploitation

The typical situation in low-energy society, in which physical goods were produced in a social matrix in which material and nonmaterial means were alike considered to have a meaning beyond their obvious characteristics or their instrumental fuctions, gave way as trade expanded to one in which goods came to be known only by their ability to perform such instrumental functions.

The great expansion of trade made Englishmen dependent upon goods produced all over the empire under conditions totally unknown (and frequently unknowable) to their consumers. In urban areas the fact that the food consumed was not locally produced broke the intimate association of consumption and production and interfered with the sanction of ritual and magic and religion which affected the volume and nature of production. These city people were frequently unaware of and unconcerned with the conditions under which food was produced. No change in their value systems was required to make it possible for them to accept food from abroad in preference to that raised in England. They chose to accept cheap food from abroad because the cheap energy of sail delivered it to them at less sacrifice of their own values than was demanded by English farmers seeking to maintain or improve their own position in relation to the urbanites. The production of goods in the city for the market rather than for consumption within a community sharing common values robbed many of the previous norms of production of any functional meaning for the buyer. Thus the rate of exchange considered to be "normal," or the "just price" agreed upon where stable conditions long endured, ceased to be an effective measure of wealth. As we have seen, the use of the ship also forced a change in the concept of the just price for money and in the attitude toward moneylending. The danger of loss of the ship and its cargo made some sort of insurance not only allowable but necessary. Conversely, the enormous gains possible with the use of the ship made their division among a number of owners seem to be more equitable than their concentration in the hands of the ship's captain or a merchant prince. Thus, while the great bulk of the people of the world continued to consume and produce in a tradition-sanctioned world, on a constant-cost, constant-price basis, a few men in the trading nations, Britain in particular, were permitted and encouraged to share the gains of the new energy system.

Although English traders did engage in what Veblen had termed conspicuous expenditure, they also invested tremendous amounts of the new energy in production goods. Consumption itself ceased among them to be the sole measure of status; since abstention from consumption could result in tremendous increases in power, which could in turn be transformed into still more power, that power rather than the ability conspicuously to consume often became the index to status.

The process was accentuated in the British realm by the system of primogeniture and entail. This gave control over all the landed estate of the family to the eldest son. The younger sons, deprived of the opportunity to rival the achievements of their elder brothers, migrated in great numbers to reestablish in the New World a system which there often yielded even greater surpluses than that of the ancestral lands. On the enormous expanse of new continents the old system was used to concentrate control over products of tremendous value. The plantation system of the Old South was extremely well adapted for the accumulation of the means to investment even if the social norms prevailing there were to cause that surplus to be largely invested elsewhere. The plantation system never resulted in a high plane of consumption by the slaves and indentured labor who cooperated in production, but it did make possible a high plane of living for the owning class and produced the dominant leaders of the United States for a considerable period.

In England the changes in technology which caused plants to be replaced by coal and falling water as the major source of surplus energy received no immediate recognition. The old patterns justifying control over surplus remained for a long time intact. When resistance to the necessary changes was encountered, and profits in England were diminished as compared with what could be gained in the colonies or other available areas, investment abroad was sanctioned. Religious conversion, cultural enlightenment, technical advance, and profitable enterprise were conceived to be necessarily related one to another. There was in those days no powerful group to contest the right of the investor to take the product of English mines and factories to the ends of the earth if he so wished. England had access to all those areas which could be reached and dominated by the use of sea power. If the value system of one area was resistant, another could be selected. At first, because the British trade was with local nabobs, there was no need to change native low-energy systems much. The still comparatively small output of high-energy converters in England could be disposed of by dealing with a small ruling class. The probing finger of trade sought out the weak spots in all the coastal cultures—situations where surpluses generated in the British Isles might be traded for raw materials, luxuries to satisfy British consumers, or promises to pay which would satisfy British capitalists whose status and prestige at home could be enhanced by such evidence of their ability to control the future flow of energy. As trade increased, however, more changes were required in the countries invaded by trade. The degree to which the trade system became acceptable among the people with whom the British traded did, of course, vary. In large parts of China no extensive break with traditional concepts of the necessary relation between production and consumption has yet occurred. Not much more was accomplished in India or in some parts of Africa. In the Americas and the Commonwealth countries, however, the social system of the native was disorganized and finally destroyed. Over most of North America, Protestant British institutions replaced those of Catholic France and Spain, which seemed less suitable to minister to the new techniques, although there do remain areas in which the older institutions still show their influence.

COMPARISONS AND CONTRASTS

The westward movement in the United States constantly re-created low-energy systems and sometimes produced enclaved regions which reverted to a subsistence economy; however, the low-energy systems established were not able, except in the South, to create a culture sufficiently rooted and stable to prevent the subsequent rise of the new pattern. The continent's resources in many cases got into the hands of those who were little bound by traditional morality, who were not moved by considerations of status or by community or family control to preserve the old ways, who felt no spirit of *noblesse oblige* to look out for those weaker than themselves. This resulted in changes in the old system undertaken in the name of "progress" and justified by the new religion, pragmatism. In rural regions, however, the Puritan spirit helped prevent the rise of any great demand for consumption goods. It provided an ethical system that was an excellent milieu for the accumulation of converters. Where resistance was encountered, the surplus produced was adequate to increase power at an unheard-of rate and at the same time to support politicians, persuade the clergy, endow schools, subsidize the press, and generally weaken the hold of old institutions. It was sufficient also to provide through public services the education, propaganda, and advertising to cause the old ways sanctioned by traditional culture to be supplanted by new ones justified by the production of new goods and services.

The advance was not even, nor was it uniformly successful, and regions vary in the degree to which urban, secular, and pragmatic sanctions have replaced the traditional ones. All the British dominions in some degree faced similar situations. New Zealand and Australia were required to make few concessions to low-energy systems of either the native or the imported variety, but Canada finds in the descendants of old-regime France many of the same problems as are presented by the Deep South of the United States.

Germany

On the other hand Germany, while deliberately copying many of the techniques used in England and, particularly, the United States to increase physical productivity, developed high-energy technology in an area where ideals and values varied considerably from those found in England.[11] Feudal landlords and the militarists with whom they were allied played a much greater role in determining what the rate of diversion of energy into converters would be and the purposes to which the new surplus would be put. Great emphasis was laid on the power produced rather than on the individual consumption good to be secured. Surpluses from the newly available energy were put into the hands of a ruling class which was not required to share power to the degree that the British aristocracy had been. These surpluses were devoted to the creation of new converters at a rate even higher than in England and, considering the size of the stock of converters and the nature of the natural resources with which they had to work, even higher than in the United States. Such concessions as were wrung from the ruling classes took the form more often of free public services than of privately selected consumers' goods. Increasingly, education became a matter of receiving training in the techniques necessary to carry out socially prescribed duties rather than of learning for self-fulfillment. The values taught in the schools justified the diversion of energy into new converters in terms of collective rather than individual gain. Most important was the diversion of energy into the tools of war. These were twice unsuccessfully gambled in the effort to create a system which would place the resources necessary for German industrialization beyond the reach of British sea power. There never was distributed in Germany the flow of privately owned consumers' goods which so successfuly justified continuous expansion of the high-energy system to the people of the United States. Nevertheless, the system worked in such a manner as to bring Germany to a level of physical productivity far above that of many other areas that subscribed to the "free enterprise" system which is so largely dependent upon increased distribution of consumers' goods to justify increased production of producers' goods.

France

The French have not been able to modify their old system sufficiently rapidly to keep pace with the areas just discussed. Their situation is similar to the other industrialized states of northern Europe. In France those who currently control much of the surplus being produced have contented themselves with agreements which hold present techniques and present prices more or less sacrosanct. They dispose of such earnings as they control by investment in the more productive areas abroad. French adherence to the international free market preserves this right to French capitalists, who have frequently invested abroad a sizable fraction of the amount which others, such as the American government, were at the same time investing in France to increase the ability and determination to defend "free enterprise" there. The French are motivated neither by the German's sense of duty nor by the American approval of hard work and high consumption of material goods. They accumulate converters at any considerable rate only under the stress of war or preparation for it; their refusal after the First and Second World Wars to increase their war potential sufficiently to keep their place as a great power portends a diminution of their ability to shape their future. The slow accumulation of surplus of the small French investor, who seeks to gain through saving the security denied him by the

limited size of the family he raises and by the absence of extensive systems of social insurance among the peasants and businessmen, has not provided nearly the flow necessary to assure France's
place in the world. The French are left free to exercise the choice
which the presumably attractive opportunity to make profits in
this country of great potential ability and low plane of material
living should, according to many economists, make very advantageous. In actual fact the freedom of choice has not produced a
great deal of investment.

Japan

The Japanese rise to power makes the traditional explanation
of the accumulation of converters seem even less plausible.
Under feudalism a few great families had gained control over an
enormous proportion of the surplus energy produced. Their control was, if possible, more effectively sanctioned by religion,
law, and morality than that of the feudal lords of Germany. Confronted with a competing system which proved to be more powerful than that which they controlled, they quickly set out to discover the sources of its power. They were not impressed by the
official explanation and the traditional structure offered by British
theorists; they found the German methods to be more congenial
to their own culture. Their success was enormous, but they failed
to understand all its roots. They took for granted the world
market which the British had built up, in which they could
function with almost no payment for the social organization which
had made it possible. But after the First World War the picture
changed. The British position of power was much impaired. The
United States and the Commonwealth had begun to produce respectable stocks of converters of their own. The resurgence of
German industry, unhampered by the burden of debt and other
obligations which was not lifted from the British, was great and
rapid. British supremacy over the investment market and over
the world market for commodities was shaken, but nationalistic
controls, established in the interest of national integrity, as opposed to free trade, now intervened to limit the international
market for Japanese products. Furthermore, the Japanese failed
to recognize that the surplus which they controlled at the outset
of the revolution was a consequence of the long-continued policies

of population control in Japan. As they shifted to high-energy converters, there was a great increase in urbanization. This changed the relationship between parents and children in terms of both productivity and opportunity in such a way that there was an enormous increase in the rate of population growth. Japan's own food resources were inadequate to meet the demand, and she could no longer expect to secure the food necessary to meet it by the export of cheap goods. In consequence a great deal of the surplus energy being produced was diverted into the means to overcome by military power the resistance of Asiatic nationalists in alliance with or dependent upon Western power to Japan's efforts to get food. Then the accumulation of converters proved to be inadequate to the tasks demanded of it. Whatever the future role of Japan may be, it becomes obvious that the cost of the necessary accumulation of converters is not going to be met from the savings of her grossly expanded and impoverished population unless a rigid system of taxation or rationing is imposed and further population growth with its increased demand on available converters is prevented. Neither step is likely to be taken under liberal auspices.

MARXIAN THEORY AND COMMUNIST PRACTICE

We have already shown why it is hard to find in the official explanation for the accumulation of converters any satisfactory account of what actually happened in the West. It is even more difficult when we come to examine the efforts of the U.S.S.R. Basically the official Marxian analysis rests on the same fallacy that we pointed out in the classical system, that is, it is founded on the labor theory of value. The English chose a logic which supported the moral right of the capitalist to the increases in productivity. The Marxians deny any such moral right to the capitalist or landowner but grant it to labor. Now if, as we insist, converters are a cost involved in the use of high-energy technics, they represent no consumable goods as such and can no more be claimed for consumption by labor than by capital. Confronted with this fact the Marxians, like the Westerners, rather than repudiate their tradition, have chosen to act on other premises than those they claim to be following.

The Bolshevists recognized fairly early the gains to be derived from high-energy technology. The communism of their first efforts, which distributed widely the land, durable consumers' goods, and control over what little stock of high-energy converters existed, soon showed itself to be a system which would rapidly regress toward a low-energy village community and family-dominated economic pattern. Like the French before them, the Russian peasants, once in control of the land, became very conservative. As a result the movement toward further progress in the direction of Bolshevist goals came to depend almost entirely upon industrial workers of the cities, who rather quickly discovered that in the absence of a workable industrial system which could quickly deliver consumers' goods they were likely to be starved by the peasants. In consequence a whole series of measures to deny to both peasants and workers control over the surplus energy they produced was reestablished. All available goods which could be used in exchange for converters from the West were taken ruthlessly from whoever controlled them and sold abroad. Population not needed on the farms or in the cities was gathered into pools and often worked to death to build the dams, canals, roads, railroads, and buildings necessary to supplement these converters. To rationalize the failure to distribute immediately the products of the stock of converters so acquired, the myth of "the workers' state" was propagated. The old IWW used to proclaim that the purpose of the church was to teach the workers "You'll get pie, in the sky, When you die," whereas the capitalists eat pie today. Marx called religion "the opium of the people." In both cases the argument was that religious means can induce men to surrender that which they have produced and therefore have a "right" to consume. The succession of Five-Year Plans was supposed to reduce the interval between performance and Utopia, but it was designed along exactly the same lines that Marxians always claimed represented a despicable effort on the part of capitalists to rob workers of their just due.

Acting under the myth that theirs is a workers' state, and within the semi-Asiatic culture of the area dominated by the U.S.S.R., Soviet leaders have in large part turned the new surpluses available to the production of converters and the durable structures required to make them work. The productivity of some of their basic industries approaches that of many areas in the West, but the worker as consumer finds only slight increase in his consumable income. From this he can save little, and what he does save is recirculated through the productive system. Like the German worker under the Nazis, he receives what gains he does get largely in the form of collective services. He cannot choose to spend this income on goods and services which reduce his capacity to produce, nor can he compel available energy to be devoted to the production of goods the technical experts think will contribute less to future productivity than those *they* propose. The Russian system of accumulation, then, depends hardly at all upon the free choice of consumers to save and invest. On the other hand, the insistence upon the ruthless use of power to increase the stock of converters makes their system resemble in many ways that which many capitalists label as "progress," for it does make the accumulation of "capital" the primary aim of public policy.

The culture of the Russians to a very great degree is a product not of high-energy but of low-energy experience. Much of what is now being done there could once have been done but no longer can be done in other areas which are now industrialized. In these areas the consequences of industrialization were such that it was impossible, once the critical point in increasing the stock of converters was reached, to continue the processes by which this point was reached. Thus it is possible that some of the inevitable consequences of the use of high-energy converters may force a change in the Russian system if it succeeds in attaining (if it has not already done so) and retaining the necessary ratio of population to available energy.

Whatever the future may hold for the Russian system and however it may be changed, we must not neglect to analyze the actual process by which the *present* stock of converters was secured. The first steps toward the accumulation of this stock were, in terms of Communist aims, very successful. The Russians were able to make use cheaply of the enormous gains in technology which the West had achieved only as the result of expensive experiment and costly errors such as the building of equipment and physical structure that was obsolescent as soon as it was completed, technologically inefficient distribution of population, and the creation of technically "inefficient" values and beliefs. The operations of the Western economic system permitted the Communists to import during the depression in the West a great deal of physical goods at considerably less than their actual cost of production. The Bolsheviks benefited from the liquidation of those in Russia who held durable consumers' goods which could be traded and from rapid exploitation of the easily secured resources which manpower could deliver. The recurring threat of war made it possible to use the values and attitudes developed in the past in "Mother Russia" to call forth heroic efforts toward industrialization to further military preparations. But this situation also diverted surplus energy from the production of converters which could have been used to produce consumers' goods to the production of planes, tanks, guns, atom bombs, and thermonuclear weapons and the equipment to make them—as well as a navy—and which must ultimately either be destroyed in battle or become obsolete. Thus it is very difficult to make any estimate of Communist success as compared with what might have been accomplished had British and American rather than Marxian and Russian ideas and institutions prevailed. Perhaps, however, a little more historical perspective will show that the actual processes involved in accumulating converters in the U.S.R.R. are not as different from those elsewhere as either capitalist or Marxist purists would hold.[12]

It is not our purpose here to try to evaluate all the consequences of either approach to the problem. Our concern is with the problem as it is to be faced in the future, and the study of the past must deal with the facts of the past regardless of the degree to which they support or contradict the myths which are officially used to explain them. It becomes clearer as we observe the actual relations between saving and investment in the West today that abstention by individuals faced with the choice between consuming and saving has much less to do with what is invested in particular industries than official explanation would hold. In fact it is, as the struggle between Keynesians and anti-Keynesians shows, the disparity between savings and investment that represents one of the crucial problems for Western economic theory.

MODERN TECHNOLOGY AND INTERNATIONAL DISEQUILIBRIUM

But of far greater import for Western theory is the fact that *the very spread of high-energy technology has so upset long-established relations between the peoples of the earth that the whole of the twentieth century has been characterized by war and the preparation for war.* The tremendous diversion of energy into the converters needed to carry on mechanized war has led to a paradoxical situation. While continuing to adhere to the official dogma that in pursuit of private profit a society will accumulate converters more rapidly than by any other method, the West, led by the United States, has embarked upon a program in which military need under political direction has greatly supplemented the consumer's choice in determining the rate of accumulation of converters. The free choice of the consumer in the market place is made subservient to the power of groups to affect public policy and to the choice of the voter in the polling booth. The fear of the spread of communism has resulted in the accumulation of converters at a rate and in forms very different from what they probably would have been in response to the demand of households for consumers' goods. This is evidenced by the reaction to taxation which reduces the opportunity to buy those consumers' goods and to rationing systems which control physical production directly. It is not widely believed that a return to private international investment undertaken in competition with domestic demand for goods which require domestic investment would suffice to put resources where they are needed to stop the trend toward communism. So by collective political decision they are put there anyway! But this state-directed system of determining the rate of accumulation and its location is parallel in many respects to the policies actually adopted in communist states. There also the demand for consumption by households is made subservient to the need of the state to fight the inroads of the "enemy."

Similarly, replacement of individual savings by "welfare" systems of collective forced savings as a means of dealing with the time preferences of the individual or of anticipating probable future needs at the present time characterizes all the areas of the old British system as well as most of the rest of the West.

The only thing about this control that is new is the degree to which political rather than economic motives govern those who exercise the choice between investing and not investing. The great corporations and the investment bankers were making just such collective judgments long before "government" played any great part in them, and before them the feudal lords and the robber barons did so. In fact, it is quite possible that it was the refusal of such as these to acquiesce in the demand for "goods now" by the consumer rather than any self-denial on their part which gave rise to the stock of converters upon which the defense of consumers' free choice rests today.

What has been said here has been an attempt not to give a thumbnail history of high-energy society but to cite some of the experiments which have been made, however blindly—and however intermingled by historians with other movements—in the accumulation of the necessary production goods. We have shown something of the modifications of the social system which are required permanently to divert from immediate consumption into production goods energy adequate for the creation and maintenance of a high-energy system. In summary we may say that high-energy technology requires the diversion of an ever mounting volume of energy into goods which are not ends but means and requires in justification of such diversion the emergence of a morality to sustain itelf. High-energy technology also requires a continuous modification of the habits, training, and occupation of enormous numbers of people: their activities, ceasing to be ends in themselves, require justification in new and different terms. As to the kind of system which best supports and sustains these operations, we have only the very limited evidence provided by the experiments which have so far been undertaken, and there are so many variations in the cases as to make any scientific demonstration of an exact character impossible.

We do know, however, that a morality which delays or obstructs these necessary operations renders a society very vulnerable. For societies which *have* made the necessary social changes and have accumulated a stock of converters have enormous surpluses which enable them to place limits upon the choices that can be made by those living in low-energy societies.

CHAPTER 9

The Organization of Productive Effort

While our present-day experience with high-energy converters yields no definitive outline of an "ideal type" of high-energy society, it does provide evidence of some of the necessary social characteristics of such societies. The direct study of converters and the limits they impose gives some additional insight as to the direction in which societies will have to move if an increase in high-energy converters comes to be accepted. One of the clearest inferences, drawn from both historic and analytical evidence, is that high-energy converters require the use of some large production units.

By *production unit* we mean all the factors necessary to produce the goods which such a unit is expected to produce. The emphasis here is upon the unity, or wholeness, of the process. In other words, if a certain minimum number of various types of machines, trained persons, raw materials, techniques, and social organizations are required to produce a good, then that complex will here be considered an indivisible whole. For other observers and other purposes, these things, persons, and relationships may also be part of other wholes, or they may function apart from one another.

REQUIREMENTS OF THE SHIP

The production unit is for our purposes defined by its functions. For example, the sailing ship was a physical unit tremendously larger than any previously developed converter. The fact that it had to function as a physical whole is quite obvious. But what is apparently not so obvious is that its use was dependent upon rela-

200

tively stable, spatially extensive *social* relationships. The ship could be built only if there were means to accumulate at one point large amounts of surplus energy which could be permanently diverted for that purpose. Copper, iron, teak, oak and pine, cotton, tar and resin, and rope fiber are not produced by nature at the same place. They must be gathered from widely scattered points. To assure that men at the building site would perform as they were expected to perform, skills and occupational codes of conduct had to be developed and maintained. Thus for the physical creation of the ship a certain degree of social integration was required. For its use in transportation other social conditions, if they did not already exist, had to be created. The ship could be used only where trade was possible. Such trade depended not only on the presence of the physical requirements for production but also on the existence of a social system that would permit the necessary goods to be produced and subsequently to be removed from the local community. To make trading possible for a period long enough to return to the builder of the ship the surplus energy which went into it, a fairly stable code that was binding on both parties to the trade had to be maintained. Arrangements between traders and other producers in the various areas cooperating in the use of the ship were also required. Unless all these general relationships—and in any specific situation many more, peculiar to the local situation—could be assured, the ship could not be used.

As has been said, the sailing ship was the first converter to break through the limits imposed upon societies primarily served by low-energy converters. Before we discuss further the conditions which its use required, it may be well to recall the characteristics arising from the limits of the low-energy society. First of all, the norms of low-energy systems generally subsumed what has in modern times been called "economic productivity" into a general configuration of expected and approved behavior. Economic values were not distinguished from the other values held, nor was economic production separated from the physical and material factors which entered into religious, familial, political, or aesthetic activity. Second, the codes which governed economic activity tended, like other codes of behavior, to become sacred. By this we mean that the ends the individual learned to seek and the means by which he sought them were of equal concern to the groups of which he was a part; violation of these codes was thought to be injurious to the group as a whole and was frequently also thought to be of concern to the gods. Third, the physical area throughout which such a system was in operation was relatively self-sustaining. Fourth, this system was limited in extent and its contact with other systems was also limited. Such contact as did exist either was stylized and formal or was sporadic and tended when it occurred to be the occasion for conflict rather than cooperation. Finally, the roles required of the members of the system were likely to be sufficiently consistent for the means regularly used to form personality in the society to serve to induce most of its members to undertake these required roles and to carry them out within acceptable limits.

The use of the ship required disruption of some of these conditions. Where the society depended upon the family or other kinship groups, or on the organized village community as a production unit, it was difficult to secure sufficient trade to justify the use of the ship. The specialization required at one point to produce parts or materials for shipbuilding or to produce large surpluses of particular items to make a cargo necessitated radical changes in the assignment of roles among members of the production group. Extensive increase in the size of the production unit was also required. The system of identification among kinship groups cannot be extended indefinitely. Only rarely in low-energy society was the customary production unit initially large enough to serve the ship successfully. Even in these cases the new method of production meant abandonment of many previously assigned roles in favor of a system in which the great body of the population played the same few roles, such as those involved in making copra, raising cotton, digging copper, producing turpentine, etc.

This assignment of identical roles for most of the working population destroyed or made unworkable the traditional varied role assignments. For example, it would have been possible for some of the largest kinship groups in China to have produced either the materials for the ship or its cargo. However, to have done so would frequently have meant violation of many of the most sacred obligations between parents and children, wives and husbands, priests and patrons, teachers and students, artisans and customers, and even war lords and those whom they protected. Consequently in many parts of China it was not possible to get the populace to engage in the kinds of production which would have made trade most profitable for the Chinese merchant and for the "foreign devil." [1] In most other places where the kinship unit was used it was just too small to serve alone as the means to produce the ship or its cargo. Surviving intact, it must interfere with seaborne trade. If, on the other hand, its members did engage in the necessary relations within a large unit that was capable of serving and being served by the ship, the old system was deprived of much of its vitality and lost much of its pragmatic reason for being.

In fact, then, a very significant limit upon the development of the ship was the inability of the trader to induce the required individuals to cooperate in a unit large enough to justify the use of the ship. The ship actually came into extensive use where, on the one hand, some social system such as feudalism or slavery operated to provide surplus energy enough to make its use feasible and where, on the other, those who would have opposed trade were not possessed of sufficient power to stop it.

What was true in connection with the ship became even more marked when other high-energy converters began to be adopted. When the freely wandering buffalo was replaced by privately owned cattle fenced in by barbed wire and shipped by rail, the Plains Indian was forced to choose between remaining attached to a system which depended upon energy supplied by the buffalo, and which became every day less capable of regeneration, and attaching himself to the iron horse at the price of the abandonment of most of his traditional way of life. The Navaho today has to choose between life in the hogan, with accompanying poverty in material things and in the services which money will buy, and the abandonment of his people's social system in favor of employment by the Santa Fe railroad or some other agent of high-energy society. His kinship unit is not adaptable to such converters as the locomotive. This conflict faces many peoples and many cultures, and most people so threatened will attempt to resist a system that will eventually destroy their social organization. But the use of high-energy converters in many cases makes such change unavoidable.

TECHNIQUE AND ORGANIZATION

The efficient size of the production unit is in part dependent upon the technological requirements of high-energy converters. Since the purpose of adopting such converters is frequently to substitute as much energy derived from low-cost fuel as possible for energy derived from food, power-driven tools must replace manpower wherever feasible. Each job must be broken down into units that some mechanical device can perform. However, some single operations may require a very expensive tool. To form an airplane wing by extrusion involves the use of a press which costs as much energy to produce as a hundred or more wings made by riveting the component pieces together. Continuous use of this press is the only means of reducing to the lowest possible point the cost per wing. This means that the production unit of which it is a part must produce enough planes to require full-time use of the press. Of course the use of the press may so greatly increase efficiency that the cost of its use even when it is used only part of the time will be less than that of any known alternative method. But economies will still be effected by using it more, until it is working all the time its maintenance will permit.

More complicated operations on a single part may be achieved by the combination in a single machine of a number of fairly cheap tools positioned and operated by high-energy converters. One such machine, for example, can perform all the operations required to change a rough casting into a finished automobile cylinder block. By means of such combinations the attention of one man can be substituted for that of a large number of men each using a power-operated tool. Once set up, this machine can produce a large number of parts with a minimum of human guidance. The machine itself, rather than the single tool or converter, becomes the unit requiring guidance and adjustment to compensate for the human qualities which cannot be built into it. Again, however, such a machine is economical only when it can be used full time. So the minimum size of the production unit is set by the full-time use of the machine performing the operation done least frequently in making the product. Other elements may be such that it takes a dozen of the machines used constantly to one of the machines used least frequently. To be economical, this may require mass production, for the prototypes of many modern production machines cost almost unbelievable amounts of energy before a single consumption good can be produced to justify that expenditure.

The efficient minimum size of the production unit becomes a matter for calculation; the point must be found at which the energy diverted into converters, plus the costs of their use, divided among the units produced becomes less than the energy required to make a unit by some alternative method. For some operations, small units may be technologically as efficient as any known larger unit. For others, it is clear that only very large production units can deliver goods at the least energy cost. When this is the case, social arrangements have to be created which will induce the needed individuals to cooperate in such large units within the sometimes very close limits technologically demanded. Also, the costs of creating and maintaining such social units must be less than the gain from the use of high-energy technology, else there is no economy. Production in such large units requires that consumption, too, must become uniform and predictable, for only if the goods produced by high-energy technology satisfy those who use them will consumption justify production. Knowledge of the immediate costs of the physical operations is not all that is required for the calculation of the most effective technological unit. There are other factors, such as research, to be considered. It may well be that only through the distribution of research costs among many production units can the energy savings produced by research be made to equal the energy costs of providing for it. In some cases the costs of research can be met only by mass marketing. It is this fact rather than production itself that requires such essentially simple products as soap to be produced in large units.

Distribution costs must also be considered. To induce a large number of consumers independently to choose a specific good rather than some alternative involves some of the same types of costs as are involved in production itself. Modern advertising and propaganda rest upon the use of high-energy converters. The costs of copy, the artist's studio, the engraver's shop, the composing room, the preparation of the initial plates, and the makeready on the press are almost the same for the first copy whether

fifty thousand or five million copies are to be run. The master
negative of a moving picture and the master record for a sound
track are similarly costly prototypes. It is as costly to prepare a
show for one TV or radio station as for a whole network. The
means of creating values via mass communication will be least
costly, then, when a production unit is large enough to supply a
market created by very widespread use of these costly prototypes.

THE "CURSE" OF BIGNESS

Some thinkers, critical of the concentration of power developed
through the use of large production units, have advocated reducing their size. From what we have said here it is clear that smaller
production units may in some cases be technically just as efficient
as larger ones. The case can only be made in specific terms, however. The decentralization of such economic empires as Unilever,
Shell, Ford, du Pont, or General Motors might serve to show that
a successful attack on bigness need not presage a diminution of
technical efficiency. It might in fact produce greater efficiency.
But the attack on bigness as such does not answer, it merely raises
the question of how large the production unit must be to be
technically most efficient.

There is proposed by some a kind of nostalgic retreat, a return
to the family or village community as a production unit. The
proposal gains plausibility through the fact of the development
of the fractional horsepower motor. With it the family can now
serve as the efficient unit for some types of use of cheap energy.
It is, however, assumed by some idealists that all or nearly all the
goods required for the family can be produced with primary
dependence upon these motors: [2] thus the family can again become the basic production unit and some of the more critical
problems of modern society can be solved.

It is true that we can now wash clothing mechanically in the
home. We can chop food, grind coffee or meal, refrigerate perish-
ables, and keep ourselves cool or warm. With a small motor we
can run a sewing machine, beat a cake, or mix drinks. But most
operations cannot be done efficiently with small units. To provide
for each family the equivalent in miniature of the textile industry,
the furniture industry, or the automobile industry, to cite only a

few industries whose products are largely consumed in family units, would be far more costly than using even the most primitive hand methods. To think of duplicating for each family such necessary services as are supplied by public utilities, railroads, steel mills, machine tool factories, and all the basic operations involved in mining, milling, smelting, refining, lumbering, and shipping would be fantastic. There is no likelihood that the family will become, in the near future, the production unit for any basic commodity other than some of the simple organic products. In fact, as has been shown, even to retain the family-sized farm requires considerable dependence upon other social units if the farmer is to use high-energy converters. We face the fact, then, that wherever high-energy converters are to be used, whether under the auspices of communism, capitalism, or socialism, large production units will have to be created.

Concentration of Control

A necessary consequence of the increase in size of the production unit is centralization of control over the actual operations of production. In low-energy society, where the bulk of production is dependent upon the work of a relatively small amount of energy, the head of a family or some other leader may personally direct production. Small functional groups of artisans such as weavers, smiths, or carpenters may be subject to immediate control by a master artist or mechanic. Alternatively, some of the work may be so highly stylized and occupational codes may be so binding that no judgment by the artisan is required or possible. By its very nature, high-energy technology frequently makes such control ineffective.

In many of the high-speed operations involved in high-energy technology the vagaries of judgment among those producing render them inadequate actually to control operations. Nor is it possible to depend upon stylized arts passed along in the training of artisans. Mass production requires scheduling that is exact to the fraction of a second and demands controls over heat, temperature, chemical constituents, and other measurements that can be maintained only by experts. The efficiency of the decisions of the experts can be judged by "amateurs" only in terms of the results obtained *after* the operations have been completed. Even if the

decisions have been wrong, they cannot be replaced by the judgments of those who see only part of the production process or only
the result in the form of the completed product. Those who plan
the organization as a whole can frequently learn much from on-
the-spot judgments of the operators of machines, section chiefs,
and others, but the integration of such knowledge into the system
is still essential.

While some concentration of control is thus a necessary consequent of high-energy technology, it is also true that concentration
may be undertaken where it is not technically required. Centralization may contribute to the ego satisfaction of power-hungry
man. It may be required in the interest of a social class or it may
be developed to secure objectives other than technical efficiency.
For example, the Russians have gone well beyond the point of
greatest technical efficiency in their control over agriculture. They
apparently seek neither the largest return of surplus energy from
their farms nor the largest total amount of food that it is possible
to produce. Their aim is to secure the largest amount of food that
can be taken from the farms to industrial sites. Much that the
land-owning peasant could and would produce under private
property is, under their present system, lost. To permit the Russian peasant to return to a hoe culture, although it might improve
his lot, make the system more stable or more democratic, and
increase the total amount of food produced in Soviet Russia,
might also force the wholesale return of workers to the farms and
the abandonment of further "progress" toward the use of high-
energy technology.

Similarly, there have been built up in the West vast aggregations of power over production, not in the interest of the greatest
possible physical production or technical efficiency [3] but in the
interest of some family, class, or group of "insiders." Certain of
these aggregations could be reduced with no loss in efficiency.
But many units must remain large, and it is impossible to retain
technical efficiency in these units and distribute control among
the amateurs who constitute the owners on the assumption that
competition among these amateurs will bring about the most
effective technical use of available resources. To all intents and
purposes, control by owner has been lost. As we shall see, partly
it was lost through abdication and partly through usurpation. But

chiefly it was lost as an inevitable consequence of high-energy technology, and the portion so lost cannot be regained by quoting strictures against collectivism or repeating the rules against conspiracy in restraint of trade. No matter what moral or legal fictions are employed to defend it, it is still true that the high degree of coordination required by high-energy technology perpetuates a high degree of centralized control. Such control may be carried out by an agent of a democratic state, by a corporate bureaucrat, or by the functionary of a Soviet trust. It cannot rise spontaneously from the common values of those who must cooperate to produce. The character of the skills and knowledge which are required to operate the system, and the costs of acquiring them, are such that only a few individuals, if any, can be trained adequately. Whether those who know and propagate this knowledge are made subordinate eventually to a referendum politically imposed by a democratic state, by organized property owners, or by the priests of a cult promoting technological efficiency—or whether management itself becomes the ruler, independent[4] of such referendums—is not determined by high-energy technology. That such a bureaucracy of experts exist and administer the system *is* required by high-energy technology.

SPECIALIZATION AND DIVISION OF LABOR

High-energy technology has another, and at first glance antithetic, consequence: in one sense it distributes rather than concentrates control. This follows from the requirement of territorial and functional division of labor. Low-energy societies cannot make extensive use of such division. Transportation costs mount as men are segregated into specialized communities to and from which they must transport a large part of the goods consumed, the raw materials processed, and the finished goods produced. Such costs cannot be met from the small surpluses produced in low-energy societies. Here every community becomes in large measure self-subsistent, and production involves the assignment of a few general roles rather than a number of specific and narrow specialties. It is not possible in low-energy society for many people to spend time and energy learning the extremely elaborate and detailed skills and knowledge that are required for such roles as that played by a modern organic chemist or nuclear physicist. Only those roles can be prescribed which when performed will return to the individual and to the community sufficient reward to compensate for the energy and time spent in training. In low-energy society the costs of acquiring an occupational role and the rewards to be secured from it are rather quickly learned. The occupational code which teaches those who play a role what they should do and what they may expect by way of compensation is likely to be tested frequently against the actual behavior of those with whom the occupational specialist must cooperate. That is to say, for example, that the local miller, even if he is supported in such an effort by millers in other communities, cannot very long maintain a code which prevents his cooperation with the local butcher, baker, and candlestick maker, for they are necessary to complete his own way of life. Similarly, if in a community the miller is so poorly rewarded that he moves away or is unable or unwilling to induce his or any other man's son to assume his role, the local system must and will, if the services are required, come to provide the means necessary to replace him. This necessity to provide locally for the regeneration of occupational controls stands in important contrast to certain elements of high-energy systems, which, as will be shown, permit codes to be set up outside the community and supported from afar which continuously disrupt the local community.

As has been pointed out, the use of high-energy converters to replace men involves the division of tasks into minute specialized operations which machines can be set up to perform. The specialists who are required to build and operate these machines depend in turn upon the makers of instruments and control devices, which involve further specialization. In consequence, high-energy technology requires many times the number of socially approved occupational alternatives that were acceptable in most low-energy systems. Moreover, as a result of the fact that the materials needed are, in their natural state, widely dispersed, specialized communities must be set up to process them. Accordingly, whole communities appear which are devoted to the assembly of the specialized products of other communities; we see communities engaged in the production of a single product such as tin, copper, lead, or mercury, or the raising of a single crop such as wheat, rice, sisal, tobacco, cotton, or coffee, and others devoted to the manufacture of products made of a single commodity such as paper, glass, or rubber.

These specialized communities are in turn composed of specialists. There are those who locally provide such goods and services as bakery products and policing. There are those who perform locally a specialty which is quite uncharacteristic either of other local groups or of the distant groups with which they, as specialists, must cooperate in order to produce. A good example is the builder of specialized machine tools. Men so situated are no longer guided adequately by the traditional codes which they learned as children. Neither are they equipped as individuals constantly to make the judgments which would serve to keep them cooperating one with another. Here, customarily, new codes of action grow up.[5] That is, common prescriptions or proscriptions based on past experience of groups who have been carrying out a given task are drawn up, and members of the group are expected to act alike when confronted with a given type of situation. These regulations may take the form of union rules, company rules, codes developed into professional "ethics," and frequently even laws. They may govern all the members of a given industry, craft, profession, or type of trade. They may deal with particular local situations such as those reflected in chambers of commerce, parent-teacher associations, trade councils, ministerial associations, etc. Each code grows out of a specialized situation, where presumably it has adequate sanction and will continue to be regenerated by experience.

Depersonalization and Disunity

What is perhaps of greatest importance here is that integration through central operations among those who deal with functional groups may interfere with integration at the local level, and vice versa. There is frequently no erosion at the local level, because of the fact that neighbors judge one another. The local farmer in the United States may live next door to the railroad engineer who operates the milk train, but frequently nothing done at the local level will affect either the wage the engineer receives or the price he pays for milk. The engineer will depend upon his union to deal with a distant railroad management, and nothing specific about milk as such will enter into the determination of his wages. In turn, the farmer may depend upon a cooperative or a great

corporation such as Borden's or National Dairy to intercede for
him in determining the price of milk. He may depend upon the
Interstate Commerce Commission or a state Public Utilities Commission to set the railroad freight rates. He may come to depend
upon the government itself to set both the price of milk and railroad rates. He may be friend or enemy to the engineer next door;
their relation in production will not be affected by their personal
relation. True, there must also be a set of codes by which the
farmer and the engineer pursue their common goals in local
church, school, and government, in recreation, sanitation, and
public health measures. There will, however, frequently be
effected "insulation," preventing the local attitude from affecting
the occupational code. During the depression college professors
generally deplored the low estate of farmers, but neither they nor
the farmers would have thought of paying or accepting other than
the market price for eggs. During inflation they join in deploring
the low estate of professors but for the most part they would
both think that there was something wrong or even degrading in
the paying or the accepting of anything other than the market
price for produce.

To repeat, in high-energy society the community ceases to be
a self-contained unit in which the codes that are produced operate
upon one another in such a manner as to make them mutually at
least tolerable. Instead it becomes a locus of interaction which
may continuously generate local conflict. The fact that conflicting
attitudes cannot serve to modify the conduct which generates
those attitudes does not mitigate the conflict; it accentuates it.
When it is apparent that no kind of persuasion can alter the acts
of an opponent, the frustration and resultant aggression are likely
to be greater, rather than less, than they would be where argument
and reason could produce altered conduct.

The significance of local conflict generated by codes not of local
origin is manifested in the many operations of modern society
which still depend upon consensus at the community level. Jury
trial, for example, is necessary for much law enforcement in the
United States. Such a system assumes that a sample of a local
community will represent the forces actively at work there to
produce values required for necessary control by law. But in the
case of a code which grew out of experience quite other than that

generally shared in a locality and was placed on the statute books by pressure on a legislature, jury trial would be almost totally unreliable as a means to enforcement of that code. Thus "functional" codes may operate to threaten or destroy the codes which support local traditional values, and vice versa. High-energy society can, then, no longer rely on locally generated values to assure control over many activities which require control. Many specialists whose activities are of the greatest importance to the local community are out of reach of local control. For example, no local jury can penalize the distant manufacturer of drugs if he neglects to take some precaution and a local child dies as a result. Only knowledge and control by some expert who knows what should be done will be effective. On the other hand, a jury composed only of those adversely affected by the enforcement of a code adopted elsewhere will be unlikely to bring a verdict against a local code violator. A whole series of devices must be set up which will provide necessary local autonomy in the face of equally necessary control by those who are responsive to the needs of occupational or other specialists for code enforcement.

CHANGING PROPERTY RIGHTS

An area in which this difficulty is most widely felt and in which it is increasingly apparent is property rights. As high-energy technology comes into wider use, the relations between property owners and other producers undergo marked change. In every property system, morality sanctions an area of conduct within which an owner of property is free to make certain disposition of goods and services which are denied to nonowners. He may, for example, determine the present use of goods. He may determine the future use of goods, in some cases even for generations after his own death. He may determine the disposition of the product of goods or the offspring of livestock. In some cases he may destroy the goods themselves. The number and importance of these rights is a measure of the degree to which private property is a significant element in a culture.

While political events, military conquest, geographic cataclysm, and even population growth have also affected property, many of the most striking changes have come from a shift in the use and source of energy. To demonstrate the point let us go back for a moment to a characterization of property as found in low-energy systems.

Broadly speaking, *property* can be classified as "land" or "personalty." Of course such a definition distorts to a certain degree when it is applied to many societies known to both historians and anthropologists. But all societies treat possessions that relate to natural resources, such as forests, arable lands, salt licks, mineral deposits, and grazing lands, differently from possessions regarded as an extension of the personality, such as tools, ornaments, articles of dress, and weapons. In the low-energy society land was only rarely, and for short periods, assumed to be as completely subject to the control of an individual owner as personalty might be. It is easy to see why. In a society dependent upon organic converters the consequence of land misuse is rather quickly apparent. If the relation between property in land and the permanent welfare of the society is not recognized in time, the society is threatened. Even in areas of abundant natural resources, the wanton destruction of nature's gifts leads to group disapproval or societal suicide. In some areas, such as the valley of the Nile, nature restores the balance upset by man, and the time of retribution is delayed until population growth forces more careful husbandry as the price of survival. Generally, however, property in land is constantly subject to control derived in part from the character of local plant and animal ecology.

Rational versus Traditional Land Rights

Development of the concept of property in land in low-energy societies takes place in terms of the interpersonal relations found there. Land is not only property, and as such a factor in economic productivity; it is also the locale within which other institutions function. We have already discussed the dependence of morals upon the interpersonal relationships which create and foster them. The relationships that have their basis in property are no exception. In low-energy systems property is likely to be coextensive with the other institutions of the community, and within the limits of low-energy converters property concepts evolve reciprocally with changes in other institutions.

The shift in the character of the field, gradient, and limits which accompanies the use of a new energy converter changes the spatial character of property relationships. When such a shift occurs, the owner of land may personally cease to be subject to the morality of the community in which the property is found. The "rights" of the owner may in turn cease to be held morally binding by the members of the community in which those rights have to be asserted. The owner sometimes loses the ability actually to carry on the functions required of him. Under absentee ownership, agents increasingly carry out the functions of the owner. These agents, while themselves subject to local interpersonal influences, are frequently unable to respond to them, being bound to pursue the values of the owners whom they represent. Thus, there is no necessary and immediate interpersonal relationship between owners and those who dwell on the land where the property rights must be respected. The automatic check which formerly protected the ecological base of the community ceases to be assured. As a matter of fact, there is frequently divergence between the morality taught in the community in which the land is situated and that taught to the children of the absentee owner. This has often led to revolt; even where it does not come to that, continuous diversion of the surpluses of the land must take place to provide the military and political coercion required to assure property rights. Corruption and widespread disrespect for the state and its agents follow. If, on the other hand, some other source of energy (such as the sea power of the Romans) reinforces the power of the owner so that he is successful in maintaining his dominance over the land, apathy and conscientious sabotage grow.

Absentee ownership is unlikely to prosper in societies where the only surplus energy available is produced by the husbandmen. In low-energy society a system of land ownership, to be successful, must impose duties upon the owner as well as the nonowner. This is not to say that "justice" prevails. The property system may sanction the transfer of all but the barest level of physical subsistence for propertyless persons. It may sanction great wastage by a few and complete exclusion and starvation for those not needed to till the land. But to retain property rights the land itself has to be kept producing. Men have to be taught as children the necessity of abiding by, if not the justice of, the property system under which they function. No matter how potent the myth by which they are rationalized, other systems of landed property are likely to be short-lived.

OWNERSHIP: PAST AND PRESENT

Personalty is subject to different limits from land. Personalty relates to goods which by their nature are limited in extent. Great castles and landscaped estates, public monuments, paintings and sculptures, barrels of rubies and emeralds, piles of gold bars, bales of silks, stables of horses, harems of wives, which represented the greatest accumulations of such property, performed their function in low-energy society largely by display or storage. Their possessor need have neither intelligence nor social insight. Only the actual wielders of tools and weapons controlled things functionally necessary for survival. What a man can do with hand tools is restricted by human physiology. Property concepts cannot enlarge these limits, but they can greatly contract them. In almost every society social rules state who can use certain tools, and under what conditions. Personal property in tools is thus limited through social definition in terms of division of labor locally held to be moral. Other types of personal property, such as ornaments and articles of dress, are likewise circumscribed by rules. These vary from some simple ones that merely require indication of the sex of the wearer to extremely complex classifications prescribing or proscribing ornamentation and dress in detail on the basis of occupation, rank, caste, class, age, religion, and other factors. Through its property system a society may deny all but a tiny fraction of the population the right to wield known tools, to consume many of the products produced, to share the rewards of increased productivity, or even to avoid personally painful consequences of socially approved arrangements. Such a society may still be stable and well organized and give little evidence that most of its members feel themselves to be ill-used. Motives which induce individuals to act seem here, as in many other elements of social organization, to be much more a function of expectations derived from experience with social myth than of an instinctive drive toward acquisition, the hedonistic calculus of the rational man, or an inherent wish to be creative. But what we have been saying about personal property does not imply that there is no functioning morality: it emphasizes that the system must provide a social definition of behavior which not only tells the property owner what he can do but also tells the nonowner what the rights of the property owner are and makes him accept them. Personalty is thus dependent, as is the concept of property in land, upon a generally observed set of controls taught to all children, defining the roles of all. It must therefore be affected no less than land by changes which change the roles required.

A shift in the energy system tends to undermine previous concepts of property in personalty just as it does in land. Ownership of a railroad, a utility, or the widely scattered resources which must be assembled in a high-energy system must be based upon a multiplicity of communities. No single community could serve as the base for operations, no community evolve all the necessary controls. Each of the communities which must serve the whole organization is bound to be in some measure different from others also functioning. There is nothing in the low-energy society to create the elements required to operate such a property system. The property rights necessary have, in fact, to be created with the aid of surpluses from new sources.

True, there were collective property concepts related to land in the old systems. For example, the English common, the Russian *mir,* and the upland pastures of Switzerland functioned under such a concept. But all this collective property, like private property, involved controls which could be generated in one small area. The centralized control necessary for more widespread cooperation to protect absent owners of land or personalty was usually lacking.

Except for goods used to establish status through display, most personal property rested on the ability of the user directly to control and use that property. He might also make provision for the inheritance or even the destruction of his property without greatly affecting the similar rights of others. The culture might, in fact, require that all his personal property be destroyed or be buried with his body. Obviously when the survival of a society comes to depend upon preservation and functional operation of goods "personally" owned, as in the case of a public utility, a great bank or railroad, or even a single factory, then it is no longer possible to permit such latitude to the private owner. If he fails to function under the prescribed rules, he may lose his property rights. Unlike simple tools or possessions created primarily for the ends sought by the individual owner, production goods are now created to serve the ends of others than their owners. It is not possible, then, to convert them, at the whim of an owner, to any desired purpose, without at the same time disturbing the means by which others may attain their own ends.

Control by Management

However the fiction of private property in production goods is maintained, the operational meaning of ownership is altered by the character of the relationships actually created in high-energy systems. The property fiction tends to obscure the new relationships, but the new facts force change. The old system could depend upon almost automatic creation of the attitudes necessary to guarantee the sanctity of property. Under widespread absentee ownership of property, no such automatic process takes place. Persuasion, conversion, and coercion become necessary. The old guidance provided by the immediate self-interest of the owner likewise proves insufficient to make the system work. New morals and new institutions are needed. They are hammered out so long as possible behind the façade provided by the current myths. These myths become less and less functional in the sense that if the individual naively accepts them he is less and less likely to achieve the results he has been taught to expect. This follows from the fact that technology sets limits on the specific operations of specific converters. To run a railroad involves specific techniques, not generalized ones. To build a plant to produce penicillin or an atom bomb we must call upon a different body of specific knowledge from that involved in producing cotton cloth or cash registers. Decisions, to be effective, must be based upon an enormous amount of information available only to specialists. To coordinate the operations of a large number of specialists is again a specific technique involving the cooperation of large numbers of persons. The great body of knowledge, skills, and techniques required is available to no one person. It becomes a function of social organization, which, to be understood, must itself be the subject of scientific study. The system cannot be operated effectively by the hunches, guesses, fears, and hopes of widely scattered amateurs who happen to be owners. Neither can it be controlled as a consequence of the collective morality of a self-contained community which is itself now merely one part of the necessary system.

Neither the old variety of collective ownership represented in such examples as the Russian *mir* nor the individual produced in a self-contained community is equipped with means or guided toward ends adequate to deal with all the factors involved in operating high-energy technology. The freedom of choice of such individuals is, in fact if not in myth, a definitely limited one. The owner is no more free of these limits in making his choices than is any other cooperator in production. The ways in which he might wish to use his property are as apt to be incompatible with the actual achievement of his goals as those of any other person involved. There is no omniscience attached to ownership. Unless we can show some divine power operating specially to provide owners with information and guidance not available to other citizens, we must assume that their choices are also subject to error.

COLLECTIVISM VERSUS INDIVIDUALISM

Under the few extensive political systems existing in low-energy societies in the past, whatever necessary coordination was required was secured either by direct political means, such as taxation, or through the extension of the idea that personal property was vested in some divinely ordained person such as the monarch. Acts which interfered with the monarch's rights were barred, and vast areas were made subject to controls not dependent upon local decision. But when a local system was made subordinate to a more extensive one, it was not necessary to alter it greatly. A wide variance in morality from region to region was consonant with production, since in each case the productive system was relatively self-contained. The only alteration that might be required was to develop the right of the sovereign to remove surpluses from the locality in which they were produced. No concept of functional interdependence and no specialized but subordinate morality was necessarily involved. Such "ownership" by kings or churches could thus provide for production with low-energy systems. The question as to whether it could supply a property system adequate for the widespread integration of specialized communities and occupations required by high-energy technology is another proposition.

This is not to say that it is impossible to create an adequate collective property concept because of some obstacle in terms of human nature. The argument that the hedonistic calculus, the instinct of property, or some other inherent characteristic of man prevents the operation of collective property concepts is fairly easily refuted. History, psychology, and anthropology demonstrate that organisms apparently anatomically indistinguishable from modern man did create systems in which the very concept of the individual as we understand it was completely unknown. Many millions of people now living are so completely identified with others in a community that the concept of private property in land, for example, is absolutely unknown. There is ample evidence that a collectivist concept of property of the old communal variety has existed, but the question as to whether it can be maintained under the conditions required for the use of high-energy converters is not answered in the affirmative by this evidence.

The old collective concept of property arose out of the close relationships between groups, the mutual support of dominant institutions, and local interdependence created by a relatively simple and self-contained system of division of labor. As was indicated earlier, it is maintained by the group processes operative in such situations. So it would seem that if these conditions are changed the old concepts will be altered. Since high-energy technology does require changes in these relations, it follows that any return to the old types of communism based on communally generated attitudes is impossible. The Marxian utopia, in which the "state will wither away" because everyone is automatically taught to want to do what he has to do is thus obviously incompatible with the use of high-energy systems.

The Modern Myth of Ownership

Nor is the case for pure individualistic exercise of the right of private owners much stronger. So long as it was assumed that there were far-off divine ends toward which the society inevitably moved, some test of the ability of the individual to contribute to those distant ends might be made. Collective morality could thus give direction to individual choice. In the absence of such a framework there is a tendency to assume the finality of end values as residing in the individual of the moment. But even assuming this, we still face the fact that the particular individual attempting to use his property to serve his own ends has often little or no knowledge of the social and technological transformation necessary to achieve them. On the other hand, if we assume the values themselves to arise in any degree out of the experience with the transitory world of which the individual is a part, then a further problem presents itself. Which of his values are emergent, which decadent? Again, obviously ownership carries with it no talisman to make judgment infallible. The owner is as likely to be confused by his conflicting loyalties, objectives, and identifications as is any other person in the society.

When we apply these generalizations to the specific operations which the owner is supposed to perform, we face a reality which makes the *de facto* dominance of the owner almost impossible. Since the accumulation of converters required to make extensive use of high-energy technology is very great, the ownership of shares in such converters must, if widespread private property is to survive, be extremely widely scattered. Very few of the investors in production goods in such a system have any intimate knowledge of the industries in which they invest. In fact the tendency in capitalist countries is, in order to spread the risk, to make investment a second- or third-hand operation by participation in retirement funds, insurance, the purchase of annuities, and other similar means. This results in a situation where the "owner" does not even know in which operations his claims are vested. In a socialist society, in which he "owns" part of everything, he is even more ignorant. He is thus stripped of all effective means of making his choices known, except for the final one of receiving the goods delivered as a result of his investment or of exchanging this claim for some other similar claim on future goods. It is obvious that this is not ownership in the old sense any more than ownership of a horse can be acquired by betting on his performance in a race. The position of a stockholder is perhaps more nearly parallel to the betting situation than it is to the earlier but still current mythical concept of private property in corporate stocks. Obviously the myth, however required by tradition, is not functional in terms of the actual determination of how the products of energy will be distributed through the society.

In the West ownership in the sight of the law is a bundle of rights which are presumably exercisable by the owner of a thing. These rights are defined by the state, which protects the owner in their exercise. But there is no way that the state can prevent that abdication of these rights by an owner, which is a common occurrence. Many property rights can be contractually waived in such a manner that their subsequent reassertion will be denied by the state. Unless these rights are closely identified with other rights considered to be inalienable, the state will even enforce a contract which operates to deprive an owner of his property rights; witness, for example, the legality of nonvoting stock or the court denial of access to the books of a corporation to one of its stockholders. This process of abdication has been pragmatically justified in that it permitted the development of the high-energy society. The myth making it moral is not widely established as yet.

THE CORPORATION

The reasons for this abdication will probably be better understood if we recall the historic process by which it came about. As already noted, during the period of dominance of sail the sharing of risk and sharing of surplus derived from the use of the ship was morally sanctioned. It became clear that in the operation of the ship there was a possibility of gain and of loss far in excess of the amount that could be regularly gained or lost through the average operations of a low-energy system. At first the captain of the ship, usually a considerable owner in his own right, made the actual operational decisions—when to sail, what to ship, when and to whom and at what price to sell. Slowly companies of owners, retired captains, or financiers assumed those of the captain's functions which could be handled by agents on land. Sound business judgment was thus made consistently available to the company of gentlemen; the best seaman and navigator would not necessarily be familiar with the market, the quality of goods, or even the social customs of all the places in which he might have to trade. Special charters were granted by European sovereigns, vesting in such companies, usually in return for a share of the profits, joint rights of operation under a common title. Property was thus made a collective right of the company. This was a modern revival of the corporation, a body as well known to Roman law as the individual. British and other Western law continued to be phrased as though it dealt only with individuals, but it did in fact endow these companies with a fictitious corporate personality. This personality exercised the actual functions of ownership, which were thus severally stripped from the persons of the owners.

The growth of these companies specially endowed with rights was rapid as British institutions (along with similar French, Dutch, Spanish, and other Western property systems) spread in all the areas engaged in trade, and it was accelerated by the advent of steam. The idea was adopted widely in the emergent social system of the United States. The corruption of legislatures by businessmen in pursuit of the special privileges that incorporation offered finally led state legislatures in the United States to set up means through which to grant charters almost automatically to all comers meeting specific requirements. Finally, under an interpretation of the Fourteenth Amendment to the Constitution, corporations were endowed with the elements of control which had been abdicated by the stockholder, and with such additional elements as the law could confer. The growth of the corporation has been similar wherever Roman law previously existed. In some cases, where the survival of feudal and familial institutions permitted vast concentration of wealth without widespread sale of stock, it was possible to concentrate adequate control without the use of the corporation. This trend was particularly marked in China and in France. In Russia the Bolsheviks were able to seize control whether it was vested in the person or in the corporation and to abolish private title to land and to producers' goods. They set out to distribute claims on consumption directly, without resort to claims based on the ownership of production goods. Here, too, trusts exercise elements of ownership similar to those exercised in the United States. Variations of these several methods of control can be found in all countries which have made any use of high-energy converters.

Capitalistic versus Communistic Ownership

Whether one examines the operations of a Russian trust or of an American corporation, it becomes clear that control is not effectively exercised by owners. How effective the average American stockholder in a giant corporation may be in exercising his rights as owner as compared with the average Russian (who presumably owns what is managed by the Orgburo and the subordinate bureaucracy) is a matter of degree. This separation of ownership from control makes it impossible for either system effectively to claim that it is in the power of the owner to make the judgments necessary to keep the system in equilibrium. Control is far more likely to rest in the hands of those who determine the ends for which the society exists and the present value of goods and services, and in the hands of the technicians who make the system serve those ends and yield those goods, than it is in the hands of most of those with legal claim to ownership. As a matter of fact, where the ends are well known and accepted almost universally and the means to attain them are known to depend on expert knowledge, as in war or education, the elimination of the whole concept of ownership is common, and definition is made only in terms of control. Who "owns" the Army, or Harvard University? For purposes of making contracts with private persons the Army or Harvard is treated as a corporation, but the relationship to the "owners" is so ephemeral that no amount of effort to get people to act as if they owned the property in question is effective. Almost identical attitudes prevail among the great majority of the "owners" of the AT&T and the TVA. What comes clear is that the ends are made to justify the means, and control rather than ownership of the means is important. That is, we ask not what the owner wants but whose ends the corporation he owns is serving. At times some of the largest corporations have operated without paying a single cent in dividends. All the producers except owners —management, labor, suppliers of materials, and government— have been rewarded, but not the stockholders. It is absurd to hold that these businesses were run for the benefit of their owners, or were serving the self-interest of property holders. If we examine the situation in Russia under the Communists or in Germany under the Nazis, we find the same paradoxical condition to exist in so far as effective control of the citizen "owner" is concerned.

Management functions to satisfy some ends. The discovery of what ends, or whose ends, is made not by definition in terms of ownership but by ascertaining who was actually served by the activities of the industry. If, in fact, it serves groups and individuals with many divergent ends, this fact cannot be disregarded in understanding the survival of the system. Close observation will show that the ends served are created by many competing groups and institutions. Management is required to serve all of them in some degree. The degree to which the ends of one or another group are served will reveal something of the strength of the values created and mediated. If a "profit-motivated" society serves the ends of the state to the amount of 40 or 50 per cent of all the goods and services produced, there is no basis for assigning "profit" as *the* motive for that production. The fact that the eventual profit taker seeks to maximize his return makes him in that respect no different from groups such as management and labor. Similarly, the Russian state, as profit taker, must consider the limits within which it may take profits if cooperation among producing groups is to be maintained.

New Forms of Organization

The separation of ownership from control involves a whole new series of relationships which the myth of ownership does not cover. The growth of corporate property has technological roots. It will not be exorcised by fleeing from one ideology to another. The emergence of a new morality and law reflecting the reality is slow, but the reality of corporate loyalty as distinguished from community identification or national patriotism constantly thrusts itself forward for recognition.

Concomitant with this development there has been an increase in organization among other groups involved in production. "Labor" has undergone many of the same kinds of change that characterized property owning. The worker, stripped of the protection previously afforded by local morality, and brought into competition with another, cheaper converter, wielded by a powerful organization of property, found himself unable alone to compete successfully for his share of the new surpluses. The old organization of artisans has not been adequate to meet these conditions. In place of the simple and limited local systems, which included the master craftsmen and owners, there have grown up, wherever high-energy technology has come into use, very extensive and powerful organizations confined to those working with their hands and brains and not engaged in supervision, planning, or the broader aspects of production. The auspices under which the new techniques were introduced have affected the rate at which labor organization has grown in numbers and in power. Nowhere, however, has some growth in one or both respects been lacking. Similar organizations of other types of producers have also made their appearance. "Functional" organization thus competes with the community to determine the values of the individual.

These substantive changes which are required in high-energy society are frequently made so quickly that the *rate* at which change occurs becomes in itself a factor affecting the kind of society which emerges. Changes in means, since they violate the codes shared, become, in fact, as difficult to alter as changes in ends. A relatively small group wielding the power of modern converters can coerce a much larger one with less energy at its command. There are, of course, limits on what can be done with power alone. Today when a powerful minority undertakes a technological revolution it is likely to change things so quickly that adjustment is made with great difficulty. Consequently there is likely to be widespread personal as well as social disorganization.

Obviously, social codes attempt to control behavior generally thought to be possible; there is little need to prohibit what it is clear to all men is impossible. However, limits to action which appear to be fixed and stable when only small amounts of energy are available become, in fact, much more fluid as the available energy increases. High-energy converters come to replace other means at those points at which they least violate old controls. This puts the old system on the defensive. It becomes necessary to accept the new means, together with the changes which this step introduces, or to *create new sanctions* which will prevent their further use. Many of the old sanctioned ways cannot be preserved if only those controls which were already internalized by early experience among the members of the population are used. Men who had agreed upon the sacred finality of the relation between means and ends must now find *reasons* for accepting or rejecting the new. The assertion that only this means will serve to attain this end collapses before demonstration that it is not so. In such cases pragmatic sanctions must replace sacred obligation, prudence replace piety. Frequently in the effort to maintain old ends in the face of this threat, new and untried means are adopted which have the effect of destroying the ends which they were invented to uphold. Militant defense of pacifism, coercion to make people democratic, the use of force to make people compete in defense of a system of thought that holds competition to be so natural that it cannot in fact be prevented, wars to end war —these and many other situations come to mind. The "sacred" elements of the culture are often undermined either by the inability of these ways directly to withstand the competition of the new means-ends relationship or by the means adopted to bolster them up.

The series, then, runs something like this: Increase in the use of high-energy converters leads to the creation of large production units. This in turn requires concentration of control. The use of high-energy technology also requires a tremendous increase in the specialization of labor, with increased development of specialized codes governing specific areas of performance. The change is likely to be rapid, forcing a reconsideration of previously sanctioned means-ends relationships. The old process by which economic production was locally sanctioned under a unified "sacred" social system thus comes under attack as soon as high-energy converters come into use. Because it is only one of many structures serving economic functions, in the high-energy society the local community can serve the larger society only by continuous connection with other specialized communities. Frequently efforts to integrate the community by interfering with other types of organization threaten the welfare of individuals, groups, and institutions which are dependent upon the wider network of relationships.[6] The reaction is apt to be sharp and ruthless, the whole power of these other groups or organizations being brought to bear upon the recalcitrant area to force it to acquiesce in the new arrangements.

Depersonalization of the Individual

Integration, then, must take place at some "higher" level, if at all. Barring this, there will be a kind of unstable equilibrium among contending groups promoting conflicting values. The individual as a focal point for these contending values frequently no longer finds in his early experience a model for behavior which will necessarily provide societal or personal integration. Rather he is forced to choose among the demands of various codes as the situation he is in brings them into competition one with another. Most of the satisfaction he receives no longer comes from socially sanctioned acts of production.

Now whatever explanations of personality are offered by the various psychological systems, all agree that early development in the family and in the neighborhood groups in which the child finds himself have much to do with the conception of the self that arises out of his experience. The roles assigned in low-energy society tended, for the reasons already given, to be more or less compatible with one another. Those who had to play a number of them and share intimately the lives of others who also played such roles had the means to bring role requirements into at least tolerable alignment. What was required of the father in his role as breadwinner, for example, could not long stand in the way of his playing the role of husband. Even if the formal code remain unchanged, sanctions must be such at least as to tolerate his defection from one or another of the mutually conflicting formal requirements. We are familiar with the pseudo maintenance of sanctions (an example is the insistence in the United States that marriage is permanent, when in fact divorce is frequent and in many areas there is almost no external consequent of divorce other than those that arise from the severance of the marriage relation itself). Similar conditions exist in low-energy society. The actual course of events which follows violation of a norm is quite other than that formally prescribed. Nevertheless, it is generally true that the roles learned by the child and the codes governing his conduct are likely to be such as to prepare him for the roles he will actually play in adult life. The process of assigning new roles to be played as he grows older is likely to be formally recognized, and an organized means to make the adjustment in roles is socially provided.

In the high-energy society only a few generalized roles, such as that of "citizen," remain. No adequate system of preparing the individual to meet the changing demands of his changing roles can be set up, for no one knows how these demands will be changed or which role will be expected of any particular individual. The most that the society can do is to teach him to be prepared without much notice to meet the requirements of new situations without disturbing others. Ultimately this fluidity will presumably decrease and stability will set in, but such equilibrium seems now to be far off.

The rapid appearance of a multiplicity of specialists produces a situation in which many of them have become completely anonymous. Thousands of occupations exist which have not even a name except on the payroll, the labor contract, or the job catalogue.[7] There is no status attached to them. They have no social meaning, save perhaps in the work group itself, and even this may not be significant. No one knows what to expect of a person performing such a role, nor can the person discover through widespread community definition what he has a right to expect of others. No general code defines for him what is "good" behavior in such a way as to provide guidance in specific situations. Emergence of a social definition of an occupational role is itself frequently interrupted by a change in or the disappearance of a job or its transference to a new geographic region, where it has a different setting. The consequence is that there is general lack of coherence among the changing roles assigned to some individuals.

It is assumed here that values develop from experience. Common values then presuppose common experience. As has just been pointed out, high-energy technology has the effect of subjecting various groups and individuals to widely varied situations and conditions. Relations between acts and their consequences are influenced by the requirements of changing technology or of the social organization by which the society is operated. In such circumstances experience becomes almost as specialized and disparate as the various processes of production and distribution. Social organization involved in production is more and more circumscribed by technological requirements and is less and less immediately derived from recognition, in the production process, of the social needs of the individuals who engage in it. Justification is not often found in the acts of production; it is found, if at all, in the contributions which such acts make to consumers of the goods or services produced.

Personal Insecurity

Put another way, what has been said implies that the individual in high-energy society has lost most of his indexes to the worth of his services. He must evaluate them in terms of the reaction of consumers who in most cases are completely unknown to him, know very little of what he does for them, and care even less. Self-evaluation in such circumstances becomes extremely difficult, and there is apt to be a lack of correspondence between the individual's conception of himself that arises from his experiences in early life and the evaluation of himself that stems from the adult roles which he plays.

The lack of coherence in the experiences of the average man has, of course, been accentuated by the appearance of high-speed communication. The coordination in time and space required for the operation of even the comparatively slow railroad traffic of the early nineteenth century made the apparent value of high-speed communication very great. Brought into use originally to serve the railroads, it was quickly adapted to other purposes. Operating with the speed of light, the telegraph made all points on a telegraph circuit as measured in time equally distant. Thus words and symbols could be used to represent events torn from the context in which they originally occurred. In low-energy society the same converter served for production, transportation, and communication: today the three are separated. Thus, stripped from its relations to things and events for which it originally stood, the symbol might now denote the same thing but connote altogether different things in the place of its origin and that of its reception. As a consequence, the stimuli to which each person effectively cooperating in a production system might have to respond became enormously more diverse, and at the same time, less surely comprehensible than would have been either necessary or possible in low-energy systems.

For many reasons, then, high-energy society tends to "build into" personality the basis for conflict between what the individual is taught to expect and what will probably happen. There is no assurance that if he follows the course socially prescribed he will achieve the goals sought. Far from having a set of prescribed courses of action certain to justify his conduct socially no matter what its results for him personally, he is constantly confronted by the necessity to make choices whose outcome is unpredictable: his decisions, even if made at the sacrifice of his immediate personal goals, may actually undermine and destroy what he is trying to defend.

The individual is part of no integrated and organic whole; rather he is intimately part of many groups, some of which are in competition with others for dominance or survival. The acts demanded by one group may be condemned by another. The system of values acquired in childhood in a local community prove inadequate as a guide to adult behavior. (Even the golden rule works only when people agree on how they would have others do to them.) Guidance by an inner voice reflecting a multitude of experiences in childhood, all part of a network of impressions creating the "subconscious mind," gives way to considered choice among competing claims. There is no certainty that the peculiar hierarchy of values which characterized the modal man in the past will be the outcome of the experiences of modal men in the future. As a consequence, it becomes ever more difficult to predict in what particular order values will emerge. Production of goods and services, since it must satisfy this shifting and disordered system of choices, ceases to be an automatic function of the community or the personality. Rather, it is based on the calculation of what is likely most closely to fit the patterns of emerging values. Production must now be justified not for its own sake but for the effects upon the consumer of the goods and services offered.

CHAPTER 10

The Distribution of Consumers' Goods

Attention must now shift from production as a socially defined and socially sanctioned act bringing its own rewards to production justified primarily by consumption. This poses a new set of considerations. In the low-energy society, as we have pointed out, the relation between producer and consumer was spatially close and likely also to be functionally intimate. But this situation is less and less characteristic of high-energy societies because of the necessity to accumulate converters and the roundabout methods of production required for the wide use of high-energy converters. Claims on the good produced lie in the hands of many, and they react to one another only derivatively and unpredictably. This makes the old concepts of "fair exchange," "just price," and "a fair day's work for a fair day's pay," which were meaningful in more stable societies, decreasingly serviceable as actual guides to conduct. In fact, conflict arises primarily because there is no agreement as to the "justice" of claims made, particularly on products of newly formed surpluses.

Two antagonistic points of view emerge in most societies confronted with the opportunity to shift from low-energy converters and their fuels to a high-energy system. One would preserve the values and stability of the old system, with its ethical justification for production, even at the sacrifice of the gains from high-energy technology. The other is willing to see most social relations disrupted if necessary in order to gain the fruits of the new energy If the first of these positions is triumphant, there is no further "advance" in the use of high-energy converters and the old ethical standards remain in force. But even where the second position prevails, there is still a drive toward keeping some kind of ethical control over production and consumption.

The slogan "Production for use" was adopted in the effort to maintain the "moral" relation. Obviously, by definition all production is for somebody's use. To have any meaning, then, the slogan must point to enhanced values or lowered costs for the consumer. Thus basically it is a reiteration of the moral claim that all have against each in society. The slogan implies that the purpose of increased production is moral only when its gains are distributed among all consumers (as opposed to being shared only by those who have actually had a part in increasing production). This, as has been emphasized elsewhere, is the very base on which rest the demands for unfettered application of the law of supply and demand. It supplies the premises from which spring strictures against that "conspiracy in restraint of trade" which presumably permits producers to hold their prices above what competition would make them. Claims made in the name of the general welfare as opposed to that of specific producers are exerted most effectively among people holding common values. They are thus most apt to be respected in the small, self-contained village community of low-energy society. In more widespread economic systems the producer is unlikely to accept passively the burdens which the exercise of this "right" imposes upon him. He tends to be more responsive to claims to his goods which are based on the offer of the exchange of something substantial for them. Thus if production for use is to come about it will result either from the universal acceptance of a single set of supreme values or from the exertion of claims by the consumer in some other fashion than the expression of a pious wish.

"Production for use" does, of course, characterize production by a single person for his own use. In this case it is precisely the ends which he has in mind as consumer that direct his activities as producer. Relations of this kind are coextensive and reciprocal: coextensive because production and consumption are centered in the same person, extend through the same time, and involve common use of space, and reciprocal because the ends achieved justify the sacrifices required. Such a system is in social equilibrium. No other factors need to be introduced to get those acts performed which must be performed. However, it is rare, if ever, that a single person constitutes a complete production-and-consumption unit. Robinson Crusoe, the perennial example of an earlier day, consumed much that he had not himself produced, both directly in the form of goods taken from the ship and indirectly in the form of ideas, techniques, skills, and knowledge learned from English society. Moreover, as a single person he could leave no progeny and thus could not replace either the consumer or the converters on which his system depended. Obviously any lasting system depends on the reproduction of both.

Inadequacy of the Kinship Group

There can, then, exist no social system of pure individualism. The smallest lasting coextensive and reciprocal social system must include at least the family. Such a kinship group can teach its members as children to assume the roles which they must play as adults to secure the goods and services necessary to perpetuate the group. The goods produced, in turn, provide through their consumption, part of the incentive necessary to stimulate further production. Reproduction of the converter is assured by the same process that recreates the consumer. Kinship groups can be set up in a wide variety of forms to meet the requirements of geographic, technical, and demographic conditions. They have sometimes survived where other forms which have temporarily supplanted them have died and disappeared. Where they have been abandoned, then, there must be some compelling reason. Part of that reason can be found in facts which we have dealt with earlier. Like other forms of social organization, the kinship group operates as a production-and-consumption unit within energy limits. The lower limit is of course easy to see. No social system can survive unless it provides regularly a daily minimum of around 2,000 Calories in the form of food for its members. The upper limit is more difficult to see clearly. It is the point where the family can no longer serve as the production unit for the number and kinds of converters necessary to produce an increase in energy. For example, if the kinship unit is incapable of providing the social relations necessary to create and maintain, say, mass-produced automobiles, then a society using only kinship organization cannot provide its members many cars. The limitation on cars curtails the amount of energy which can be used, even where an abundance of fuel exists. Thus the amount of energy available to the kinship group is limited by the use of the kinship system. It is seldom, however, that a small unit such as this is permitted to operate up to its potential maximum. Before it reaches that point it usually has to compete with some other form of organization more effective in providing the social means to operate high-energy technology. The kinship unit may thus be confined to more limited operations than it is inherently capable of performing, but in general, as we have seen, the very extensive and intensive coordination required for high-energy technology exceeds the capacity of kinship and communally organized structures to serve as production units.

THE HIGH-ENERGY CONSUMPTION UNIT

But this is only part of the story. The kinship unit is also too small a consumption unit to serve some of the functions necessary to high-energy society. By a *consumption unit* we mean all those persons who derive sufficient satisfaction from a particular act of consumption to act so that such consumption can be repeated. As has been stated, it is assumed here that humans make repeated choices in the light of the consequences of their previous experience. That is, the consequences of previous acts either reinforce or inhibit future acts. The repetition of an act serves as an indicator to the observer that the factors affecting choice are operating in such a way that the "consummatory response" of the performer is adequate to induce repetition.

It is the ends sought by individuals that provide the means by which a society is maintained, but the ends sought by individuals arise from socially directed experiences. Thus, if the society is capable of providing experiences such that the individuals who successively make it up regularly choose to do what is expected of them, the social structure is maintained and reinforced. The cycle, from some early consummatory response which reinforces the experience giving rise to it, to a situation in which the individual actively seeks the conditions which are expected again to give rise to that response, may be "explained" in terms of a number of psychological systems. The choice between these systems need not here be made, for it is from the observed fact of repeated act that the values necessary to reproduce the act are here inferred. *Value* here denotes the factors that within physical and physiological limits affect choice. The nature of these factors can be examined introspectively by any individual and the inference drawn that similar acts by others derive from similar subjective experiences. From such self-analysis, or by other means, a hypothesis that a particular factor affects choice can be made; this can subsequently be tested by altering that factor and discovering whether or not choice *is* altered. Something of the nature of the factors affecting choice in given types of situations may be so revealed. But, in whatever manner the factors affecting choice are revealed, the fact of repeated choice serves to show that the experience to which the choice gave rise was adequate to reinforce that choice.

"To Each according to His Need"

We return to our definition of the consumption unit. The repeated action which perpetuates such a unit is brought about when the individuals who comprise it are so affected by some act of consumption—which falls within the category of acts necessary to secure the end sought by the group—as to want to repeat the act. The effects of consumption upon the consumer, whether or not he is a physical participant in the act of consumption, determine how he will act in similar situations in the future. An individual may be so identified with others, or with an idea or ideal, that he will "find satisfaction" in consumption by others who act in the name of, or are thought to be perpetuating, an idea or ideal. For example, in the family, the most common and pervasive consumption unit, parents are often so identified with their children that they commonly regard the food and clothing and other goods and services consumed by their children as sufficient justification to repeat whatever acts are necessary to make it possible for them again to consume. (They may also do this in particular instances for other reasons.) In fact it is relatively common to discover parents, at some stage in their relations with their children, doing without goods and services which they themeslves might have consumed in order to provide these for their children. It is likewise true that at another period the children may make similar sacrifices in favor of their parents. This identification of self with the activities of others is of course typical of all consumption units larger than the single individual. The self must be identified with a unit if consumption by that unit or any member of it is to justify to the self its activities in behalf of that unit. Men sacrifice for the perpetuation of corporations, unions, lodges, fraternities, political parties, churches, states, and nations time and energy which might be spent in the attainment of such satisfactions as leisure, opulent living, or aesthetic enjoyment because they place the values so derived higher than the values sacrified to attain them. The most extreme form of this identification of self is found in the sacrifice of life itself to perpetuate some social unit such as the family, the nation, or the church. In making this sacrifice the individual seeks to assure the achievements and/or the perpetuation of ends more significant to him than the survival of the body, which is offered as a sacrifice to maintain these ends.[1]

The processes by which such values are created and maintained are not mysterious or unknown. They constitute the means by which most of the repeated action of the human organism is secured, and are common practices in every family and existing social group. In some cases such repetitive acts are immediately related to the necessary physiological functions and hence may be called "biologically adequate" for survival. In others these acts are only remotely connected with the physiological needs of the organism and can be connected with such needs only by assertion. But whether or not such acts are biologically adequate, they must be socially adequate. Thus one proof of the fitness of a group, movement, or institution to survive is its ability to command energy sufficient to carry out the acts necessary to that survival. Diversion of energy to this end must go on in competition with diversion to all the other ends which the associated groups and individuals are seeking. Thus, as he grows older the individual discovers the competing claims of all the groups in which he must or may function. Each group attempts to assure that the emerging individual will have experiences that will subsequently result in the choices necessary to achieve group ends.

In every society the claims of the family must first be met, else the family will disappear and with it the society. Beyond that, the order primacy of other types of claims, for the perpetuation of other groups or institutions, varies widely. Demand also exists to preserve the relations socially necessary to create and serve particular personality types, to secure particular physical ends, or to meet needs which arise because some socially approved end is sought. The appearance or disappearance of social structures takes place as these necessary conditions are met or fail to be met. What is primarily demonstrated here is that the conditions imposed by high-energy society require varieties of social organization which rest on value-creating experiences in many ways different from those which are apt to take place in low-energy society. It is this that makes the realization of many of the utopian dreams derived from a pastoral world improbable.

If it were possible to extend the process of identification characteristic of experience in the family to include all producers and all consumers, the production unit would in every case be coextensive and reciprocal with a consumer group. The problem of securing social coordination of production and consumption would then be solved. Morality would automatically assure that each would produce "according to his ability" and would be permitted to consume "according to his need." Ability and need would be socially defined, and socially created norms would be so related as to produce the choices necessary to secure the required repeated action. Since each individual would want to do what he had to do, nobody would have to be forced to do anything.

Primary groups do sometimes act in this way in low-energy societies. Moreover, during at least part of the life of the child every family today operates on this basis, else children would die before they could become producers of what they must first consume. Many idealists argue that since this "proves" there is nothing in human nature to prevent society's operating on this basis there is nothing anywhere to prevent it. They would expand the family to include all the people of the world and thus assure the production necessary to satisfy all man's needs. Because most men spend some years as children in families where this kind of primitive communism exists there is a recurring pervasive longing to "return" to it. Whether this is a search for a "father substitute" or a symbolic return to childhood in some other sense, it is clear that for many, beset by a world which seems harsh and cruel as contrasted with the security of their early childhood, an economic system based on experience with the altruism of their parents is appealing. It is likely to be particularly appealing to those who cast themselves in the role of the child who receives rather than of the parent who gives.

The Family Commune

However, as we have seen, the conditions which favor an expanded family system are themselves unlikely to exist together with the use of high-energy converters. The family is an inadequate unit for some kinds of production. Examination will show that it is also an inadequate unit for some kinds of necessary consumption. Family life involves close interpersonal relations. Such experiences must by their nature be shared by only a few persons, for human beings in such relations demand responses, each of which takes time; time being limited, interpersonal response is therefore also limited. Aside from interpersonal experience with actual people, identification of the self with a cause, idea, or ideal comes to be made through symbols. But symbols stand for experience and gain their meaning from it. To an individual raised in a democratic family "fatherland" means something different from what it means to one raised in an autocratic patriarchy. "Mother country" evokes no nostalgic response in an individual raised without the affection of a real mother (who apparently need not be a biological relation). Thus the experience of children provide the base upon which many loyalties rest. Subsequent interpersonal relations provide further experience, which may redintegrate or disintegrate the patterns developed in childhood.

In low-energy society, as we have seen, the necessity to operate with little energy-wasting conflict and the necessity for local interaction among groups claiming individual loyalty result in some kind of accommodation among the claims of the groups in which the child will normally function. But in high-energy society there is no necessary accommodation at the structural or cultural level among these claims. Moreover, the goals or ends sought by various groups come into conflict or competition at many points with the family-maintaining codes which were earlier taught to the child. The tremendous emphasis upon those personal qualities which perpetuate the family, qualities idealized in the Christian religion among others, seems to the child to offer a means to solve all subsequent moral problems. But as he confronts adult life many of the passive and altruistic attitudes which he has been taught are seen to produce results (at least immediately in his world) quite other than those which lead to success in terms of his role as a provider or protector of his family. What is more, even when it is recognized that all men are brothers and all children God's children, the claims of a man's own family must in many cases transcend those of another family if the goals sought for his own family are to be realized. He chooses to put a coat on *his* child's back before he provides a shirt for someone known to him only as the child of another American or of a fellow Christian in some remote place. He chooses to stay at home and defend his immediate family rather than to leave them to face danger while he protects his fellow countrymen on some distant battlefield. But this may endanger the state, the nation, or some other unit of which he is a part. In a very large part of the world today men are able to secure even the necessities of family living only if they are able to defend their territory with military means, and exploit their resources with the aid of extensive social, economic, and political organization. Loyalty to the family is by itself not enough; loyalty to such organizations as the company, the union, the state must at times come to take precedence over the claims of the family. These units must be able to justify their claims through generating appropriate values in individuals. A given form of the family cannot survive unless it provides means whereby children learn that it is sometimes necessary to sacrifice the primary group values to those supporting more extensive organization.

The Communal State

High-energy technology has resulted in the aggregation of such huge amounts of power that small social units operating alone are often ruthlessly and unheedingly swept aside if their ends are antithetic to the purposes of those who control the power. This increase in power has forced changes in the value hierarchies obtaining among the world's population. It is possible for each small unit, acting alone, to induce its members to act in its defense in collaboration with members of a large number of similar small units, in such a way as to control power adequate for their defense. Such confederations have served in special situations; Switzerland is perhaps the best example. But this kind of collaboration for defense is rare. In fact, it is only where ideas such as the supremacy of nationality over other aspects of the personality have become characteristic of very large numbers of people that the necessary military and political efforts have been effective in protecting all the groups included in the nation. To obtain the immense amount of power required for its defense the national state must compete as a consumption unit with the family, the church, and other institutions. It must control enough of the value-creating system continuously to justify that flow of energy. Unless the hierarchy of values is such as to assure this, the state will be unable to carry on its defense function and the people of the state will become subordinate to any other state which seeks, and has the means, to control it.

This is not to say that the fundamental requirement for survival for all societies everywhere is the subordination of all other values to military and political ends. It is merely to point out that when one powerful agency seeks to dominate another, only adequate force will deter it. To secure adequate force to protect itself, the national state must become a consumption unit for such things as tanks, battleships, bombers, and bombs. Only as a sufficient number of men take satisfaction in seeing these made available to the armed forces of the state will they provide the means necessary to get the implements of war reproduced. Not only in military but in other activities the state pursues ends that require large units. Sanitation, flood control, conservation, research and education, and many other types of production can be justifed only if the great body of the citizenry accept these kinds of activities as ends which to them justify the necessary costs. If a society fails to stir men from the limited attitude that only such consumption as is participated in by members of the kinship group or the local community is justifiable, it may fall before the more effective techniques possible to those who have succeeded in inducing men to take satisfaction in activities involving larger consumption units.

It is clear, then, that the state can for some purposes serve both as a large production unit and as a large consumption unit. On the basis of this fact, it has been assumed that if the state can serve some values it can serve all values. But just as it is necessary to realize that the family, while it is adequate and necessary for some purposes, is limited in its capacity to serve, so also it is necessary to recognize the limitations of the state as a consumption unit. First of all, of course, is the fact that the state as such cannot provide the interpersonal experience which the family provides for the begetting and rearing of children. No state can make love or bear offspring. Unless there is some rewarding experience to justify it, parents will not rear children, and unless someone responds to the child many of the very qualities upon which the state will later depend, such as altruism, idealism, willing cooperation, are unlikely to appear among its citizens. If, on the other hand, parents provide these responses, they will also tend to prefer their own children to children unknown to them. A man who willingly pays taxes to put arms into the hands of a neighbor as he goes off to defend the country will much less willingly take bread from his own mouth and put it into the mouth of an improvident neighbor who remains at home. Some acts of consumption remain immediate, sensual, personal. Some are symbolic and relate to larger groups of which the consumer is a part. Nowhere is mass consumption all of consumption. If there are circuses, there must also be bread. Between such extremes as self-immolation in war and self-indulgence in love-making lies a whole range of possible acts of consumption. These acts may serve one family rather than another, the employees instead of the stockholders of a corporation, a nearby school, library, gymnasium or park or one far away, a hospital for us or a tank for an ally. Identification with various groups competing for preference forces the creation of a hierarchy of the claims made by different social structures. The demands of the union may during a strike require sacrifices in respect to the demands of the family. The demands of the church may require forswearing marriage. Within the same personality the demands of the veteran may compete with the resistance of the taxpayer to those demands. Neither the state alone nor the family alone can serve all the values of men equally well everywhere, nor can either provide experiences assuring that the ends sought by all men, everywhere, will be such that each man will develop precisely that hierarchy of values which would make him choose to perform the very acts required to meet the expected demands.

It is in households that many of the goods and services which high-energy technology can deliver are apt to be consumed. Paradoxically, the household becomes smaller as the high-energy society develops; thus the size of the consumption unit for many goods becomes smaller as the size of the required production unit for the same goods and services is enlarged. Hence the "ideal" situation—that in which consumption and production units are coextensive and reciprocal—becomes less likely as high-energy technology develops. In high-energy society the values developed in the consumption unit are not likely directly to justify production, and experience in production roles will not directly serve to create those values redintegrated by consumption of the goods produced. Increasingly production must be undertaken for the purpose of exchange. The dreams of the primitive communist become less attainable as high-energy technology develops. The parallel dream of the utopian who sees in the omniscient and omnicompetent state the means to realize all man's hopes meets no better fate. Rather it seems that a multiplicity of social structures, each of which is justified by the achievement of only part of the values of the individual will appear, and/or that some system must emerge which permits each individual to try to achieve some of the goods he seeks—regardless of their origin or effects—through exchange for them of whatever he controls which is to himself less valuable.

THE MARKET PLACE

In fact, of course, all high-energy societies have produced both of these conditions. The market has emerged as a place in which the variations in value can be given maximum range. A multitude of forms of social organizations—groups, associations, and institutions—have at the same time come into being, each seeking to serve only a few of the values of those who make them up. The price system, operating alone, permits the individual to act independently of all the groups of which he is a part. At the same time each group seeks controls over him which will prevent his acting in the market in a way thought to be dangerous to the survival of the group or likely to interfere with the achievement of its goals. It is in the West that the use of price as a means to mediate values has become most widespread. It is so widespread that in many case value is frequently equated with price. Other values

than those measured in the market are conceived to be of less
significance. Their pursuit, if it interferes with the maximization of
price-measured values, is often thought to be unnatural and dangerous to society. Only price mechanics are considered to be legitimate means to secure those values which price currently
mediates. A slight acquaintance with the history of the West will
show that many goods and services once "in" the market, such
as titles, commissions, and slaves, are no longer considered legitimately to be so. Other goods and services now mediated through
price have only recently been otherwise provided. Many of what
are now called the "economic" functions were in the medieval world
defined and controlled by the religious, moral, political, and legal
system: they were not mediated in the market. This is typical of
low-energy systems. There the individual consumer-producer has
little reason to question whether the average operation of the system provides for each of those who cooperates in it specific opportunity for consumption "commensurate" with his effort in production. There is neither need nor opportunity for him to ask whether
the value of the goods and services he gives is greater or less than
the value of the services and goods he gets. Only rarely does the
special situation in which an individual finds himself as a result
of luck or disaster justify an unusual reward or penalty. When
scarcity might induce price rise, to the producer the traditional
reward is felt to be enough, and disaster is compensated for by
unusual types of aid to the afflicted. This changes with increased
use of high-energy technology. The fact that money will serve
in a variety of groups, regions, and situations as a common denominator of many values gives it peculiar advantages here. These
advantages include the fact that such values as can be translated
into monetary terms are then subject to mathematical manipulation and statistical treatment. This quantifiability has in turn
given a kind of seeming reliability to price-measured values which
does not appear to exist for other values.

Price

Price served the early trader well, for he sought to deal with
only those values which *did* enter the price system. But the success
of trade provided support for the belief that all values [2] could be
brought under the same sort of calculus as is represented by price.

What had been "political economy," became "economics." The former had concerned itself largely with the question of the proper sphere for the operation of various value-mediating institutions, particularly the state and the market; the latter word sometimes has presumed to mean that the calculation of all significant values could be made in terms of price and market considerations. Such economics concerns itself exclusively with the study of price mechanisms. From what is happening in the market it infers what would happen in a world with no values other than those finding expression in price terms and with no locus for judgment about the ordering of values other than the mind of the individual buyer or seller. The economist who confines himself to the examination of this kind of evidence and makes this kind of inference obviously deals with only part of what really happens at any place and time. Seemingly there will always be a choice between values which can be expressed in terms of price and values which are not so expressed. There will always be not only the exercise of choice by the individual but also the organized operations of groups whcse objectives frequently represent an ordering of values altogether different from the individual value hierarchy of many of their members. Predictions that events *will* follow a pattern like that which *would* result if all values *were* expressed in the market as a consequence of choice by individuals frequently are at variance with the events which actually follow. There are apparent limitations on the use of price as a measure of value and as a determinant of action. While the unfettered operation of price might have many advantages, it also has consequences which lead men constantly to seek to avoid its use.

The advantage of price lies in its flexibility and its universality. These characteristics permit the price system to bridge the gaps between producer and consumer in a world where they are likely to be unknown to one another and seldom share all the same values or seek them in the same order. Cooperation comes to be mediated by rates of exchange determined through price rather than specific performance ethically, politically, or legally sanctioned. This facilitates the ordering of individual hierarchies of value in terms of the costs of gaining the cooperation of those who control the goods and services necessary to achieve those values. But it must not be forgotten that many values are not measurable in terms of price: the love of children by parents, patriotic devotion, religious conviction, and numerous others. Much of the cooperation necessary for the functioning of price mechanics is secured by means other than those operated by the market. It thus measures only part of the factors necessary to its own existence. A "pure" market economy would immediately destroy itself.

The proper sphere of pecuniary valuation is not, then, to be discovered by some a priori discussion about its merits as a universal means to mediate value; it can be determined only by examination of the probable consequences of its operations upon given groups and individuals and of the probable reaction by the affected groups and individuals as they contemplate or experience these consequences.

Price in the early years of limited trade was a relatively stable factor. As we have seen, the limits on productivity change only slowly in low-energy society. Consequently the "just" price or "normal" exchange value could be worked out over time by trial and error and the social controls necessary to stabilize values could be developed. Such a system deals inadequately with the rapid alterations in the proportion of the factors used in production and the rapid changes in the hierarchy of values which characterize high-energy technology. The old slogans cease to be statements of generally accepted norms and become instead exhortations designed to assert the claim that a particular group, class, or region *should*, on the basis of some position held in the past, continue to share the results of increased use of surplus energy or other gains resulting from change.

Market Maldistribution

As a consequence of the individual's increasing inability to determine his own worth otherwise, price comes increasingly to measure some of the costs of his cooperation. The consumer, seeking to minimize his costs, chooses between combinations of factors to find those which involve the least sacrifice of his values. Frequently he thus forces men who have only their own bodies to serve as converters into competition with others offering the same goods who are equipped to produce it with the help of cheap energy. The price system then may have the effect of threatening to destroy many of the values of those who operate under it. They in turn may seek to avoid the use of the price system because of these very consequences. To say that action of this kind is contrary to nature, that is, deprives man of his freedom to choose, or that it reduces his efficiency, is merely to reassert the assumption that he ought to want to use price rather than some other system of evaluation and that he ought to want to maximize his gains as a consumer of priced goods and services rather than in some other way. The "oughts," in this case, derive from assumptions that are not currently accepted by all men everywhere.

Price is generally thought to bring about the kind of equality of opportunity which has been the aim of many democratic thinkers. In operation it has frequently produced no such result. In fact, a man who has the opportunity to buy and sell freely even in a world market can cooperate only in terms of *his* alternatives. He who buys an automobile tire, for example, pays for the cooperation of all those who combined to produce it, in so far as their cooperation became a charge in the market. The costs of the services of the Malayan rubber worker, the Mississippi cotton hand, the Akron tire builder, and the vocalist on the radio program which sells the tire are among the factors that help determine the price of tires. But the cost of the service of the Malayan is set in price terms based on the cost of *his* alternatives. If he owns no land he may have the choice of near starvation in the jungle or employment on the plantation at a wage set by the willingness of his neighbors or of a synthetic-rubber worker in Texas to take his place. The "worth" of the cotton hand in Mississippi reflects *his* alternatives, which are quite different from those which the rubber workers' union has been able to provide for the Akron worker in a market where other employment opportunities in other industries supply *his* alternatives. The consumer of tires in turn pays a total bill which represents a choice among *his* alternatives. What the various producers receive out of the tire is a measure only of the alternatives open to them. To say that each has been paid according to his productivity is merely to define his worth as being identical with whatever he had to be paid. The tremendous variation among these payments indicates how completely price is divorced from need, effort, skill, or discomfort on the part of the producer. Under such circumstances "worth" loses for the performer of a task most of its meaning. He is put in the position of saying that since he is able to demand more he is worth more; and for him the increased price resulting from restriction of production is in the same category as increased payment arising from increases in physical output.

The range of alternatives open to those who cooperate in production reflects differences between low- and high-energy production as well as differences in social organization and in skill, training, and ability. The consumer of a good or service seeking to minimize the costs to himself may force workers into competition with other men, equipped with high-energy converters, who are able with little effort to produce many times as much as they. The consumer could, in a pure, completely free price system, exploit these differences to reduce some men to penury. The proponent of the free market, who assigns to the consumer the "right" to demand all the gains made possible by such situations, faces the same dilemma as the Marxist, who solves the dilemma by insisting that it is labor, as producer, that has the right. Each has to choose between seeking to reduce the human energy costs of production—even if in so doing he denies to many men the opportunity to exchange labor, the only thing they have to exchange— and limiting the substitution of other converters for men by guaranteeing "full employment"—thereby guaranteeing that some men will continue to live only by labor for which a machine could be more cheaply substituted. Whichever choice an onlooker makes, he should anticipate that there will be resistance by those who are thus denied what might otherwise be theirs.

INSTABILITY OF THE FREE MARKET

Price represents one means of measuring value. Many of the goods measured in this way can also be measured in others. Two hundred pounds of pork always weighs more than one hundred pounds, but it is possible that sometimes one hundred pounds of pork will sell for more than two hundred. Thus the goal of increased production as measured in pounds is not always compatible with the goal of increased production as measured in dollars. If increased production results in decreased price, those who impede achievement may be rewarded more highly than those who promote it. The very nature of price relations is likely, except under very carefully controlled conditions, to produce this paradoxical situation. Price always measures both scarcity and value, and it does not distinguish between limitations on supply that spring from "natural" causes such as the shortage of materials, converters, tools, or manpower and those that reflect the deliberate policy of men to refrain from or to hamper production. Thus deliberate restriction may be as well or better rewarded than "full" production. In these circumstances cooperation to limit supply is as normal as cooperation under other circumstances to increase it. In fact, then, it is only by deliberate *intervention to prevent group action* that the supposed beneficence of the free price system can be maintained. It must not be forgotten that although some goods and services may be freely exchanged in terms of price alone other goods and services will continue to be sanctioned by the reciprocal obligations of the family, the duties imposed by the state or the church, the exercise of "rights" which are believed to imply no exchange of thing or service in return, and the multiplicity of agreements, understandings, codes, and customary privileges that characterizes every society.

Value continues to be a consequence of many experiences. Only some of these are reflected in terms of price. The law of supply and demand is merely a statistical statement of the outcome of the factors at work in a situation to the degree to which they are expressed in price terms. Exchange reveals the location of values that relate to the market, but the individual who holds them may at the same time seek through other institutional arrangements to achieve other aims. The pursuit of these goals may have the result of preventing his achievement of what he seeks through the market. Price mechanics permit the individual to exchange those goods and services placed low in his own hierarchy for those placed higher and thus to minimize the frustrations arising from his inability simultaneously to satisfy all his wishes, needs, and wants. By thus revealing the order of his values the market makes it possible to anticipate what the order of his future choices is apt to be. Action by others in anticipation of persistently repeated patterns of choice permits the fulfillment of those choices. But this is possible only if, on the average, choices remain consistent. That is to say, unless it is known that tomorrow the average individual will choose goods in about the order he does today, no basis exists for making the kinds of investments which will pay off only over long periods of time. If the individual is too "free" or too capricious in his choices, high-energy technology becomes impossible. Yet the operations of high-energy technology produce change, and change affects values. Knowledge of the experimental or tentative character of the market becomes extremely important in carrying out the process of discovering changing values and so allocating resources that they will not be used wastefully or destroyed. A market too "liquid" is, however, likely to destroy the stability necessary to induce investment. A market too "sticky" may allocate resources in such a manner as to become a relatively inefficient means to certain ends as compared with some other institution such as the corporation,[3] the the state, or the family.

Some Consequences of Market Operations

The free market, dependent upon the limited knowledge and experience of individuals, is always subject to the danger that they will choose on the basis of temporary or fleeting emotions or on the basis of incomplete or inadequate foreknowledge of the consequences of their choices, and will subsequently refuse to repeat those choices. Rapid oscillation in choice may destroy much of the value of some of the fixed assets necessary for high-energy technology. Moreover, if the market is the locus for choice among the basic needs of all, extreme fluctuation in the market may make it impossible for the individual to meet the demands of other roles he plays in other institutions. Thus unemployment created by the operations of the market may threaten the existence of the family, the state, or some other institution, and reaction will set in to limit the sphere of the market. For its own survival, then, a modern firm may be required to spend a good deal of its effort "normalizing" demand, that is, *creating those values by which its existence is justified.* To affirm that in satisfying those demands which it has created it is responding to the free operation of the law of supply and demand is, at the least, confusing. In the early days of the trader the market revealed areas of possible change which could have been discovered by no less delicate instrument. In modern societies some men are equipped with the power to override the established values of weak groups and have the means to create the values which will justify further "advance" in terms of the values they seek. They may find such a delicate arrangement as the free market to be unnecessary. In fact, in the "monopolistic competition" of this day it is often possible to predict rather accurately where and when a market will arise under the stimulus of modern means of advertising and propaganda. This kind of manipulation of course has its limits, but there is no question that creating wants makes them easier to anticipate than merely discovering them.

Whatever the "proper" role of the market may be, the very fact that its functions change produces reactions among the individuals and groups which make up the society in which it operates. Some of these changes may be extremely far-reaching and productive of revolution in its true sense. In high-energy society the sphere of the market has grown in competition with all the other institutions. To it have been transferred functions previously carried out by the church, the family, the community, and the state. In the process some of these institutions have had their ability to carry out their remaining functions weakened. For example, when the head of a household who is dependent upon the market to assure bread for his children becomes unemployed for reasons which in the market are considered good and adequate, he ceases to be capable of performing his role as breadwinner. Because of his inability to carry out this function he frequently becomes incapable of carrying on other functions which the market is totally incapable of absorbing, for example, the discipline of his children.[4] His diminished capacity to serve in this role may lead to increases in delinquency or dependency, giving rise in turn to increased function by the state, both to supply bread and to provide a substitute for parental care. Thus increased emphasis upon the free right to hire and fire in the market may give rise to increased use of coercion elsewhere in the system in order to protect those institutions upon which the very operation of the market itself depends.

THE BUSINESSMAN VERSUS THE POLITICIAN

We might summarize this in another way. Around the points in the economy where the use of new converters permits the utilization of the surplus energy of coal, oil, and water power, there form pools of unclaimed surplus energy. The effort to claim this energy itself involves a reformation of previously sanctioned behavior. The nature of the property system, the concept of "rights" currently held, the degree of collective consumption, the rate of expansion of new converters will all modify the results, but in any case modification of codes will take place. Much of the new surplus energy itself may be distributed in the process of changing these codes. Where the price nexus is used, this distribution of surplus will be reflected in prices. On the other hand, the state may draw off all but a small part of the available energy for some purpose of its own, and the sphere of the market remain relatively undisturbed. A case in point is the industrial experience of the United States during the Second World War. The enormous expenditures for war were almost wholly offset by increased productivity. A larger portion of the American population was permitted to man machines which, under the administered price policies which represented labor and management codes in "normal" times, probably would not have been produced, or having been built would have stood idle much of the time. During the war the surplus productivity of these machines was claimed either through taxes or through bonds. It was delivered in the form of war goods. At the same time there was also a definite increase in consumption of consumers' goods by the population. The pool of increased energy available was not large enough to maintain permanently both streams of goods because, during the war, in the civilian economy converters were being worn out faster than they were being replaced. It is probable, however, that forty or fifty billions of dollars' worth of goods could have been produced, to be consumed by the government continuously, without much affecting the expectancies in the form of consumption goods which were developed, previous to the war, among the various groups cooperating. However, postwar inflation created claims in excess even of the increased capacity to produce. To a lesser degree this was the case in Canada and in other areas where war did not destroy the basic converters. But in Britain, Germany, and Russia the downward spiral of production created by the destruction of basic converters created great difficulties for those seeking to restore cooperation induced by price. There the economy was incapable of delivering goods in the volume adequate to meet the demands customarily made on it and to supply what was necessary to maintain the codes of the groups required to cooperate in production. Thus the sphere of pecuniary valuation was reduced and the area of coercion increased by inability to maintain the necessary rate of production.

These examples illustrate the fact that the sphere within which price operates expands and contracts in accordance with the ability of the society to develop codes of behavior adequate to induce *cooperation* through *price*. Which brings us to a discussion of another element of the system of pecuniary valuation—its effects on the process of value creation.

In earlier societies the church or the state usually had control of the surpluses. Vast wealth was accumulated during the Middle Ages for the greater glory of God. In huge cathedrals costly works of art and jeweled treasures were held before the eyes of the people as examples of the use to which surplus should be put. The standards of the old regime in France were demonstrated by its magnificent palaces.

Business changed all this. It expanded the production of *things*, through new converters, beyond the level previously thought possible or considered desirable. It was the merchant salesmen who opened up new avenues of productivity—and who were therefore in a position to determine in large part the uses to which the newly created surpluses would be put. The support of the arts, of the church, and even of government passed to them because they controlled these surpluses. Great emphasis upon the possession of *things* as evidence of success was one consequence. Advertising and education created new values dependent upon the possession and the rapid obsolescence of things. If they did not wear out fast enough, "fashion" could be created to destroy old values and inaugurate new ones. Competitive relationships were extended into areas where status had long been fixed. For example, the significance of costume as an indication of status was destroyed by the mass production of cheap clothing from "upper-class" models. Milady now had constantly to buy the new to demonstrate her superiority over those who could not afford to discard clothing until it was at least partially worn out. Similarly, rapid obsolescence of automobiles, houses, and furniture became characteristic. (Of course, as was said earlier, it is perfectly possible for the modern state, seizing upon the surpluses, to give an entirely new direction to the society. It is also possible that, with scientific research replacing profit-motivated exploration, the state may be able to advance with more certainty and less loss than business has in the past without the benefit of such research.)

Wherever events follow this pattern—that is, where the market serves to introduce new methods of production and the trader consequently gets the first claim on any new surpluses—the use of pecuniary symbols and standards will grow. The peculiar explanation given to this development in the United States under the heading "profit motive" fits the actual happenings no better than the collectivist jargon used in Russia explains what goes on there. In fact, in both places a large portion of the people's activities is incomprehensible in terms of the official explanation, and all kinds of rationalizations are given to explain, or expletives uttered to abjure, the "normal" behavior of many persons in the society. During the Second World War, "profit-motivated" America used fixed prices for consumers' goods as a base upon which increased productivity actually took place, whereas the Russians, heralds of the virtues of the "planned state," resorted to free prices for much of the product of the peasant to get their results.

Both the advertiser and the socialist agitator, in their roles as value creators, frequently overreach themselves. They set up expectations in excess of those which the system of production can satisfy. Their efforts to increase the value of the goods which they have to offer, when compounded with the efforts of others along the same line, may succeed only in disturbing those relationships between services and things which have hitherto been accepted. The process of creating value without definite knowledge either of what the probable increases in the volume of things will be or of the prices they will sell at, invites miscalculation. At the moment, knowledge is probably not sufficient to form a basis for predicting just what the controls would have to be in order to keep a continuously harmonious relation between, on the one hand, increased volume of consumption goods produced and increased use of high-energy converters and, on the other hand, the necessary stimulus value of the things produced. Certainly there is little in the record of planned states to indicate that they have learned the secret. They have had to revert to coercive controls whenever price-induced cooperation broke down, and have rarely restored the price mechanism over any large sector of human relations after such a resort to coercion. It must of course be remembered that since it is a matter of ideological pride in some cases that the price mechanism should not be restored, the fact that it *has not* been done is not conclusive evidence that it *could not* be done.

From the evidence at hand we can conclude that a cooperative relationship between highly diversified groups and individuals can be carried on through price if at the same time and place supplementary means, including the use of the state to enforce contracts and to police the other codes developed, are used to secure the necessary coordination. There are cooperative systems serving a limited area without the use of either price or statute; the rise of unions, trade associations, professional societies, better business and similar bureaus, as well as informal controls by agencies of the party in one-party states, indicates that there exists a whole set of values which neither the state nor the market is well equipped to implement. The groups which have built and which serve such codes act continuously to prevent the operation both of the free market and of the total state. The number of situations that demand this growth of groups and codes increases with the increasing use of energy, and this growth in turn presents new problems solved neither by the omnipotent state nor by the free market.

CHAPTER **11**

The Enlargement and Concentration of Political Power

With the transition to high-energy society there is increasing use of the state. As we shall see, in part the increase represents the taking over of functions previously performed by other institutions and in part it represents the exercise of types of social control which were unnecessary in the low-energy society. What will be attempted here is a clarification of the connections between increased energy use and increased state function, with special reference to the future course of these interrelated trends.

The developments already cited made it less and less possible for traditional codes of conduct, interpreted by traditional means and implemented by existing administrative agencies, to meet the needs that arose in the high-energy society. The price system supplanted many of the old ways of meeting needs. The use of contracts in which the subscribing parties agreed upon a code to govern part of their relations during a specific period of time was another such development. The enforcement of these agreements required the power of the state. But the numerous consequences of the new relationships emerging from high-energy technology were of great concern to many besides those immediately involved in a contract or a sale. To guard their interests further controls both on the market and on the nature of the contract were needed. When these groups demanded protection, it was often supplied by the state.

One of the groups most adversely affected by the appearance of the contract and price systems was the family. It is not possible, since there are so many variations of the kinship unit, to show just how each type would be affected by each change in converters or by a specific change in the market. However, there are some general propositions which have already been presented here, and others which can be made, which will now be brought together to make clearer the cumulative effects of high-energy technology upon the family.

Some changes were due to the limited effectiveness of the family both as a consumption and as a production unit. As was shown earlier, the use of the flowing stream and the sailing ship led, in some places, to replacement of the family as an economic unit by the feudal system or some type of slavery. With the use of coal, oil, gas, and hydroelectricity the family became even less capable of competing successfully with other social groups in performing some of its functions. One of the principal factors which affected it was change in the relationship between production, consumption, and land ownership.

Where private ownership and inheritance of land prevail in the low-energy society, and land is scarce, control over land can become the basis for exploitation of children by their parents or of siblings by one of their number. The power of the patriarch to determine which of his children shall inherit land enables him to make the welfare of the head of the family the primary object of family activity. Primogeniture, by guaranteeing to the first-born that he will inherit, regardless of whether or not he makes any contribution to the welfare of the rest of the family, similarly lends itself to exploitation. Thus, viewed historically the family exhibits, in addition to the affectional and reciprocal arrangements so widely approved, definite compulsive and exploitative aspects. In Christian countries, particularly in the United States, the family is idealized. It is regarded as being almost totally a beneficent institution for all its members throughout their lives, and its negative aspects, which frequently prevail even in Christian society, are overlooked.

By shaping his early experience, parents can inculcate in a child the values on which their welfare depends. Family control over land and over surplus energy, which might be used to create or secure tools and additional converters, increases the certainty that if parents "train up a child in the way he should go," he will

not, as an adult, "depart from it." The emergence of forms of
energy which did not depend upon control over arable land provided the exploited members of the family with alternatives to
family control. They could now survive without their. father's
blessing or the cooperation of other members of the family; they
could escape from what had been in the low-energy society ines-
capable. The way out often entailed migration.

Migration robbed the community of origin, in turn, of its hold
over its members. Between them, the family and the other groups
rooted in the local community had held a monopoly on the development of skills and had exercised control over the vocational
codes which limited access to and performance within occupations. With the development of the new skills involved in the
use of high-energy converters, the family lost some of its capacity
to develop in its members the attitudes which assured that family
values would be given a high place in a well-defined complex
including the values of other competing groups. In low-energy
society the interplay of institutions provided a network of controls
which supported one another. There was no such thing as an
"economic man," for, whether making war, worshiping, or partici-
pating in the acts necessary to secure sustenance, the individual
was constantly made aware of the sanctions that might be applied by other groups to which he belonged if in one endeavor
he should violate the code of another group. The sacred rites
through which he was endowed with his innermost personality
were not separable from the mundane habits by which he secured
food, shelter, and clothing. The removal of some acts from the
matrix in which they had functioned robbed the system of the
means by which balance among the various claims on the individual was obtained and security for each group and institution
was assured. The deviant could no longer be required to conform
to group standards on pain of punishment or expulsion. He might
now attach himself to some independent organization which
existed to serve the new converters, such as a ship's company or
a corporation, and there survive and prosper even while his one-
time superiors declined in prestige and the system they served
disintegrated.

The family thus lost some of its capacity to carry on those of
its functions which depended upon its ability to discipline its

members. In the kinship system the protection of the weak and ill-favored was secured by placing bonds on the strong and well-favored. Divested of such control, the family could no longer protect those unable to fend for themselves. But the groups which made use of the more productive or valuable individuals of the family seldom assumed responsibility for those whom the family could no longer provide with care. There was bound to be a searching and sifting of alternatives to determine who now should assume old family responsibilities. Changes in the family thus gave rise to changes in other social arrangements. Loss of family control over its younger members results in a situation in which there is no surety that care and affection lavished upon children will be reciprocated in the declining years of parents. Those anticipating their own declining years are therefore required to look elsewhere for assurance that they will not become a "burden" to their children. It is also apparent that in high-energy society children are no longer a potent source of aid to parents in their efforts to accumulate the means to provide old-age security. A tractor frequently costs less than rearing a child to the age at which he can be useful, and the cost of a child's food alone is greater than that of the fuel which would supply more than the equivalent of his mechanical energy. Children in the urban home perform few functions which a machine cannot perform more cheaply: the mounting cost of urban housing, clothing, recreation, and education makes the cost of child rearing very much greater than any financial gain which is likely to result from his services to the family. Parents therefore increasingly seek means to escape the costs which child rearing entails. This results in declining fertility and in increasing demands that family burdens be shared by other institutions.

EXPANDING FUNCTIONS OF THE STATE

As a consequence of the family's declining ability to perform what were once family functions, a number of other associations and institutions have had to assume them. In the West labor unions have been required to provide pensions and disability and burial funds. Corporations are forced to set aside reserves to provide similar services. Fraternal and benefit societies are organized specifically to perform such functions, and "private" insurance against the vicissitudes of life takes a multitude of forms. But all together these take on only a small part as compared with the number of functions assumed by the state. In every high-energy society the state is required to bear at least part of the cost of educating children, and the care of the aged is a mounting burden on the taxpayer. Even in the United States, where ideology officially frowns on "socialized medicine," the care of the mentally ill is assumed for the most part to be a responsibility of the state, and the cost of the care of men injured or killed in wars no longer falls entirely on the families of these men. Where the family is broken, the state more frequently than the relatives assumes responsibility for the care of the dependent children. In most high-energy societies part of the burden of caring for the sick and the injured falls upon the state instead of the family of the disabled. It is the state as often as the family that attempts to reform the delinquent. The state arrogates to itself the duty of punishing the criminal. If the market fails to provide the means whereby the family can secure the means to subsistence, the state attempts to supply it. These functions have been assumed even where they are hardly defended, let alone encouraged, by official ideology. Whatever explanation is offered, it is clear that the increased activity of the state in areas previously covered by the family is neither fortuitous nor entirely the outgrowth of ideological roots.

In democratic states privately organized groups are continually being formed to fill the gaps between what emerging values demand and what already existing organization can do. In the course of time many functions originating in such private organization have been transferred to the state. In the socialist states government has directly assumed many functions previously performed by the family.

Loss of Local Autonomy

To the functions of the state there have also been added some which were previously carried on by locally centered organizations. These agencies are frequently unable to cope with the power wielded by such giant entities as the corporations of the West or the trusts and other agencies of the totalitarian states. In the high-energy society a decision to alter the whole character of an area can be made without the consent or even the knowledge of the local population; the economic base of the community thus becomes subject to the vagaries of the market or to decisions made in some distant directors' meeting or by some government bureaucrats as to whether or not a particular undertaking should be discouraged, encouraged, permitted, or prohibited. When such a decision is made, the state usually has to take on a number of new functions, for the organizations which carry on the changed economic functions often are without the authority, and frequently have no motive, to supply the new services which are now required. The provision of schools, roads, streets, lighting, hospitals, sanitary systems, public transportation, and other necessities is sometimes left completely out of the calculations of those who introduce the new productive facilities.[1] Moreover, whether unemployment, collapse, prosperity, or boom follows, only limited modifying action is possible within the local community.

It has also become apparent that sometimes decisions made locally will not be tolerated by others who have more power than can be wielded by local groups. The conflict between what has been considered moral in a particular place and what is demanded by outside force has probably been most frequent and most crucial when codes connected with property have come into conflict with other codes which demand conduct in opposition to that required by property rights. Values learned in the family from elders and neighbors sometimes preclude the relations necessary to high-energy technology. Such norms may interfere with the efficient operations of enterprise; if followed absolutely they might make the new technique unworkable. Conversely, the adoption of new rules made necessary by new techniques frequently will completely destroy the existing social system. In such circumstances a close relation between morality and law, between what is taught in the family and neighborhood and what is demanded by the state, is almost impossible. What people have been trained to want to do clashes with what they subsequently discover they have to do. The freedom of those imbued by the traditional morality with one set of values interferes with the freedom of those acting on the basis of another set of values. For example, a worker who, in response to the demands of groups in the local community, fulfills such obligations as those of breadwinner, husband, and father may, in the struggle over the terms of a collective bargaining contract, be required to remain on strike and thus be unable to fulfill the demands of his other roles. Similarly, the manager of a local plant owned by a distant corporation may be required to shut the plant down, causing great losses to all his local friends who are in business as well as to his employees. Again, local resources may be purchased and taken out of production by an owner who seeks either to remove a competitor from the market or to establish a reserve for future use. The whole basis of community life may thus be destroyed.

In situations like this, it will be a rare community in which locally responsible officers will willingly act to preserve the interests of distant property owners against those of their constituents. Usually the locally elected administrative officials conveniently fail to note trespass, and local juries do not find evidence on which to indict or convict. The enforcement of contract under these circumstances may require the fullest use of the centralized power of the state. To protect property rights the central state has frequently authorized police action by officers actually selected and paid by, and responsible to, the property owner. Government has made this use of power in many places and at many times. Examples abound, among them the Hudson's Bay Company, the Coal and Iron Police, and the Carboneri. The evidence here suggests that, whether or not the particular parties to the contracts (sometimes called "treaties" when a small and "primitive" party is being dealt with) entered them willingly, a great many of those affected accepted the consequences unwillingly and only in the face of overpowering force brought to bear by the state.

Political Control of Production

The separation of the site of production from that of consumption has similarly involved an increase in state power. If food is prepared in a distant packing plant the consumer no longer is in a position to judge whether his health is being adequately protected by those who prepare and process that food. If drugs, serums, and vaccines for which only the very carefully trained technician can set adequate standards (and detect deviations from them), are manufactured in a remote plant, the old adage

"Let the buyer beware" provides no basis for effective control. Where standards can be set and policed only through state agencies, increased use of the state is essential.

In the same way specialization has contributed to the multiplication of state function: the determination of individual competence in many specialized fields has been added to the state's obligations. The consumer is no longer expected to risk his life or his property in uncertified hands until such time as the competence of the specialist he needs has been demonstrated, and, on the other hand, the competent practitioner is afforded a means by which he can be freed from the competition of the charlatan. Judgment in the market place is supplemented by examination of the credentials offered and of the results of tests designed by those in a position to pass on competence, responsibility, and integrity. A study made in 23 states of this country as early as 1929 found more than 1,200 occupations [2] entry to which was limited by government. Today, following a quarter century of increasing governmental power, the number is legion. This in what is probably the least regulated of the societies extensively using high-energy technology!

The effects of competition between areas well advanced in the accumulation of converters, and in the social and technical conditions required to make use of high-energy technology, and those not so well equipped has led to continuous effort by groups in the "backward" states to preserve the integrity of their regional culture. Tariffs, quotas, rationing, favorable and unfavorable exchange rates for goods and services thought to protect one group against another or one nation against another have multiplied with the spread of industrialism. Often these rules regulate what it was previously impossible or unnecessary to regulate. In particular, regions dominated by food raisers have clamored for a means to escape the consequence of unregulated competition between high- and low-energy converters.

Political Distribution of Surpluses

As has been noted, such competition has had the effect of demoralizing the food raiser and frequently of destroying a long-established culture. Confronted in the market by a colossus in the form of the agent of a corporation or an industrial state, the farmer has turned to his government for help in making the struggle more equal. Every food-raising area has sought some kind of political protection against domination in the uncontrolled market. Efforts have proceeded along two lines. One is the use of the power of the state, supplemented by that of such organizations as cooperatives, to match the power of the organized industrialist worker and management. To this end the state is expected to extend to the farmer special privileges in organization and special concessions in taxation. Farmers demand special forms of credit and monetary and fiscal policies favorable to farm groups. In some cases specific protection for farm prices as against those of other goods has also been obtained. Methods of assuring "fair" prices have included "dumping" surplus abroad and subsidizing special classes at home who can consume what will not be bought at the protected price. There has also been deliberate destruction of crops and farm products, in addition, of course, to tariffs and other barriers to imported food. A second line of effort is pursued by farmers, along with other groups who are able to exercise more power in the political than in the economic realm, in demanding a redistribution of national income. Their success in this effort has grown out of the conditions under which high-energy technology has come into use. In most of the places where it developed, high-energy technology was achieved only at the price of political compromise. Coalition of a number of groups with somewhat differing values and purposes but all interested in using the new converters was necessary to wrest power from the old rulers. In the struggle the aid of many men was needed. The myth most successful in bringing about the required political changes was dependent on a successful appeal to the "common man."

Put more exactly, perhaps, the appeal was in terms of those values most widely shared in the society. Whether the liberal democratic state is regarded as being run by a succession of contending power groups, who appeal for support in the name of the values they are prepared to enhance and protect, or as being run by the masses, who seek leaders willing to pursue the values to which "common men" are devoted, it must necessarily serve values widely held. In states of this type a referendum is occasionally held to determine whether the existing government serves more of the widely held values than it is currently believed some alternative coalition might do. But even if no such method is used, the state must either serve widely held and significant values or devote endless energy to coercing those whose choices are frustrated.[3] Thus the consequences of the dogma "One man, one vote" makes the democratic state far more responsive to the wishes of the man in the street with limited wealth than is either the oligarchic corporation or the market, wherein "One dollar, one vote" may prevail. As we have seen, the new converters required concentration of power in the hands of management. In democratic states this clashed with the dispersed power of the people. Such states, possessing the power to limit and coerce, are required by their voters to undo the "injustice" which arises from the "abuse" of great power of wealth and position in the corporation and the market.

Government by Administration

The compromise which was required to bring about the transition to high energy in England, and in some degree elsewhere in the West, gave power to the voter, the laborer, and the consumer. The increase in the power of these groups was not so extensive in Germany, Russia, and Japan. There the power of high-energy technology fell more largely into the hands of those already influential in government. In these countries government, being less subject to the demands of the multitude, could retain control over the new surpluses. Instead of distributing the surpluses, politicians appealed to tradition, patriotism, racism, and similar values to justify state control over them. The power developed was used to make the position of the elite more secure; only such concessions were made to values revealed by or created in the market or the local community, or to the democratic tendency, as were thought necessary to consolidate that position. Thus both the democratic and the nondemocratic state have shown a tendency to turn away from the most widespread possible use of the market to determine the "just" allocation of goods and services produced. To many the state represents a more equitable distributor of some valued goods and services than the market.

The "judicial" functions of the state also increase with the increased use of energy. As the number of conflicts between the codes which governed the old institutions and the codes found necessary and desirable under high-energy usage multiplies, the old means become less and less adequate for settling disputes. In the low-energy society conflicts between husband and wife, parents and children, neighbors, employees and employers, and fellow workers are often settled by relatively informal means; appeal to a higher authority to bring about a settlement is infrequent. Where there is widespread adherence to a religion, a priest may be called in to give the "just" answer. For the most part the individual is left to make his decision in contemplation of its probable results. Thus, for example, where divorce may be unilaterally invoked, its possible consequences in terms of repayment of dowry or bride price, shame and humiliation for the whole clan, ostracism and denial of religious consolation, or loss of the affection and services of children may prevent it in all but the most unusual circumstances. Again, the local reputation of the worker and the employer with whom he may be involved in a dispute may be altered by a decision locally thought to violate justice, and the subsequent effects on ability to hire or be hired may greatly temper the position of both parties to a labor dispute.

Sanctions such as these continue to modify this kind of relationship in high-energy society. However, the growing mobility required for increased use of high-energy technology, and the inability to modify by local action decisions and codes made at a distance, rob the local system of many of its sanctions and render some of the remaining ones inoperable. As the rate of change increases, there is a growing diversity of values among members of families and an increased disparity between the values of succeeding generations. Alterations in role requirements, as between husbands and wives, parents and children, make formal action by the state more and more necessary. Laws to enforce the care of parents by children and children by parents, regulations concerning joint and community property by husbands and wives, decisions concerning inheritance, all these become more subject to state action when there is the widespread and rapid change which accompanies an increased use of new converters. As in the cases noted earlier, this involves the state in operations very different from those foreseen by the founding fathers. Instead of serving as a referee in a game with well-established rules, the politician is required at once to discover emerging norms, enunciate and implement them, and enforce sanctions against violators.

WAR AND THE MODERN STATE

In such circumstances a "government of laws" loses most of its meaning. If when circumstances change, decisions previously made are repeated verbatim, the consequences of the restated decisions are nonetheless different from the consequences of the original decisions. If new decisions are made in the light of differing circumstances, the surety which once characterized "the law" is replaced by uncertainty. The rapid growth of administrative law in all high-energy societies reflects the necessity to control even the controllers, so that their decisions will have at least the similitude of consistency. The continuous alteration of constitutional law in all those countries which claim to be bound by constitutional limits, even though the changes are made in such fashion that the duties of the agents of the state can be carried on behind a façade of continuity, amounts in fact to change in fundamental law.

Perhaps none of these changes—nor all of them put together—has had as much effect on the state as has the use of high-energy technology in warfare. For reasons some of which are already apparent and some of which we shall discuss in the next chapter, increased warfare has accompanied the emergence of high-energy technology. But whatever the reasons for war, preparation for it and its execution involve entirely different social consequences under high-energy technology from those seen in low-energy society.

The tremendous emphasis upon manpower directly engaged on the field of battle which was characteristic even of the First World War made population as such a much more significant factor in determining victory than it currently is or is subsequently likely to be. A regiment of Napoleon's troops could be equipped for war for less energy than it costs to provide the pilot of one jet fighter-bomber with the tools he commands. The energy costs of the first atomic bomb were probably in excess of the energy expended in many a whole battle in previous wars. Techniques of command in the field and techniques of preparing for war have become so different as a consequence of changes in the converters used that the whole matter of determining what weapons shall be invented and who shall command them must be reconsidered. While it is still possible to give nominal command to the members of some ancient class or caste, such as the samurai or the Junkers, control in fact passes to those who can design, produce, and handle tanks, planes, radar and sonar gear, and other new converters. Much of the actual power wielded by the state is thus transferred to those who are technically competent. No state has been able to find within the limits of its hereditary aristocracy all the individuals who can and will develop an understanding of new techniques. Failure to discover and educate those with the capacity to invent and operate high-energy technology makes a state vulnerable to attack by technically more competent states. With a change in converters there is bound to be a shift in the locus of actual power both within states and between them.

The arbitrament of war forces the abandonment of much of the old façade which hides this shift. War frequently brings to power men who have not been educated to defend the values highly prized by the older ruling groups and who are willing to use energy in any way that will obtain results. Among the means they use will be some previously not considered to be moral. Because the ability to command technical resources is only infrequently developed along with a thorough understanding of the relationship between technology and the values which it is designed to serve or is capable of serving, ends-destroying use of means becomes probable. Nevertheless the military man must be given wide latitude in choosing his means, else the whole existence of the state may be jeopardized. Moreover, because of the continuous threat of war a great deal of control over research and the development of new knowledge and new techniques must fall into the hands of the military. States which attain great military competence develop, in the process, the ability to achieve many values which depend upon the use of force. In such cases it is undoubtedly true that if the new technical knowledge had been developed under other auspices, much more time, effort, and thought would have been directed toward the achievement of values which are not dependent on force.

POLITICAL BUREAUCRACY

The state—whether as an administrator of "welfare programs," as a provider of norms and standards, as an adjudicator of disputes, as a developer of new knowledge, or as a war-making agency—develops great bureaucratic structures. For many of those who serve in such structures the activities which they pursue become both important ends in themselves and also significant means to achieve other ends, such as personal power and prestige or security. As in the case of those using other institutions, the groups that serve the state come to be concerned about the maintenance of the values which their own ideas, ideals, and purposes serve. They compete with groups promoting the activities of older institutions like the family and the church and newer ones like the market and the corporation. They do not assume that the state must stand aside and permit others to create values which will take precedence over those which the individuals who serve the state wish, in its behalf, to maintain.

In Education

The state has become, in every high-energy society, the major institution providing training for children in the instrumental arts and sciences. It competes with other institutions for determining the ends to which these arts and sciences are to be devoted. It also is the largest assembler of statistical evidence as to the significant developments in society, and through its emphasis in the selection of the data collected it can, to a degree, determine the interpretation of the society which emerges. Through its machinery are collected the "secret" data about other states which are used to justify its actions in "foreign" affairs. Judicious manipulation both in collecting and in presenting such data gives the agent of the state a tremendous advantage over others who may be attempting to determine the purposes and abilities of those in control of other states. Propaganda issued by government bureaucrats in the attempt to justify their past actions and to prepare the way for their future actions is backed by resources not available to any but the largest corporations and the most powerful churches. As a consequence of these and other factors, the values which the state seeks to develop come more and more to be those furthering the aims of the elites which govern the state, as differentiated from the elites which pursue their aims through indoctrination within the family, the community, the church, the market, and the corporation. Perhaps most significant: when all other actions fail, those who control the state have the right "legitimately" to utilize physical coercion to achieve their aims.

In Business

It is a consequence of the realization of the tremendous strategic advantage of those who govern the state that the relation between "politics" and "economics" has undergone such a reversal in high-energy societies during the last half century. As we have seen, the businessman of the nineteenth century found himself possessed of so much power through the use of the concept of private property and the surplus energy it permitted him to control that he made great efforts to confine the state to the performance of a very limited set of functions. "Economic" considerations became dominant, and businessmen eschewed politics and values politically served. But, as we have noted, partly in reaction to the consequences of businessmen's decisions there was subsequently great increase in the power of the state. Today, as a result, more and more power-seeking men are to be found taking positions in government. From here they can direct many of the value-creating and value-mediating relationships which they could not influence even as heads of great corporations. In the United States, for example, there were, before the Second World War and the New Deal, a number of corporations which produced goods with a greater money value, employed more workers, or controlled more physical property than many of the state governments. A few rivaled even the national government in respect to the power and influence which they wielded. Today the operations of the Department of Defense or even of the Atomic Energy Commission make even the largest of the corporations seem small by comparison. It is little wonder that men long since provided with every status-giving symbol attainable by possessors of wealth are turning to the state to further their power and prestige. In so doing they elevate the status of government office, for government service is shown to compare favorably with the top positions in private business which they abandon to join it.

It is now recognized that in large part the consequences of economic acts can be altered as easily and as surely by direct political control, that is, by fiscal, monetary, and taxing policies, as they can by such economic measures as changes in methods of production, advertising, and marketing practices. The proper sphere of the market comes thus to be discovered as well through political as through economic experiment and experience. In place of a fixed concept of the legitimate sphere of government there develops a poorly defined zone whose limits are hardly ascertainable by even the most erudite scholar and are certainly not definite enough to be pointed out with any exactitude to a new generation.

THE FUTURE OF GOVERNMENT

This brings to the forefront the central problem of political science, that of determining the limits on legitimate acts of government and the means by which such limits are worked out. Speculation about where the process of increasing state function will stop has been accompanied by numerous pronouncements about where it should stop.[4] Functions regarded in one area at a particular time as being legitimately performed by government have there been regarded at another time as belonging "naturally" to the individual, the family, the market, the church, or some local agency. Divine Providence is regarded in some places as having sanctioned the allocation to the state of functions which in other places are not considered to be within the province of the state at all. Decisions as to the legitimate distribution of functions among various institutions which may be in conflict over the issue puts a heavy burden on the agents of the state. They must, to a degree, share in determining the range in which it is legitimately the function of the state itself to perform.

The Consent of the Governed

It is hard to account for the fact that men will acquiesce in the exercise of power by other men, acting in the name of government, which may deprive them of their liberty, take from them part of the product of their labor, seize gains resulting from the ownership of property, order them into situations where they face injury and death, and deprive those most dear to them of their property and their lives. The theory of divine right, which was widespread in old, stable, and well-established societies in the past, has ceased to be accepted as an adequate explanation for this phenomenon in modern, secular, industrial societies. Accounting for the state by an explanation based on the crude theory of force—that is, the position that some men have the capacity physically to force their will on others—fares little better. Government officials attempting new functions which appear to the impartial observer to be no more injurious or dangerous than many of the acts which they are regularly permitted to carry out, sometimes meet with resistance, even including the use of force. Why, if the power of government is great enough to intimidate the subject so that he does not resist one of its acts, is that power insufficient to force him to acquiesce in another? Inability to find an adequate answer to this question has led many political theorists to abandon the doctrine that explains the legitimacy of state power in terms of physical force alone. But these theorists have found it very hard to locate the factors which do determine in each case which functions of government will be accepted as legitimate. Within the state formal structure provides an answer of sorts. It shows how and where the decision is to be made as to which functions the state will perform. It also shows what the state is at the moment prepared to do, if not the limits upon what it might conceivably do. A body of usage, treaty, and international law serves similarly as a rough indicator of what is to be expected between states. But, as we have seen, efforts to increase the use of energy have been accompanied by a series of efforts to change the functions which the state will be expected to perform.

Western theory generally assumes the proposition that government is legitimate only when it proceeds from "the consent of the governed." If this position is accepted, it requires both the statesman and the political scientist to determine which acts, done in the name of the state by whom, to whom, under what conditions, will willingly be assented to. Law is not to be regarded as being static and fixed. The conditions producing changes in the law then become subject to scrutiny: the whole body of values existing and emergent in a society, as well as the social organization and controls which are used to create and mediate them, must be examined. No attempt will be made here to carry out such a complete examination. It may be possible, however, for us to indicate the nature of the influence that changes in the converters in use are apt to have on the determination of just which functions will be considered legitimately undertaken by the state.

The means used in a society to attain the ends pursued there—including the means of production of physical goods—often come to be considered ends in themselves. In the United States, for example, the government guarantees that no person shall be made subject to penalty except by "due process of law." But there can be no "due process" which robs the citizen of his property rights or requires him to undergo "involuntary servitude" except in the armed services or as a punishment for the commission of a crime. Thus, not only the means by which the state regulates the productive activities of the individual prescribed but also the institutions through which production is regularly undertaken are protected. Other states similarly assert the final value of their established ways. This identity of ends and means may be disturbed if the existence of a society is so patently threatened that a choice must be made between sacrificing the whole system and allowing changes to be made in some parts of it in order to preserve the rest. The introduction of new converters frequently poses such a threat. In these situations some ways of doing things that had come to be considered ends in themselves may come again to be regarded as means only, and as subject to alteration if this will serve to maintain other values. Once it is felt that the security of the society against the threatened loss of its most significant values has been attained, scrutiny of the system will again be undertaken. Some will seek to continue those means which were found to be successful in meeting the threat, while others will seek to return to the old ways. War or depression, for example, may require the adoption of many new types of institutional control. Those who feel that they have gained more by these new arrangements than they will gain from a return to the older setup will seek to sanctify the more recent as against the traditional system. Very often the crisis which requires a shift in means-ends relationship results in the relocation of control over physical power in the society and alters the relative influence of the various groups in determining the new hierarchy of values. A new equilibrium of power emerges over time. As this new equilibrium, backed by the new order of values, comes to be commonly accepted in the society, the more important values become so significant that even coercion will be given sanction if it is required to preserve them. When the state acts in support of such values, it acts "legitimately" even if it resorts to force. But by the same token the emergent system of values will be setting limits both upon the means which those who act for the state may use and on the ends for which they may legitimately use those means.

"Pressure" Politics

While the power of various groups within the state is shifting, as a result of the adoption of new converters, the agents of the state are confronted with a dilemma. One group may demand that it receive aid or protection from the state and another group deny that the state has any right to provide such aid. If those who govern fail to respond to the first group they may be confronted with the threat of civil disobedience, civil war, or a coup d'état, whereas if they accede to this demand they may be confronted by a reactionary revolution. The range of legitimate governmental action falls between these extremes. Government acting under the political influence of one party may approach the limit of what another party will, though grudgingly, acquiesce in—or vice versa, again up to the limit permitted. So long as there exists assurance that government will use only those means which the ultimate values of most of the citizens justify, and will use even these means only in spheres of activity similarly justified, government is legitimate. The older democratic societies all passed through periods of civil strife that arose when the government in power did not recognize these limits. But these older democratic states made the transition to high-energy society under conditions which held the rate of change in check and permitted new value hierarchies justifying the new functions of government to become widespread before new areas of power were carved out. In some of the states now going through the transition the flow of energy has increased so rapidly that coercion of great numbers of people is possible at such a rate that no corresponding rate of change in the value system can be made. For it is not easy to get adults to accept basic values that are different from or contrary to those that held sway in childhood. While increased knowledge about psychology has permitted us to hurry somewhat the processes of psychic change, and particularly to modify the specific objectives valued by men, there is much evidence that it is still very difficult to alter the basic personality structure shaped by a culture in the child's early years. It is in part upon this fact that the continuity of morality, religion, and law depends. Thus the state is able to change its legitimate range of activities only slowly. In addition, since one of the first consequences of the adoption of high-energy technology in a region is an increase in longevity there, high-energy societies face the difficulty of dealing with a continually increasing inertia resulting from the existence in their midst of a growing proportion of old people. At the same time, as we have seen, increased use of high-energy converters is also accompanied by demands that the state assume new functions. It is not uncommon to find groups urging extension of the functions of government in their own behalf and concurrently opposing the enlargement of state function in any other direction. The result has been a good deal of ideological double talk, accompanied by sporadic enlargement of the scope of the state to include functions not justified by the moral convictions of many of the groups brought under the new controls.

Political Theory versus Political Practice

Various means of assuring the legitimacy of state policy in the midst of this confusing interplay of forces have been attempted in the democratic states. In most of them, however, there have been periods of stalemate and vacillation followed by periods when the party in power rode roughshod over the protests of many minorities, disregarding the fact that such action was not legitimatized by traditional morality. To pick an example from American history, it was thus that the South was forced, following its unsuccessful attempt at secession, to accept a government which was not legitimatized by Southern morality. The government which was regarded as legitimate by authorities in Washington had to be defended by the use, or threatened use, of Union armies. The acts of the Confederacy, regarded as legitimate in the South, were specifically repudiated by the national government, and any effort to conform with the obligations undertaken in its name was enjoined. Following the withdrawal of Northern troops, the legitimate governments of the states of the South openly denied to their colored citizens rights which were supposed to be guaranteed them by the Constitution. In many other ways these state governments revised the effective law of the nation as it affected the South. History reveals many such denials of the rights of minorities as a consequence of changes in the power position of various groups. Such acts have, in turn, decreased the probability that the basic morality of the minority recently deprived of power will sanction the acts of these governments.

A government acting under the control of those who have recently gained power through a shift in the energy system is not often immediately considered to be legitimate. It cannot always be foreseen whether in fact it will ever become legitimate, for much depends upon the conditions which surround the new state and the use to which the new surplus is put. So when the defenders of a modern dictatorship assert that theirs is but a temporary autocracy, which will serve only until conditions favorable for democratic government have arisen, their position cannot be dismissed out of hand. Actually, such a course was pursued by the United States in the Philippines, and the British in India and elsewhere, to say nothing of its being the basis of the mandate system of the League of Nations. The claim that a dictatorship is temporary can best be tested by discovering whether the acts of the dictator are such that a value system including a morality to support the kind of regime planned is in fact likely to grow up, given time. A brief period will suffice in many cases to make it clear that democratic government is not possible in the foreseeable future. In other cases it will become clear that an oligarchy which controls and increases the surplus energy derived from high-energy technology is not likely to be dethroned by the resistance of angry, disgusted, demoralized but comparatively weak proponents of government based on values derived from and dependent upon the operations of low-energy society.

Our short survey has shown how the increased power of the state derived from the transition to high-energy technology, and indicated some of the areas into which it is likely to go. There is no clear answer as to what the range of legitimate power of the state may be in the high-energy society, for as yet the ability to legitimatize the functions which many groups demand of government is not established. But it does appear more and more clearly that the high concentration of control over physical energy which the new converters make possible upsets many of the factors entering into the balance of power within and between states under which democratic government emerged and survived.

CHAPTER **12**

Not One World, But Many

Many issues are raised by the alteration in the functions of institutions which accompanies transition to high-energy technology. The difficulty of prescribing the legitimate role of an institution as it concerns events taking place within the borders of a single state is compounded by difficulties arising from relations between states and between individuals and groups in different states. In domestic relations there has come to be general acceptance of the idea that government should indicate the limits within which each institution, including the state itself, should function. In interstate relations no such agreement exists. Far-reaching institutions such as churches, corporations, labor organizations, international public unions, and administrative agencies claim the right to control certain functions without let or hindrance by the national state. Yet sovereignty implies that the state implicitly or explicitly sanction every legal act within its borders. So if the state has the obligation to set limits on acts within its own territory, having unilaterally determined what those limits are, then the claims of "outsiders" must become subordinate to the power of the state. This requires that the state actually be able to enforce its edicts if and where other controls which the state might use have proved to be inadequate. Each state, then, must control *sufficient energy* to overcome the efforts of any group, originating within or without the state, which seeks to resist or to evade its legitimate power.

ENERGY AND INTERNATIONAL POSITION

One set of limits on the power of a state is imposed by the amount and kinds of energy which can be converted at the will

278

of those subject to the state's control. Another results from the factors which determine what portion of the energy so converted the state can legitimately command. Some theorists have been so concerned about how the power of government is to be confined to its legitimate sphere and made responsive to the desires of its citizens that they have neglected to investigate whether the result may not be to deprive the state of its ability to achieve what is demanded of it, either domestically or in its relations with other, sometimes inimical, powers. If the state does not have the power to enforce its edicts, it can no longer guarantee that what is commanded in its name will actually come to pass. Law then ceases to be a statement of what will be and becomes merely a pious hope. Let us then examine the theory of legitimate power developed in certain states to see whether it has rendered those states incapable of performing some of their necessary functions.

Democratic theory holds that the power of government is legitimatized by the values of the people it governs. It assumes that in practically every case the hierarchy of values motivating the individual has the same supreme values; these, the values which will be sought at the sacrifice of any others held by those individuals, constitute the pattern identified with nationality. The theory recognizes that there are values attached to lesser areas such as the feudal domain and to smaller units such as the tribe, kinship groups like the family, and functional groups like the union or the corporation; loyalty to larger and more universal units such as the church or an international labor organization is also taken for granted. Nevertheless, it is expected that wherever national welfare requires it any such obligation will be subordinated.

This ideology accompanied the rise of the political organizations which became supreme in the West. In the name of the nation old empires were overturned. Centuries-old allegiances proved inadequate to ensure the survival of feudal principalities and ancient provinces: nationality replaced ultimate fealty to clan and tribe. But this concept or ideal sets limits on the size of the state, as efforts to establish multinational states in Europe have shown. Within the borders of one state it was not possible for more than one nationality to achieve its supreme values. Given two or three different supreme values, each regarded as being final by one segment of the population, subordination of one or another segment was inevitable. The subordinated minority immediately denied the legitimacy of the government which subjected it. Since in democratic theory it is the nation that must serve as the unit in which evidence of consent to government is to be demonstrated, the area of the legitimate state must coincide with that in which a national group has in the past developed. Such areas are frequently small and it is possible within their borders to generate only limited amounts of energy. As has been shown, high-energy technology requires for its efficient operation extensive land areas and sizable populations. Therefore small states are often unable to produce the force necessary to carry out their edicts when confronted by the power of a large aggregation, whether such power takes the form of an agency of a great corporation, a church, or another state. If they remain weak they are unable to guarantee the enforcement of law which is their fundamental reason for being; if they seek to enlarge their power they must come to govern areas in which that power will by their own principles be illegitimate. Countries like Sweden, Denmark, and Norway, who have abided by these principles and remained nation-states, have slowly lost the ability to determine their own power position. Other democratic European states like France have at times disregarded the limits on their legitimate exercise of power and in so doing have produced conflict between their professed principles and their actions.

The Role of Nationalism

The fallacy in the principle of national self-determination is shown by the decline of power in the West. In part this decline is attributable to the geographic location of the resources necessary to the use of high-energy technology, but to a much greater extent it is due to the paralyzing dilemma which arises from the idea of the finality of nationalism as the basis of the state. Strengthened by its early success, the idea of the supremacy and finality of nationalism has been so reified that the continuing economic and military disasters which have often followed its pursuit have not succeeded in destroying it. Conflict has continued for centuries among the states which once made up the Austro-Hungarian empire, Poland, Germany, Holland, Belgium, and France, which together occupy an area geographically adequate for a very powerful state. Few if any legislative acts made in the name of any one of these nationalities would be considered legitimate in the area where another of them governs, and efforts to integrate them by political or military means have produced resistance which, when the opportunity arose, took the form of the reemergence of a "nationalist" party.

The effort to integrate these nations economically by insisting that price considerations should override all other factors, and that each state be required to sanction all international acts which would result in profit to the trader or industrialist has met with equally strong or even greater resistance. In many cases the consequence of the operations of the free international market may be as disastrous to some groups and regions as would any contemplated political act.

In areas other than Western Europe the difficulties of using nationalism as a basis for legitimate government are greatly multiplied. Very large areas of the world have not as yet developed anything comparable to what is called nationality in the West. In these areas the simple village systems based on prevailing low-energy techniques are unable to maintain for long the relations among peoples from which national self-consciousness seems to emerge. Nor have they been able to utilize successfully either the territorial and functional division of labor or the political integration and centralization which capitalizes on such consciousness. Centralization of power in low-energy societies seldom adds much to the prospect for local survival. Moreover, as has been shown, the growth of population, necessitating the use of very infertile land and decreasing the surplus energy available from plants, reduces the likelihood that in the future the kind of system of production that benefits from centralized control will appear.

Outside Europe much of the nationalism which exists stems from the European origin of the dominant elements of the population. The present governments of the United States, Canada, and some of the Latin American countries became legitimate only after the Indians had been exterminated, forced to migrate, or assimilated into the culture of the whites. In these states little is left of the Indian cultures which for a long time characterized those who governed in the Western Hemisphere. European conquerors brought their own cultures. Such cultures became the

primary basis of emerging nationalities which serve to legitimatize present American governments. Other American states are
based on nationality which depends more closely on the Indian
cultures of the pre-Columbian era. Many of these states are so
weak that their sovereignty is only a convenient fiction supported
by such devices as the Monroe Doctrine. In others, tribal and
church organization and the operations of foreign corporations,
acting without the sanction of nationality, actually determine
what government does.

The new nationalities in the Western Hemisphere are the
result of forced growth sustained by new technology and stimulated by modern means of communication, education, and propaganda. In many cases national self-consciousness, as contrasted
with a kind of nostalgic identification with the mother country,
has only recently developed.

The Western idea that nationality is the only legitimate basis
for statehood is of fairly recent origin. As we have indicated, it is
an outgrowth of the proposition that only democratic government
is legitimate and that nationality represents the highest values of
man. In most places in the world, the state government antedated
nationality and contributed much of the emergence of the nationality which later legitimatized it. This has been conveniently
overlooked by those who regard the continued existence of small
European nationalities as an end justifying any cost entailed in
maintaining them but look on the demise of long-established
non-European civilizations as a mere incident in the history of
"progress."

In some of the Balkan states, in the Near East, in India, in
China, in fact in most of Asia and Africa, the idea of nationality
has no such supremacy as that which made it a successful base
for the legitimacy of state power in the West. Here religion,
caste, tribe, and other units of identification are often more effective than is nationality in securing supreme allegiance from persons and groups. These communities still endow their members
with such values that the national state is not able to make a
successful claim to legitimacy for any very large range of functions. In these areas the assertion that a government speaks for
the nation may have very little significance in determining, for
example, whether or not treaties which the government makes

will be honored by those over whom it claims sovereignty, and whether the government can enforce its laws or the contracts made under its presumed protection. Assumption by the state of functions previously considered to be within the sphere of some other institution may produce the same kind of reaction as the claims made in the name of the English monarch once aroused in the American colonies.

So when the national state calls upon its citizenry to sacrifice some value which is higher in the hierarchy of many than is the survival of that state itself, the result is a refusal to perform as the state has ordered. Those who govern are then faced with the alternative of abandoning their position or attempting to use physical coercion.

Even in areas where national consciousness exists and its supremacy is not questioned, problems in regard to values arise, for there may be disagreement as to the ordering of the values placed just below those upon whose supremacy there is general agreement. What constitutes a legitimate function of the state is a concept that varies from group to group. For some the protection of the rights of the property owner are the most significant obligation of government; for others the efforts of the state to provide for the common defense or the general welfare justifies whatever invasion of property rights may be required. For some the preservation of racial or religious distinction is an obligation of the state; for others the presence of segregation is itself evidence that the state has failed to protect those values which justify its existence. Demands are made by one group for state intervention to prevent the financial disaster which may otherwise fall upon them as a consequence of the operations of the market. These demands are countered by the insistence of another group that such intervention is outside the legitimate sphere of the state's functions. The claims of such international organizations as churches, corporations, and cartels present further complications. Through them, power originating outside the state may be brought to bear to alter the decisions which otherwise would be reached through the interplay of forces within the state. Thus the nationality which represents an old agreement on values may fail as a means of defining legitimate state power when as a consequence of new and differing experiences there are widespread changes in values. It becomes less and less possible at any given time to generalize as to what will be considered legitimate by the people said to constitute a nation, and therefore less and less possible to predict whether or not the agents of a state will meet with resistance or acquiescence if they attempt to carry out a given pattern of acts. This applies both internally and externally.

The demands for services such as communication and transportation have frequently resulted in the formation of international bodies, like the Universal Postal Union, which to all intents and purposes enact the legislation necessary to carry out their functions. Agents of the state may then be held remiss if their failure to enforce the international code results in disruption of a desired service. States acquiesced for years in the gold standard, which effectively deprived them of the ability to determine the value and character of the money in use within their boundaries. The increasing use of technological standards in various fields has similarly required abdication by the national state of its otherwise legitimate power. At present, the requirements of military alliances have even standardized the weapons and the tactics by which the state is to be defended. Many of those who recognize that nationality can no longer serve as the basis for setting the legitimate geographic boundaries for some functions performed by the state have seized upon these developments as evidence that a world state is not only immediately necessary but ultimately inevitable. Using generalizations derived from experience in the areas where high-energy converters have already had wide use, they project the limitless diffusion of high-energy technology as a basis for the universal state, the appearance of which they consider to be merely a matter of time.

THE WORLD STATE

This work has shown that there is no such inevitability connected with high-energy technology. The changes which low-energy societies must undergo in the process of adopting that technology affect everything from the functions of the family and the nature of personality to the rate of population growth, the ratio of land to population, and the character of groups in political control. Almost nothing that gives life meaning in low-energy society is left undisturbed by the transition to high-energy converters. The introduction of these conditions means disaster to some of the strongest and most deeply entrenched groups in the community. Since the traditional right to control lies with them and not with the would-be innovators, it is unreasonable to expect that they will teach respect for and devotion to those who are destroying them. Rather they can be expected to exert great efforts to expel the disturbing agents of high-energy society and to reaffirm all the values connected with the old way of life. Acts of government which repudiate these values will be rejected by the people with scorn and derision and, if there is thought to be the least chance for success, with armed rebellion. Where peaceful transition appears to be taking place, it sometimes means only that successful physical resistance is thought to be impossible. In these cases, instead of open organized opposition the state may be confronted with anxiety accompanied by apathy and the complete failure on the part of individuals to take any action that they are not specifically ordered to take. The spontaneous and willing effort of the individual seeking to make a "success" of himself in terms of internalized goals is completely lost, and the cost of change is increased by the inefficiency with which new roles are carried out and new converters used.

It is true that the effectiveness with which low-energy societies can directly oppose with physical force the power that can be brought to bear against them by those possessed of high-energy converters is declining. If all that they seek is subordination or extermination of a people, a few individuals wielding great industrial power can impose their rule on many equipped only with the products of low-energy converters. It is no longer conceivable, for example, that natives no better equipped than were the Maori could force the British to a stalemate on the battlefield. Industrialists are no longer under the necessity of making such concessions as those which accompanied their rise in England. But this does not mean that there are no effective limits to the use of physical coercion. The growing "humanitarianism" of civilized people sets some limits on the methods they can use, or at least on the methods which they can use on other people whom they consider also to be civilized. But the ends sought by the industrialists themselves impose limits that are probably more certain and effective on the means which they can use. These ends frequently require the perpetuation of trade, and trade remains profitable only if the resistance of the native does not become too great or his productivity too low. Similarly, if low-energy peoples are expected to provide manpower for armies, their way of life must not be too much disrupted lest they become unfit for that use.

The great advantages which those who live near surplus-producing natural resources have gained from high-energy technology are not always available to induce people less advantageously situated to abandon their current methods of production. As has been pointed out, in many areas it would be foolish for the people to attempt the transition, for they would sacrifice surplus energy in hand for doubtful returns in the future. There is nothing, then, about high-energy technology itself that guarantees its universal adoption, and it cannot be assumed as a sure base for the universal culture that would legitimatize the power of a world state.

IDEOLOGICAL UNIFICATION

There are other advocates of the world state who are willing to concede that nothing so "materialistic" as technology will serve to provide universal values but who insist that certain great ideas can do this. They view culture as composed entirely of symbols which are manifestations of these ideas. Some among them hold that the culture of the future revolves around the ideas which they regard as having been solely responsible for capitalism, democracy, and Christianity. Science and technology, though they are frequently regarded as being antithetic to those ideas, are nevertheless included in the pattern of these ideologists: they can "prove" to their own satisfaction that because modern means of communication permit the ideas to be diffused they must result in a universal culture. There are, however, other people in other parts of the world for whom other ideas, such as communism and Buddhism, provide the answer for the new tomorrow. For these idealists the future of the world is foreordained. It must first of all go through some holocaust which will cleanse it of all those who hold the ideas which represent error, after which all the world will live under the beneficent control of the idea which they hold to represent self-evident truth.

Even accepting the premise that any one set of ideas, if universally taught by mass communication, can become the basis for all societies, it does not at present appear probable that the people adhering to any one of the great ideologies now claiming to be universal will be able to secure the controls necessary to impose a single set of values upon the world. Of the contending forces now existing *several* have within their power the ability to establish those values which can be created by means of mass communication. Because communication agencies must act from some secure political and geographic base, located at some point or points supplied with resources that include large amounts of energy, it is likely that future control over communication will coincide with the existing distribution of power in the world. To secure uniform results from communication, one agency would have to control all the territory in the world to prevent rival communication agencies from being set up. Moreover such an agency would have to know what everybody must be made to think and believe in order to act in all the various ways that people must act to keep a high-energy society going. Given the limited knowledge man possesses concerning the necessary relations between ideas, ideals, morals, social structure, and technology, achieving this hardly seems conceivable. So it seems improbable that "one world" will be created through propaganda and other means of spreading an ideology. If this is true, it cannot be presumed that common values created by a universal ideology will so operate as to induce those who now control large amounts of energy to distribute it and its products equally throughout the earth. Thus ideology seems to offer no more certainty of creating the conditions necessary to make world government legitimate than does the automatic spread of technology.

REGIONAL BASES OF ENERGY USE

A good deal of evidence has been presented at various points in this work to show that the conditions required to cause a people or culture to move along the continuum from low- to high-energy society involve more than common desire on the part of a people to make such a move. It is necessary to ascertain whether or not the energy required to make the transition possible is available and what are the values of those who control that energy. In the case of a region which contains the sources of energy within its boundaries, transition depends on whether dominant groups will aid or prevent the rise to power of those favoring a technology that would unseat many of them. In some areas it is clear that local resources are inadequate to provide a base either for the transition to high-energy technology or for its subsequent maintenance; here low-energy technology will continue to prevail unless some outside agency provides the means. In such cases transition depends on whether groups which have such means can be discovered, whether their values are such as to induce them to make the means available, and whether their power and influence in their own society are sufficient for them to be permitted to carry out the necessary transfers of energy and/or its products.

Decline of International Trade

In England in the nineteenth century those who wanted to "export capital" were free to do so, that is, they could, in exchange for claims on the future productivity of foreigners, transfer their own claims on current English goods and services to individuals who could exercise the claims to accumulate converters abroad. This is not always true of England today, nor is it true in many other cases. The size of the share of production going to "capitalists" has been greatly reduced in the course of the development of the modern industrial society. Labor organization and management now appropriate much of what once could have been claimed as profits, and governments tax away a large part of this source of investment. In addition, states regulate foreign investment as part of the implementation of their foreign policies. Domestic groups have put first claim on investable funds by forcing governments to issue debentures, the funds from which go to maintain "full employment" in the industrial state, or to carry out some other function such as investment for national defense. Even the portion then left to the saver cannot always be invested at will, for groups within his own state may have succeeded in having restrictions placed on the import and export of specific goods, which restrictions may reduce the probability that a specific investment can be made to pay.

The attractiveness of an area as a field for investment is also affected by the government of the state of which it is a part. When a government is controlled by groups which seek to preserve the existing order or to reserve future opportunities for their own citizens, it can make investment very unattractive to foreigners. Even where the government itself is friendly, investment is not necessarily secure, for great damage can be done to industrial installations by minorities which have active support among the population.

Changes in technology itself are also constantly affecting the profitability of foreign trade with low-energy areas. The organic products which once were staples of trade are increasingly subject to competition from products synthesized from raw materials found within the areas currently controlled by industrialized states. Indigo gave way to analine dies, nylon has taken much of the market once supplied by silk. Orlon and other substitutes threaten wool,[1] and rayon and its sister fibers are displacing cotton. Shellac, varnish, linseed, and tung oils are being supplanted by synthetic lacquers and plastics. Paper takes the place of jute in some types of bagging. Hennequin, in less demand for cordage, must also compete with wire rope and nylon. The preserving function of spices has been rendered obsolete by modern methods of canning and refrigeration, and many flavorings are now made synthetically. Perfumes are being made from coal-tar residues. The list is long and growing, and there is a constant decrease in opportunities for profit arising from the differences in plant and animal life that justified trade at a distance in the days of the supremacy of sail.

An increasing proportion of the goods imported by industrial states is in the form of minerals. Since most of these are not found in great quantities in the alluvial plains which support large populations using low-energy technology, mining usually takes place where the native population is small and its members are not able to demand much for their labor or for the exhaustion of "their" natural resources. Minerals found at sites where a considerable portion of the proceeds has to be turned over to the local population must compete for development with rich sources in unpopulated areas and with less rich deposits so located that high-energy technology reduces the economic cost of the product made from them. If foreign ores cost too much, they may be replaced through the concentration and beneficiation of domestic ores, or the discovery of new alloy substitutes. Even if the costs of foreign ores

are low enough for transportation to be added without making
them higher than the costs of goods from local sources, the fact
that local production in the industrial state will help provide
"full employment" or meet some other political goal may prevent
the export of the capital required to secure the exploitation of
distant mineral resources.

Food itself once represented a large part of the product exported from low-energy societies to compensate for their imports.
The export of food was frequently possible only because slavery
or feudalism or the abundance of land served to create a ratio of
land to population such that surplus food was available. Many of
these areas have undergone revolutions which destroyed the
power of slaveowners and landlords and have as a consequence—
witness Japan, Eastern Europe, the West Indies, and parts of the
old Portuguese, Spanish, and Dutch empires—seen so great an
increase in their populations that the local demand for food could
now absorb almost if not all the food that they can produce. The
surplus of food in the United States will decrease as the demand
which results from population growth and from the rising standard of living among industrial workers increases. The British
Commonwealth is hard put to it to supply all the food required to
maintain the plane of living of the population of Britain and the
other member nations; because of the demands of its own populations, the Commonwealth finds it necessary to obtain increasingly expensive food from Africa, India, and the Indies. On the
other hand, the increased use of machine cultivation and of irrigation, synthetic fertilizers, new methods of selecting and breeding plants and animals, hybridization, insect and pest control, and
other improvements more easily adopted in the commercial farms
of the industrial states than in those of the low-energy societies
have made it possible for some of the Western nations to raise
their own food economically if and as the mounting cost of imported food makes this desirable. The fact that dependence on
imported food renders a state vulnerable to those who can cut off
its food supply has led some states to subsidize their food raisers
instead of using comparable amounts of energy to protect distant
food-producing areas.

The very high profits which once inspired foreign investment
have become increasingly evanescent as the consequences of

nationalistic movements have revealed themselves. On the other hand, the great profits to be had from the sale of new products in the very extensive market created by the use of high-energy technology become more attractive. Capital increasingly tends to be invested near existing industrialized areas. For example, to get the "recapitalization" of Europe demanded by its foreign policy, the United States had to seize by taxation or guarantee, with bonds to be paid off from future taxation, most of the wealth required. There is apparently even less appeal to the private investor in such shaky enterprises as the industrialization of India or the Argentine.

Growth of Domestic Trade

There is considerable effort on the part of certain schools of economists and businessmen to parallel the policies which apparently made the British so successful in the Victorian age. It is questionable that they will succeed. International finance is as much a mystery to most people as is national finance. Free trade and free export of capital are not opposed on theoretical grounds; resistance arises from the reaction of specific groups to the specific results which are expected to follow from the adoption of these policies. To illustrate: the contrast between the continued prosperity and employment that the Mesabi region of Michigan has long provided (which would continue with the exploitation of the low-grade ores remaining in that vicinity) and the unemployment, tax delinquency, and general demoralization which would result from abandonment of these ores in favor of the increased investment of American capital to obtain ores in Venezuela or Labrador can be appreciated by men with no knowledge whatever of the theoretical advantages and drawbacks of free trade and free foreign investment. If the attitudes of these men are not taken into account by the management of the steel corporations, then they will probably be taken into account by representatives sent to Congress, who will attempt to control policy in their interest. Of course if these Congressmen are met by others from New York, New Jersey, and Pennsylvania who hope to benefit from development based on ore from Labrador or Venezuela, the legislative result will reflect that attitude too. But at least there will be no representative from Canada or Venezuela in Congress. The Mesabi situation has many counterparts in the industrial states.

The costs of establishing and protecting foreign investment in low-energy societies are reflected in taxes, subsidies, and credit. Whatever the hope may be for their future liquidation, immediately such costs must be met from the surpluses being produced in currently industrialized states. Within these states, however, increased support is given to those policies which result in increases in present goods and services. Those able to produce goods with high-energy converters, and without encountering the costs of maintaining long lines of communication and sustaining locally weak or unpopular governments, are more likely to be supported than are those who depend on the problematic gains to be made by retaining old trade relations which involve such costs.

Rubber, which used to be cited as one of the products which made world trade absolutely necessary, can now be made synthetically. A Texas company producing such rubber can pay wages that permit its workers to educate their children, secure good medical care, provide for their old age, and enjoy automobiles, modern plumbing, telephones, refrigerators, and similar conveniences. Yet it can sell this rubber at a price so low that the Malayan rubber plantation owner, if he is to remain competitive, can afford to pay his workers little more than bare subsistence. If Malayan rubber is traded for Arkansas rice, neither the rice grower nor the rubber tapper can live very well. On the other hand, if there was a switch in Arkansas to raising beef to be sold to American industrial workers—thus releasing to other industries the labor, machinery, and power used in rice farming—the beef raiser, the Texas rubber producers, and the industrial workers who supplied the housing, refrigerators, automobiles, and other industrial products the rubber workers bought could all enjoy a higher plane of living. In Texas there would be no need to furnish guards to protect the rubber worker from guerrilla Reds or to maintain the long sea lanes, naval bases, air strips, and other costly apparatus now required to keep Malaya supplying the West with rubber.

In the final analysis, the decision as to whether Americans will continue buying Malayan rubber will be made in the United

States, where Texas and Arkansas workers and owners have a vote—which is true neither of the Malayan worker nor of the British plantation owner. Unless some strong American groups find very convincing arguments of an ideological or strategic nature which will persuade other American groups to support a policy of subsidizing the Malayan plantation system, it appears probable that domestically produced synthetic rubber will replace the natural product in the United States market. It is possible that the savings from such a development would be large enough not only to provide our allies with rubber but also to permit giving compensation to the Malayan plantation owner which would induce him to turn the land back to local food production by the Malayans. This is not a conclusion: it is a statement that the possibility warrants calculation. Such calculations may have to be made by the British and American governments, since they find it increasingly difficult to secure the means to underwrite all the endeavors which the various citizen groups call upon them to support.

There are a great many parallel situations. In each case one of the factors necessary for rational choice of policy is the computation of the energy costs and gains of alternative courses of action. We have repeatedly alluded to the fact that many of the geopolitical arrangements that now obtain in the world are a consequence of the distribution of power during an era when the use of organic converters and trade carried on by means of the sailing ship set up a pattern which is in many cases not the most efficient one for exploiting high-energy technology. The acceptance of these arrangements as being "natural" and final has frequently been tied up with the concept that the supremacy of nationality as a set of values is final and that the center of world power is still to be found in the national states of Western Europe, who thus will be able in the future to make the kind of decisions which they made in earlier centuries. Twice the strength of the United States was added to that of England, France, and other countries to secure the preservation of that pattern. In each case the result was abortive: the outcome was a strengthening of forces outside Europe which made the old pattern even more difficult morally, politically, economically, and militarily to sustain. It has become increasingly apparent that the center of physical power is no longer to be found in Western Europe. It further appears that national supremacy also restricts the legitimate power of the Western states in such ways as to make them very vulnerable before the aggregation of power that can be delivered under the control of the United States or the U.S.S.R. and its satellites. A new power pattern is emerging; the old models are outmoded from the point of view of understanding as well as of administering high-energy society.

GEOGRAPHY AND REGIONALISM

Many variables enter into any consideration of the future character of political organization. Neither the survival of the sovereignty of the national state, as it is found in Europe, nor the immediate achievement of a world state seems probable, but it is not apparent just what the state of the future will be like. Federal systems like those found in the United States and the British Commonwealth offer models for examination, and the poorly defined relationship that prevails among the peoples of the Soviet Union and their neighbors provides material at least for speculation. These three structures differ in some very important ways. It is not easy to say whether the characteristics that they have in common are the reason for their survival or whether it is the differences between them that make it possible for each to survive in its own environment.

It may be possible, however, to determine some of the future characteristics of political organization by starting from the fact that whatever other qualities the state of tomorrow may have, by definition it must control sufficient energy to carry out its edicts in the face of resistance or the threat of resistance. If we trace energy back to its sources, we can estimate which are the possible geographical bases for the organization of states actually capable of generating power enough to sustain themselves. Given an area (or several areas combined) that seems to offer the basis for a viable state based on high-energy technology, it should be apparent from the way the inhabitants are acting whether or not such a state is likely to emerge. The very preliminary observations made in this book indicate some of the conditions required for the transition to high-energy society; research along the lines here indicated will show whether or not the necessary steps are likely to be taken. The pertinent facts will include population trends in terms of numbers, composition, distribution, and rate of growth; the rate of accumulation of converters; and evidences of the existence of the values necessary for the emergence of new social structures which can effectively organize high-energy society.

The Crucial Factor: Coal

The geographic facts about most parts of the world are pretty well agreed upon, but there is considerable difference of opinion about the significance of these facts. In the framework offered here energy sources have great significance. We hold that coal is the basic fuel for high-energy society. Any political system based on high-energy technology must, then, either be possessed of coal or operate in a world which guarantees continuous access to coal-bearing regions. Coal is the largest single source of energy being used in the world today; in 1950, for example,[2] coal and lignite supplied 47.5 per cent of all the energy, exclusive of feed and food, which was consumed in the world. Moreover, coal promises to remain for a long time to come the largest single source of energy in use. An estimate made in 1937 [3] placed the reserves of petroleum at 0.1 per cent of the visible reserves of all fuel, peat at 0.9 per cent, fuel wood at 8.8 per cent, water power at 26.7 per cent, and coal at 63.5 per cent. Since there is considerable disagreement about the specific size of reserves, these figures [4] are cited only to show the relative position of the various fuels. The significance of coal is enhanced, as we have seen, by the fact that it is used in steel making. The cost of steel enters into the cost of producing so many products that other fuels and their products are apt to move toward coal-mining regions, rather than the reverse. Further, since it was coal which was the base on which England built the first true high-energy society, those using the English system as a model for increased power have for the most part built around coal even where another fuel might possibly have sufficed. So scientific and technical development based on the exploitation of coal and the metals its use makes available gives great advantages to people using this fuel.

It appears, then, that knowledge of the location of great beds of coking coal provides a means of predicting where, if a society does make use of high-energy technology, its power is likely to be geographically centered. Coal is not evenly distributed in the world. Between them, the United States and Canada, the United Kingdom, Germany, France, and the U.S.S.R. have almost 65 per cent of the world's visible reserves of all kinds of energy sources and about 86 per cent of the visible reserves of coal and lignite. It is primarily in these states also that the bulk of the world's stock of converters is concentrated; thus the means are present for making available the potential energy of their coal beds. In 1950 North America, Europe, and the U.S.S.R. consumed 88.5 per cent of all the energy from commercial sources which was used in the world. Europe—exclusive of the U.S.S.R.—plus the United States and Canada consumed about 75 per cent of all such energy.

In 1950 North America used more than the equivalent of 6 metric tons of coal per capita. Only Luxemburg matched this. Norway, Sweden, and the nations of the British Commonwealth used the equivalent of between 3 and 6 tons per capita. In all of Africa and Asia only the Union of South Africa, Japan, and the U.S.S.R.[5] used more than ¾ ton per capita. Only about half of the area of South America used this much. These figures do not reveal the specific location of power in the larger political units; in such areas more specific designations are needed. In Western Europe actual centers of great use of energy are to be found near the Ruhr, the Saar, and the British Midlands. In the United States, important coking coal areas are found in Pennsylvania, West Virginia, Tennessee, Illinois, Alabama, Colorado, and Utah. The Kharkov, Kuznetsk, Karaganda, and Silesian regions furnish this material for the U.S.S.R. and its satellites. There is considerable unexploited coal in Manchuria and in South Africa, some in Japan. China and India have reserves comparable to those of England and Germany, but these are at present largely unusable owing to the absence of the geographic, technological, and social factors which permit coal to play so important a role in existing high-energy societies.

Coal and the Concentration of Industry

It will be recalled that with existing high-energy converters there is considerable advantage to be gained from locating industry within a few hundred miles of the coal fields. The concentration of industry in such areas reduces the amount of energy required to transport all the coal used in the whole elaborate process extending from extraction to consumption. Since transportation costs are kept to a minimum by transporting the heaviest goods the least distance, the great preponderance of heavy industry can be most efficiently located in terms of the energy costs of transporting coal and iron. The resulting concentration of market in turn leads to advantages for secondary industries, and tertiary industries increase in answer to the demands of those serving the primary and secondary industries. For these reasons, among others, no large part of the coal produced in any major field is today shipped very far from its point of origin.

It should be remembered in dealing with the effects of energy costs on industrial location that it is energy, not distance, that must be measured. In some areas climatic conditions result in savings in the energy costs of space heating which more than compensate for the added distance which coal must be transported to reach those sites, as compared with sites geographically nearer but energywise more "distant." This differential operates, for example, in favor of Los Angeles, where blast furnaces are fueled with Utah coal, over sites in Utah where the cost of space heating is higher because of the climate. Other factors, such as an abundant water supply and local supplies of cheap gas and petroleum which can be used in processing once the iron is freed from the ore, also enter here, as does the existence in southern California of a much larger market for the product of the steel mills. In other cases savings may be effected by the use of low-cost pipeline and maritime and river transport in competition with truck and railroad traffic; these differentials may make a geographically more distant point less costly to reach than one fewer miles away. Such facts as these must be weighed, along with the costs of moving populations located at points set by the earlier influence of low-energy converters. Since these people provide a market for goods produced by the new technology, and it would be extremely costly to change their location, the actual pattern of distribution in many high-energy societies is different from what it presumably would be if men could start from scratch, without having to consider existing structure. For particular industries using special techniques and special materials, the centripetal effects of the use of coal are reduced below those of other factors. Thus, industries using large amounts of power and relatively small amounts of steel and other heavy products—for example, aluminum refineries, which often are located near hydroelectric power plants, or plants using a special material like petrochemicals, which get both their energy and their raw materials from petroleum—have a different pattern from those which make use of coal alone. Despite the differences, however, they too bear witness to the significance of energy in influencing the location of industry and population and hence of the physical power which governments have at their command.

IDEOLOGICAL UNITY AND ECONOMIC REGIONALISM

Much of what has been presented here has been set forth with the purpose of making it possible to recognize the signs which indicate that a given region will in the future reveal a pattern showing that men are there seeking to use more high-energy converters. Such efforts are characteristic where men are seeking to reduce production costs; the product might be anything from a cathedral to a machine gun. Thus it would not be necessary to posit "power-mad" or "materialistic" man to account for the fact that energy is being sought in ever greater amounts. But it has been shown that some values, particularly those that depend on close permanent interpersonal relations, fare badly in the social systems which facilitate the use of high-energy converters. Where these values are strongly entrenched, high-energy technology is less likely to be adopted than in areas where achievements depending on the increased use of energy are paramount in the modal personality.

Some idealists assert the proposition that equality among men— that is, equality of status and of power, not only "equal opportunity to become unequal"—is of such significance that the concentration of wealth, influence, and power which accompanies high-energy technology is abhorrent. Where high-energy technology develops in the face of such idealism, the efficacy of energy as compared with other means affecting the survival of values comes into focus. If, in spite of ideological opposition supported by the deep-seated values that are threatened, high-energy converters come into wider use, it is evident that those who implement their desires by means of these converters are becoming dominant over those who would ideally prefer another world but are forced to retreat before their more powerful opponents. This is not the same, however, as saying that it is evident that more individuals prefer such a world. It may mean only that a small elite, themselves convinced of the superiority of the values which arise with and can be served only by high-energy technology, have the power to shape their world in the image of their values despite popular opposition. On the other hand, it might also be evidence that men generally accept the idea that "progress" consists of increasing the amount of energy brought under man's control, and that this justifies whatever sacrifice of other values may be required.

The position taken here is that the values in any particular region to some degree affect and to some degree are affected by the social structure to be found there. We also hold that there is constant reciprocity between the technological relationships that are sanctioned and the values which they help to promote or destroy. This would imply nothing about "final" or supreme values; in any society investigation could reveal the directions in which it was currently moving. It should be noted that it will be precisely in those societies where increasing amounts of energy are being used that groups favoring values which require more energy for their achievement will be able to promote those values. For example, states in which large amounts of energy are now used can utilize advertising, propaganda, and education to promote the use of means of communication and transportation such as newspapers, magazines, railways, airplanes, television, and radio. The use of these will in turn sustain increased demand for them and for goods whose use can be promoted by them. By the same token, in low-energy society values which do not depend upon the increasing possession of things are, perhaps, more likely to survive because they do not have to compete with mass-produced effort promoting things as an evidence of worth.

An examination of the ideologies contending for supremacy today makes clear that some of them require action opposed to that which would maximize the availability of energy and its products among *present* users of high-energy technology. For example, the ideology being promoted by the Cominform demands the transportation of great amounts of industrial products

from Ural and other Russian industrial plants to Korea and
various parts of China. These products are needed to help the
outlying holders of that ideology resist the efforts of those with
other values seeking to take another course. But the energy used
in transporting goods to China or Korea from the Moscow complex might, if used in production at or near Moscow, produce far
more goods for Russian consumption than can be returned to
Moscow from the product of Chinese and Korean coolie labor.
Furthermore, the use of the Transsiberian Railway in this way
wears out its physical equipment without supplying anything that
can be used to replace it. In the meantime, the population which
must be served by rail is growing in both China and Russia as a
result of policies which increase the population and at the same
time lessen the possibility of using coastal and maritime traffic.
Moreover, inclusion within the Russian sphere of five or six hundred million low-energy users adds to the difficulty of increasing
the accumulation of converters at a rate greater than the rate of
growth of population dependent on them. The persistence of this
policy will be an interesting test of the strength of Cominform
ideology, since other values being promoted within Russia call
for an increase in Russian productivity that can only come from
an increase in the ratio of converter capacity to population.

In communist theory the great achievement of Marxism was
that it taught men the true relation between technology and
society. To many Russian engineers and economists who are daily
made aware of the barriers which Cominform policy puts between
them and the achievement of maximum physical productivity, the
contrast between the ideal and the results of its application must
make the acceptance of ideological considerations rationally difficult.

Some of the values widely held in the West pose similar problems for the democratic states. The French and British seek, on
ideological grounds, to defend democracy and free enterprise in
East Asia. Taxes imposed to carry out this effort use part of the
income of businessmen in ways which the owners of free enterprises in the home countries would not otherwise have used it.
Many of the products sought in the Far East, or substitutes for
them, could probably be produced with the aid of Midlands,
Ruhr, and Saar coal at less cost than they can be secured from

Asia under existing conditions. On the other hand, certain policies of the NATO operate in accord with technological efficiency. Those who support the Schuman plan urge the use of the state to promote policies which will result in concentration of industrial production in areas near the Ruhr and the Saar. If European farmers use any considerable inputs of energy from the new surplus, the effect will be the release and almost certain migration of population from areas thus made "sub marginal" to others nearer the mines. Exchange of goods between England and Germany may demonstrate that such trade can result in a higher plane of living on both sides of the Channel than would be possible by trade between either of them and a low-energy area such as India or China. Where this proves to be true, those groups within each of these states which succeed in promoting production near energy sources save the surplus energy that would be used in transportation to a distant site. The energy saved may in turn be used to promote the extension of their policies. Thus, those who insist on ideological grounds on policies which operate against the gradient of the field being generated by the converters in use reduce the physical productivity of the area they control. In sum, *high-energy technology operates in favor of regional and against universal diffusion of that technology and the values which it serves and which sustain it.*

UNDEVELOPED AREAS AND THE WELFARE STATE

The present overpopulation of Western Europe [in terms of the standards of living prevailing and the farming techniques used] will probably continue for some time to justify the sale of industrial products to countries like Argentina and Uruguay in return for food produced there. The export of food from these regions continues to be possible because of the ratio of population to arable land and the existence of social arrangements which justify food export. For the rulers of these Latin American states the importation of industrial products makes worthwhile the continuance of these relationships. Few industrial investments made by Europeans in these regions would, however, be likely to result in the rate of physical productivity that similar investment in increased mechanization of British, French, and German industry would achieve. Industrialization of Latin America would threaten existing conditions, including, very probably, the rate of population growth. Thus as industrial investment took place it would probably result in diminished food export. This would decrease the likelihood of further investment by Europeans, since earnings from Latin American firms—in the absence of food for export and in face of the necessity to dispose of industrial products in competition with those of Europe and other well-favored industrial areas—could only represent such exploitation of labor as would also be likely to be productive of nationalist repercussions.

As has been shown, many of the conditions which once made foreign trade between the West and the rest of the world profitable in monetary terms have been upset. Not to be overlooked is the growing tendency of the people of a region in the West to set minumum standards of living for all: any group whose plane of living is reduced below acceptable standards will be subsidized. The subsidy may take the form of minimum-wage legislation, which usually requires that the consumer pay more for a product than he would otherwise, a tariff, which may have the same effect, or some system of direct free services, such as education and medical and dental care, or "relief," to supplement what is received from the market. Thus, a source of profit which once came from the necessity for some groups in a state to accept a standard of living set by competition in a world market, while other groups were offered various kinds of protection, has tended to disappear, and with it one of the foundations of foreign trade.

The more even spread of the product of high-energy technology among all those near the surplus-producing sources has been promoted by the necessity for military protection, if for no other reason. The provision of military equipment can be made a first claim on industry, and more equal sharing of consumable wealth is sometimes demanded as a prerequisite to universal participation in military service. Increasingly, values not measured by the market are brought into play through the state to interfere with the kind of international specialization demanded by the operations of the law of supply and demand. The consequence may not be the maximization of "economic" values in price terms. In a war-minded world maximization of energy may prove to be more important than maximization of private economic gain.

In the early days of capitalism investment was more in the hands of traders and bankers than of governments and industrialists. The investment banker took his profit from the sale of securities. Sometimes his gain was directly proportional to the risk which investors took. Since he was often not himself an investor in the securities he sold, he might prefer to float loans in areas where the risks involved brought him great profits. Similarly, trade was often profitable only if the trader could depend upon a great navy to aid him in supporting a merchant class against the efforts of other groups seeking to recover the regional integrity which trade continually upset. Trade was sometimes the result of the dumping abroad of the surpluses resulting from fixed prices at home. Such trade cannot be countenanced by a government able to dispose of those surpluses among those whom it would otherwise have to support out of taxes. Governments seeking to develop industry where in time of war it can be depended upon, or seeking funds which can be used to provide local employment, find allies among domestic groups which benefit from these policies. Industrialists now create a good deal of the capital they need for expansion. They are no longer required to turn it over to owners who would determine whether or not to reinvest it. Many industrialists seem to be more aware of the apparently unlimited demand which is created among well-paid industrial workers using high-energy technology than they are aware of, and responsive to, the restricted markets provided by low-energy societies. The bankers and traders have lost control of much of what they once could have invested abroad. Instead, government and industrial managers make the decisions.

These conditions have produced a kind of world that hardly represents what capitalistic ideology or the demands of *laissez faire* require. In spite of great ideological effort to achieve it, the actual world looks less and less like one big market in which goods, money, and men move freely. The world is now probably confronted by more socially enacted economic controls than it has seen in a hundred years. Events have not followed the course that should have been the outcome of what many have held to be unchangeable human nature. Nor do present trends indicate that "in the long run" things will come any closer to what liberal ideology requires.

REGIONAL HIGH-ENERGY SYSTEMS

Great regional movements like those which characterized the development of the United States and Canada are now emerging as dominant. Increase in the physical productivity of the North American system has more than kept pace with its population growth. Most of the resources required to maintain that system lie within it or within the area which can effectively be protected by the available military resources. The present rate of accumulation of converters, the present immigration policy, and present birth and survival rates seem to provide assurance that this will continue to be true for some time. Thus, in general, the effective ideas, ideals, social structure, and values of the North American people seem, in domestic affairs, to provide no barrier to the adjustments likely to be required by technology. It is at least questionable, however, whether this is equally true in those policies pursued and likely to be pursued in international affairs.

There has been a great transfer of United States products to other parts of the world to support our ideological aims. The flow to Europe, the Mediterranean, and the Near East has continued to the point at which prewar physical productivity in those areas has been reached and surpassed. The United States government in collaboration with European groups seeking similar goals have made it possible for the total productivity of Western Europe to rise to the point where it now apparently exceeds that generated beyond the Iron Curtain.[6] It must be remembered that this result was only secured by keeping in office governments favorable to the policy favored by the United States. What this policy required was governments abroad which would take a certain military posture in reference to the U.S.S.R. In many cases this posture required the backing of great quantities of physical goods, which could be produced only with the expenditure of great amounts of energy. At the same time many groups in Europe demanded the revival of a flow of consumers' goods and services, which also required energy in amounts much greater than could be supplied from European sources. To assure the survival of these governments the United States supplied the materials, the energy, and frequently the services to secure the necessary production. In this way the United States maintained the support of groups abroad which otherwise would have had to abandon the policies arising from values they jointly shared with the makers of United States policy. A subsidy was required, in the form not of money or credit but of energy and its products. A reduction in the flow of energy and products would in many cases have been accompanied by a change in those governments and the adoption by them of a different policy. The continued existence of these governments and the successful pursuit of their policies are thus not evidence of European ideological convictions alone; they also demonstrate how the use of energy may affect the survival of one set of values and the rejection of another.

The American System

There has been a general assumption that such countries as England and the Latin American states are safely in the hands of groups who would pursue the kind of course that United States policy requires of them. Goods from the United States have been offered there in great quantities only in exchange for other goods. At some future point it may become necessary for the United States to bolster up the groups in these countries which favor its policies if these groups are to remain in power.

The drain involved in the effort to maintain those favorable to United States policy in areas such as China became prohibitive, and the responsible government refused to increase the flow of goods to that unknown point at which it might have sufficed to keep in power groups who would promote American ideals in China. The choice between using or not using things in support of ideas and values seems in this case, as in others, to have affected the survival of ideas and values.

Some of the measures required by the United States policy in Europe now hinder certain groups in the achievement of their goals. They are able to pursue these goals today as a consequence of the past flow of energy from America, and they resent the limits which current American policy imposes on them. They are in a position to reject further aid if the cost of following United States policy is felt to be too high. On the other hand, some groups who are committed to the support of that policy will have less influence if and as the flow of energy and its products from the United States is diminished. The goverments in power have received military goods for which they did not have to tax their nationals. In addition, they got great stocks of consumers' goods which they sold to their own people; the revenue from these sales was used to carry out many projects which were necessary to maintain the policy approved by the United States. If they are now required to pay for American goods or supply their own military equipment, they must either increase taxes, abandon projects which would eventually increase their physical productivity but which at present require expenditure, reduce the actual rate of consumption by their people through inflation, and/or change their foreign policy. Thus a rising insistence by the United States on a return to "Trade, not aid" sacrifices one ideological objective, that of "stopping Communism," for another, the return to profit as the criterion for foreign expenditure and investment. The efficient use of energy to maximize physical productivity using North American assets requires the withdrawal of subsidy from Europe; but the achievement of this objective is incompatible with the achievement of "freedom" for capitalistic enterprise all over the world. This, too, provides a test as to which policy is the more likely to survive or become dominant.

The European and Russian Systems

Certain elements of American and European geography and culture are likely to alter the future relations of Western Europe and America. Since the American realm includes such great geographical resources, and since the great body of the sparse native population which once could lay claim to these resources has now been liquidated or assimilated, Americans can do without trade with "colonial" areas in which populations based on low-energy technology survive in large numbers. Thus the American can afford ostensibly to operate on a set of nonimperialistic ideals because he is in a position to abandon these areas as sources of materials or markets if the costs of holding them are too great or involve the corecion of too many people. But Europeans face a different set of alternatives, and in many cases they can abandon these sources only if new ones become available. A fertile source of disagreement is this area between what American ideals demand and what Europeans are likely to acquiesce to. There will be a mounting resistance by various European groups if they are forced to abandon present resources without compensation. Unless and until great surpluses exist in Europe which make possible substitution for the raw materials lost, these groups are likely to oppose a foreign policy of "appeasement" of native nationalists in Asia, Africa, the Near East, and other colonial regions. To maintain its European alliances the United States government will have either to continue a flow of energy adequate to replace the losses sustained by acquiescence in the colonial policy it demands of Europe, or to modify that policy. But the present policy of the United States is partially supported by idealists who urge the self-determination of colonial areas, and as the United States government apparently yields to the "power politics" of its allies, it will lose the support of these voters and groups. Thus the political party which favors policies that will increasingly use the energy of North America "at home" is more likely to find allies among the voters and stockholders than that party which persists in pursuing more elaborate systems of international organization. Energy will be used nearer its source rather than farther away, and the distribution of its product within a limited range will probably gain more domestic supporters than policies dictated by universal ideals.

Similarly, in Western Europe and the United Kingdom the policies which effectively utilize energy to provide domestic employment and reduce the costs of transportation and of defending distant governments will be able to find more supporters than the policies of imperialists or of the proponents of a world market and a world state. Abandonment of India as a colonial area has apparently been a prelude to its loss as a market and as a source of raw materials (which are now required by the Indian government in its program of industrialization). The effort to industrialize parts of the African continent has forced the colonial powers to acquiesce in the creation of semiautonomous governments which are being pressed to adopt policies inimical to foreign investment and trade. Only the Belgians, who have carefully prevented the rise in their colonies of indigenous groups supporting Western political and economic ideals, seem for the time to be secure.[7] The great growth of the native populations and the apparent failure of industrialized agriculture make the continued use of these areas expensive. Danish experience in increased food output indicates that it will be possible for Western Europe to confine its food trade to areas like those in South America that are equipped to export food and to raise the rest of the food needed where they can defend it successfully without too great expenditure.

The same kinds of alternatives confront the Soviet government. The official ideology holds that ultimately all the world will be Communist. Also it requires that it be directed from Moscow. The conflict between what it is possible to do with Russian resources and what is demanded by Cominform ideology is not the first instance of a clash between that ideology and the power it commands. Time and time again the ideals of the revolution have been sacrificed to the realities of technology. The ideal "From each according to his ability, to each according to his need" disappeared in favor of a system paying off in terms of "productivity" as measured by the Russian taskmaster. Repeated switches in the party line, which now supports foreign Communist parties and then sacrifices them to Russian national interests, provide evidence that here too ideology struggles with other values in determining the use of limited power. In spite of the fact that communist ideology demands even distribution of industry and its products both regionally and in terms of social classes, the facts are that the product of industry and industry itself have been concentrated in both respects. To an increasing degree it becomes apparent that the "success of the revolution" is dependent upon the accumulation of productive facilities. It should be obvious both at home and abroad that if population with its demands on energy increases faster than other converters, the productivity must fall so low as to make chimerical the achievements foreseen by the fathers of the revolution. Even a limited knowledge of the demographic facts about China, Poland, and Eastern Europe makes it clear that the chances of increasing per capita converter capacity for these populations are very dim. So a choice between geographic expansion and increased per capita productivity will have to be made—and soon.

If our analysis is correct there is, then, considerable evidence that values which require greater use of energy are increasing in North America, Northwest Europe, and the U.S.S.R. There is thus created a mounting conflict between universal ideological objectives and regional achievement of a higher plane of material well-being. Regionalism is favored by many aspects of high-energy technology, and more energy becomes available to support it as regional values come to guide policy. For much of the rest of the world we have little evidence as to the character of emergent values. But there is in many of these areas, as we have seen, a presumption favoring the survival of traditional ways of living. The inertia of these societies is less likely to be subject to the efforts of industrialists to upset it than it was fifty years ago because there are now more effective claims on industrial energy "at home" than there were then. Many demographic factors, some of which are not too well understood, seem to make the further advance of these areas along the continuum from low to high energy at least highly improbable. Some sociological and technological propositions seem to lead to the same conclusion, but others can be cited to the contrary. Thus the future course of industrialialism in India, China, Brazil, or Japan is not as clear as further research may make it.

SHORT-TERM AND LONG-TERM PROSPECTS

What does appear to be probable, in the short run, is the emergence of at least three geographically fairly well defined systems using high-energy technology. North America will be the base for one of these, England and Germany for the second, and Russia for the third. How many satellites each of these "suns" may be able to hold in its orbit depends on many things. It is not certain whether Germany or England will predominate in the second, and possibly Germany may compete with Russia for hegemony over a Communist Continental system. The lines representing the boundaries of the regions will depend on factors that range from the skill of diplomats to the accidents of domestic politics. The effects of new weapons have given many of the old factors that helped to determine where boundaries lay a different meaning from what they previously had, what we know about this is still largely speculative. It *is* clear, however, that a system which would permanently weld two of these three bases together would be far stronger than the remaining one, so the stakes of organization are very high. As Western Europe regains its previous military and industrial stature, that fact will become of increasing significance in both the other camps. Thus an unstable equilibrium may serve to force compromises less destructive to the attainment of the ideals of any of the societies than would be likely to result if one system became completely dominant. Continued over time, such a balance of power has in the past produced a way of living which required tolerance, compromise, and agreements with which no one was completely satisfied. It has also given rise to confederacies or federal systems in which power was distributed and certain functions were carried on by one agency, or from one center, and others by another. Thus in the long run there could emerge a loose federal system making arrangements that would obviate the necessity for war and provide for the implementation of such values as became universal.

The UN, like its predecessors, is the repository of some of the things human beings commonly hold to be sacred. Enlargement of these ideals is most likely to come about if no one power achieves the means to destroy the others. In this respect a balance of power resulting from the widespread distance between the centers of energy, the centripetal effect these centers have on those using them, and the practical impossibility of bringing them all into one system dominated by a single elite may provide a surer base for a tolerable world than would some of the idealistic schemes which might be possible were the geographic foundations of energy closer together or more easily subject to a single control.

Because its use is supplemental to rather than a substitute for other forms of energy, the advent of atomic power has not given any society the power to create "one world" by threat and domination; rather it has heightened the prospect that any one industrial elite will find itself weaker at the end of a war than it was at the beginning. This is particularly true on the Continent, where the balance between population and energy is not so heavily weighted on the side of the use of high-energy converters as to assure their re-creation were any great proportion of them to be destroyed. A prolonged and destructive war would probably leave much of the world with a ratio of population to land and capital such that no elite could stop "regression" toward low-energy society. In Russia, at least the engineers and economists, if they have any real grasp of the nature of the revolution they are trying to effect, must be aware of this. It is possible also that many groups of Europeans and Americans know the danger to the survival of the world they want to preserve which might come from such a regression.

Any attempt to deal with such a complex of variables as is involved in predicting the course of civilization must be to some degree a failure. The method of perception and the locus of attention developed here lead to no sure conclusions: perhaps the contribution of this essay lies chiefly in the fact that it suggests whole areas of ignorance whose exploration might increase the accuracy of our thinking about the future development of human society. If it does succeed in providing a framework for research of a kind that will reduce error, it will be justified, for certainly we must believe that more of man's ills are due to his ignorance than to his evil intent.

References

CHAPTER 1

1. Zipf, George Kingsley: *Human Behavior and the Principle of Least Effort,* Cambridge, Mass.: Addison-Wesley Press Inc., 1949.

This work examines man's behavior from a somewhat different point of view and uses another type of evidence than that relied on here. For further information the reader should consult the book itself; even extended treatment would not do Zipf justice.

CHAPTER 2

1. Daniels, Farrington: "Solar Energy," *Science,* vol. 109, no. 2821, p. 51, Jan. 21, 1949.
2. Daniels, *cited,* p. 52.
3. Willcox, O. W.: *Nations Can Live at Home,* p. 119, New York: W. W. Norton & Company, Inc., 1935.

Willcox sets out to prove that it is easily possible to feed a very much larger population than that found in the world today through selection of the proper plants and their cultivation in approved ways. To my knowledge no large area has as yet succeeded in producing even a considerable fraction of what Willcox holds to be theoretically possible.

4. Daniels, *cited,* p. 55.
5. Willcox, *cited,* p. 98.
6. Tolley, Howard Ross: "Population and Food Supply," *Chronica Botanica,* vol. 11, no. 4, p. 219, Summer, 1948.
7. Morrison, F. B.: *Feeds and Feeding,* 21st ed., p. 909, Ithaca, N. Y.: Morrison Publishing Co., 1950.
8. Forde, C. Daryll: *Habitat, Economy and Society: A Geographical Introduction to Ethnology,* 5th ed., p. 38, New York: E. P. Dutton & Co., Inc., 1946.
9. Forde, *cited,* pp. 46f.

10. Mishkin, Bernard: *Rank and Warfare among the Plains Indians,* chap. 2, American Ethnological Society Monograph 3, New York: J. J. Augustin, 1940.
11. Curwen, E. Cecil: *Plough and Pasture,* p. 76, London: Cobbett Press, 1946.
    An expanded version of this book, containing a section by Gudmund Hatt, has been published in this country (New York: Abelard Press, Inc., 1953).
12. Thurnwald, Richard: *Economics in Primitive Communities,* p. 95, International Institute of African Languages and Cultures, London: Oxford University Press, 1932.
13. Forde, *cited,* p. 378.
14. Childe, V. Gordon: *Social Evolution,* p. 161, New York: Abelard Press, Inc., 1951.
15. Thurnwald, *cited.* This is a general theme repeated at various points.
16. Fei, Hsiao-tung, and Chih-i Chiang: *Earthbound China: A Study of Rural Economy in Yunnan,* p. 11, Chicago: University of Chicago Press, 1945.
17. Buck, John Lossing: *Land Utilization in China,* p. 6, Chicago: University of Chicago Press, 1937.
    Some of the findings in this work are criticized in the later book by Fei and Chiang cited just above. Because of this lack of agreement, no extensive use has here been made of figures on Chinese productivity.
18. Ghosh, D.: *Pressure of Population and Economic Efficiency in India,* p. 43, Indian Council of World Affairs, London: Oxford University Press, 1946.
19. Goodfellow, D. M.: *Principles of Economic Sociology,* p. 76, New York: McGraw-Hill Book Company, Inc., Blakiston Division, 1939.

CHAPTER 3

1. Gilfillan, S. C.: *Inventing the Ship,* Chicago: Follett Publishing Company, 1935.
2. Clowes, G. S. Laird: *Sailing Ships: Their History & Development,* London: His Majesty's Stationery Office, 1930.
3. Van Loon, Hendrik Willem: *Ships & How They Sailed the Seven Seas (5000 B.C. – A.D. 1935),* p. 27, New York: Simon and Schuster, Inc., 1935.
4. Van Loon, *cited,* p. 31.
5. Clowes, *cited,* part II, p. 13.
6. Van Loon, *cited,* pp. 65–70.
7. Van Loon, *cited,* p. 37.

CHAPTER 5

1. Ayres, Eugene and Charles A. Scarlott: *Energy Sources: The Wealth of the World,* p. 18, New York: McGraw-Hill Book Company, Inc., 1952.

   This work pulls together an immense amount of information heretofore obtainable only by consulting a great many sources. It deals—in a way that clears the air of wishful thinking, wild speculation, and misapprehension—with a number of the proposals for using various kinds of energy. This and the State Department's volume *Energy Resources of the World,* cited below, constitute a point of departure for almost any future study.

2. Ayres and Scarlott, *cited.* This general position is also supported by Palmer Cosslett Putnam, in *Energy in the Future,* New York, D. Van Nostrand Company, Inc., 1953.

3. Ayers and Scarlott, *cited,* p. 293.

4. Department of State Publication 3428, *Energy Resources of the World, 1949.*

   It is to be hoped that a revision of this work will be undertaken, since the basic figures used were compiled for the most part in 1937. Such a revision would reveal current trends in the use of power and, if our thesis applies, provide a simpler means of determining other trends in society than the elaborate techniques now required.

5. Isard, Walter: "Distance Inputs and the Space-economy." *The Quarterly Journal of Economics,* vol. 65, no. 2 May, 1951, pp. 181–198, no. 3 (August, 1951), pp. 373–399.

   This provides an interesting and probably a fruitful method of evaluating and computing the factors that operate in determining the location of industry.

6. Schurr, Sam H. and Jacob Marschak: *Economic Aspects of Atomic Power,* Cowles Commission for Research in Economics Princeton, N. J.: Princeton University Press, 1950.

   This study gets down to earth and examines closely the possibilities of atomic power in competition with other known energy sources. The authors, though handicapped by the secrecy surrounding the subject, indicate the kind of computations which must be made and the probable outcomes of various attempts to substitute this for another source of power. Together with the discussion to be found in Ayres and Scarlott, this work makes it possible to dispose of most of the roseate dreams of the utopians and consider the practical probabilities.

7. Ayres and Scarlott, *cited,* p. 138.

8. Ayres and Scarlott, *cited,* p. 144.

9. Bogue, Don J.: *The Structure of the Metropolitan Community,* Ann Arbor, Mich., Horace H. Rackham School of Graduate Studies University of Michigan, 1949.

In this work Bogue presents empirical evidence revealing actual movements under way in the American population and offers a plausible theory as to the reasons therefor.

CHAPTER 6

1. Arrow, Kenneth J.: *Social Choice and Individual Values,* Cowles Commission for Research in Economics Monograph no. 12, New York: John Wiley & Sons, Inc., 1951.

This monograph presents a discussion of the logic required to support the use of the individual as a model for predicting emergent values. I have been more interested in evaluating trends in social structure and spatial location as evidence of emergent values than I have been in presenting an orderly discussion of the way in which changes in personality structure are related to values and to social and spatial relationships. The connections between theory based on this kind of evidence and theory based on intensive study of group and personality dynamics must, however, be established, and Arrow's presentation of the logic involved is as good for this purpose as any with which I am familiar.

2. Knight, Frank H.: *Freedom and Reform: Essays in Economics and Social Philosophy,* New York: Harper & Brothers, 1947.

Of the economists, Knight's theory of the relation of power to value most nearly approaches my own. If my attempt to use Knight's thinking to make a connection between energy theory and value theory distorts what Knight intended to convey, only I am responsible, since I have not discussed the matter with him. This particular work, rather than some of Knight's earlier ones, is cited because it shows the consistent position which he has taken.

3. Polanyi, Karl: *The Great Transformation,* New York: Farrar & Rinehart, Inc., 1944.

Polanyi's description of the way in which the traders divested themselves of responsibility for the fate of those demoralized by the energy revolution they were carrying on provides thought-provoking evidence of the nature of economic liberalism. The documentation is thorough, and Polanyi's evidence as to what was happening may well be used to supplement the simplified version of English history here presented. Polanyi does not deal at all extensively with the energy aspects of the shifts in power which he discusses.

4. Lamartine Yates, Paul, and D. Warriner: *Food and Farming in Post War Europe,* p. 39, New York: Oxford University Press, 1943.

The kind of living provided by the use of plants in Europe is to my knowledge nowhere presented so forcefully and succinctly as in these studies. Combined with short case histories giving typical life patterns of farmers, they make Europe and its problems come alive in a way which statistics alone are unable to do.

5. Davis, Kingsley: "Population and the Further Spread of Industrial Society," *Proceedings of the American Philosophical Society*, vol. 95, p. 12, 1951.
6. Ghosh, *Pressure of Population and Economic Efficiency in India*, p. 43.
7. Fei and Chiang, *Earthbound China: A Study of Rural Economy in Yunnan*, p. 6.
8. Ghosh, *cited*, p. 89.
9. Kindelberger, C. P.: "Group Behavior and International Trade," *Journal of Political Economy*, vol. 59, no. 1, February, 1951. pp. 30–46
10. Moore, Wilbert Ellis, *Economic Demography of Eastern and Southern Europe*, League of Nations Publication II A 9, 1935.

CHAPTER 7

1. Moore, Wilbert Ellis: *Industrialization and Labor*, published for New School for Social Research, Institute of World Affairs, Ithaca, N. Y.: Cornell University Press, 1951.

This book discusses at length and with full documentation the social consequences of industrializing a number of low-energy societies. It shows how resistance arises, the forms it takes, and some of the results. The case material on special situations in Mexico provides a means of estimating roughly the energy which would be required to alter some of the blocks encountered.

2. Lewis, Oscar: *Life in a Mexican Village: Tepoztlán Revisited* Urbana, Ill.: University of Illinois Press, 1951.

This is a reexamination of Tepoztlán, one of the villages studied by Redfield in the course of his work on the folk-urban classification of societies. For the characterization of the societies here called "low-energy" societies I have of course drawn largely on such studies as these. Lewis's book is particularly valuable because the "economic" base of the community is revealed so painstakingly in quantified terms which make comparison with other systems possible. The general tenor of his work and that of Redfield seems to be based upon the idea that industrialization will continue indefinitely in Mexico. Of this I am not nearly so certain as they.

3. Lewis, *cited*, p. 156.
4. Curwen, *cited*, pp. 48–49.
5. Fei and Chiang, *Earthbound China: A Study of Rural Economy in Yunnan*.
6. Mullins, Troy and M. W. Slusher: *Comparison of Farming Systems for Large Rice Farms in Arkansas*, June 1951, University of Arkansas, College of Agriculture, Agricultural Experiment Station, cooperating with the U. S. Department of Agriculture, Bureau of Agricultural Economics, Fayetteville, Ark., Bulletin 509, p. 36.

This is one of the very few reports which I was able to locate that provided all the data required to measure operations in energy terms. Undoubtedly a great deal of the field data basic to a very large number of other reports published in terms of monetary costs exist in terms which can be measured energywise. Should this approach prove fruitful, particularly in connection with such propositions as the Point Four program, publication of these data may be enlightening.

7. Buck, *Land Utilization in China,* p. 26.

8. Lewis, *cited,* p. 143.

9. *Low Cost Labor Power and Machinery Set-ups for Indiana Farms.* Purdue University Agricultural Experiment Station cooperating with the Bureau of Agricultural Economics U.S. Dept. of Agriculture. Bulletin 502, February, 1944.

10. Jaffe, Abram J. and C. D. Stewart: *Manpower Resources and Utilization,* New York, John Wiley & Sons, Inc., 1951.

The discussion shows how the number and kinds of workers are modified by changing social conditions.

11. Keynes, John Maynard: *The General Theory of Employment, Interest and Money,* New York: Harcourt, Brace and Company, Inc., 1936.

Since Keynes's work has been so widely discussed, it is almost supererogation to cite it here. However, the struggle between Keynesian and anti-Keynsian is not resolved. Connection was made here chiefly to show how a shift in social objective from the championship of the theory that maximization of profits is an adequate measure of social welfare to the championship of the theory that practically puts "employment" in that position is related to the use of energy.

12. Fei and Chiang, *cited,* p. 6.

13. Schultz, Theodore W.: *Production and Welfare of Agriculture,* pp. 87, 94, New York: The Macmillan Company, 1949.

Schultz urges the substitution or supplementation of price as a means of regulating argricultural production. Emphasis is on the effects that market operations are likely to have on the achievement of the social goal "to preserve agriculture as a way of life." The relative effectiveness with which farmers, as compared with their competitors, can deal with the events that control their fate as mediated in the market is given thoughtful treatment; it deserves wider consideration than it seems to have received.

14. "Farm Horsepower," *Fortune,* vol. 38, no. 4, p. 198, October, 1948.

15. Bachman, Kenneth L.: "Changes in Scale in Commercial Farming and Their Implications," *Journal of Farm Economics,* vol. 34, no. 2, pp. 157–172. May, 1952.

16. Schultz, *cited,* p. 138.

CHAPTER 8

1. Barnett, Harold J.: *Energy Uses and Supplies,* U.S. Bureau of Mines Information Circular 7852, October, 1950.

Barnett shows that the total BTU per unit of national product has fallen consistently during a period of about 35 years. The rate of fall has been about 1 per cent a year compounded. Thus the energy requirements for 1965 for motive power will be about the same as in 1947 and the total energy requirements will only be about 30 per cent greater than in 1947.

2. Clark, Colin: *The Conditions of Economic Progress,* 2d ed., London: Macmillan & Co., Ltd. 1951.

If the listings of real income given by Clark are placed in descending order compared with the figures shown in the UN series showing per capita energy consumed, it will be seen that there is almost no case where the class interval in standard of living differs from that in energy consumed.

3. Spengler, Joseph J.: "Economic Factors in the Development of Densely Populated Areas," *Proceedings of the American Philosophical Society,* vol. 95, no. 1, pp. 20–53. 1951.

4. Hatt, Paul K. (ed.): *World Population and Future Resources,* New York: American Book Company, 1952.

This work is of particular interest as giving a succinct summary of recent findings in this field; it shows how slight the evidence is that a fertility rate such as will result in stability exists even in the West.

5. Clark, *cited.*

6. Graham, Frank D.: *The Theory of International Values,* Princeton, N. J.: Princeton University Press, 1948.

The explanation of international trade as a simple matter of class interest is certainly inadequate. Graham's book expresses in economic terms what I think happens in terms of energy. His emphasis on the supply side of the problem of international trade is expressed always in monetary units but emphasizes opportunity costs, which are, I think, always a function of energy costs, though rarely if ever identical with them. His introduction, showing the relation between what in fact happens and what should according to classical theory happen, should serve to bridge the gap between the facts here emphasized and those emphasized in most works on international trade.

7. Slichter, Sumner H.: *Towards Stability,* New York: Henry Holt and Company, Inc., 1934.

Slichter's treatment of equilibrium as a general social phenomenon is much more nearly what we are talking about here than the "equilibrium" of those economists who express it in price terms alone. In all his books Slichter treats values given in price terms within the same framework as other values. For this reason his works are better fitted to explain the process here being described than are those of the classical or neoclassical school.

8. Mumford, Lewis: *Technics and Civilization,* New York: Harcourt, Brace and Company, Inc.

This is one of the most complete, and to me most satisfying, discussions of the effects of culture on the way in which a thing is perceived. I undoubtedly owe much more to Mumford than the number of direct references would indicate. This discrepancy is due to the fact that the frame which he uses involves the discussion of a much larger number of variables than we here undertake to examine.

9. Moore, *Industrialization and Labor*.

Moore shows, for example, how the efforts of "outsiders" in Mexico have been instrumental in setting up conditions which are viewed in two quite different ways. One view is stated in terms of the innovator, the other in terms of those affected by the innovation. The outcome of the interaction is not what either side would have sought or would have predicted.

10. Tawney, Richard Henry: *Religion and the Rise of Capitalism,* New York: Harcourt, Brace and Company, 1926.

Weber, Max: *The Protestant Ethic and the Spirit of Capitalism,* London: George Allen & Unwin, Ltd., Second Impression, 1948.

These classics deal extensively with the relation between economic values and the supreme values represented by "religion." Whether these values are "inherently superior" to others is a matter to be argued by theologians. Here we are emphasizing the instrumental value, or the effects that Protestantism has had upon a society—and presumably might have again if set down in a society resembling that from which it historically emerged.

11. Veblen, Thorstein: *Imperial Germany and the Industrial Revolution,* New York: The Macmillan Company, 1915.

In many of his references Veblen was obscure and difficult to understand. In dealing with imperial Germany he foresaw with great clarity, however, and indicated with simplicity the outcome of the adoption of high-energy technology in a feudal setting dominated largely by military values. Apparently even after the experience of the First World War and its aftermath neither German thinkers nor others took his prognostications seriously.

12. Chamberlin, William Henry: *Russia's Iron Age,* Boston: Little Brown & Company, 1937.

Compare this work, for example, with a work like Disraeli's *The Two Nations* (London: Longmans, Green & Co., Ltd., 1855).

CHAPTER 9

1. Moore, *Industrialization and Labor,* p. 169.
2. Borsodi, Ralph: *Flight from the City,* New York: Harper & Brothers, 1933.

The attempt to adopt this approach must have resembled the "back to the country" movement of French royalty just before the Revolution. Seemingly, housewives who tried to do all the things suggested, even with the aid of machines, lost interest after a short time. The subsistence homestead movement, epitomized perhaps in the experiments at Arthurdale, quickly demonstrated that to be efficient the unit for spinning or weaving modern style would require consumption of at least 10,000 yards of cloth a year. Similarly, most other units using high-energy technology required social organization beyond the reach of the family on a homestead.

3. The reports of the Temporary National Economic Committee, which

revealed the extent of this concentration, have recently been reviewed in a study by the Brookings Institution. While concentration is still characteristic, according to this report (for a summary see *Fortune*, vol. 47, February, 1953), countervailing power in the form of both political and business organization now offsets it. For a fuller expression of this point of view, see John Kenneth Galbraith, *American Capitalism: The Concept of Countervailing Power*, Boston: Houghton Mifflin Company, 1952.

4. Burnham, James: *The Managerial Revolution*, New York: The John Day Company, Inc., 1941.

The thesis developed in this work that management has become a "law unto itself" is, in our judgment, an oversimplification. Management, rather than owners, now frequently has the responsibility of distributing output among claimants and of assigning functions among those who must cooperate in production. The fact that it initiates policy, and therefore has a range of choice which is not possible to others engaged with it in production, does not mean that it can make whatever choices it wishes to make in its own interest. It still must find a way to motivate all its partners, and frequently this involves setting up patterns of function and reward very different from those it would set up if only the values of management were to be fulfilled.

5. Slichter, Sumner H.: *Union Policies and Industrial Management*, Institute of Economics Publication 85, Washington, D.C.: Brookings Institution, 1941.

Although Slichter has developed the thesis presented in this book considerably since it was first initiated, I know of no clearer statement of the way in which codes of action develop among workers and find institutional expression (see particularly the early chapters). There is a great body of literature on this, but it would serve no germane purpose to make detailed reference to it here.

6. Zipf, George Kingsley: *National Unity and Disunity*, Bloomington, Ind.: Principia Press, Inc., 1941.

The general empirical findings cited here might be "explained" by a number of theories. What Zipf emphasizes that is of greatest concern to us is the fact that an optimum size for the society seems to be related to the energy available and the techniques by which it is administered. Thus the attempt to preserve the integrity of the community or region which is below this optimum is bound to result in failure. As is clear from our discussion above, we could give no such finality as does Zipf to one series of events resulting in one measure corresponding to a single curve, but the facts he presents need adequately to be accounted for somewhere in any definitive theory of society.

7. Roethlisberger, Fritz Jules: *Management and Morale*, Cambridge, Mass.: Harvard University Press, 1943.

This is another pioneering work which has been followed by more definitive studies by its author and by others. But probably none expresses better the need to use tools developed by other branches of social science to explain much of what used to be thought the province of the "economist."

As in earlier instances, it is not felt necessary to provide here a bibliography on the subject.

CHAPTER 10

1. Durkheim, Emile: *The Division of Labor in Society*, Glencor, Ill.: The Free Press, 1949.

    The whole question of the relation between mind and body, self and society, has received much attention in the past few years, but much of what has been said seems to stem from the work of Durkheim, who was the first of the moderns to explore these relationships systematically. It is in his line of thinking that these few paragraphs on the subject find more extensive and systematic exploration.

2. Schumpeter, Joseph Alois: *Capitalism, Socialism and Democracy*, 2d ed., New York: Harper & Brothers, 1950.

3. Schumpeter, *cited*, p. 106. See also, for another point of view, Alvin Harvey Hansen: *Economic Policy and Full Employment*, New York: McGraw-Hill Book Company, Inc., 1947.

4. Stouffer, Samuel Andrew: Research Memorandum on *The Family in the Depression*, New York: Social Science Research Council (studies in the social aspects of the depression, Bull. 29, 1937), 1937.

    This is one of many works which might be cited to show how far-reaching are the results of unemployment.

CHAPTER 11

1. Carr, L. J., and J. E. Stermer: *Willow Run*, New York: Harper & Brothers, 1952.

    This and similar community studies show clearly how many functions clearly necessary for living were disregarded in planning for war production. That somebody would have to supply these amenities was obvious, but it was apparently not so obvious that failure to plan for them might endanger the whole production program, adding to its cost more than the expense of initially planning for them.

2. Wall, Hugo: Occupational Licenses and Permits, Their History and Administration. Doctoral dissertation Stanford University, Stanford, Calif., 1928.

3. Neumann, F. L.: "Approaches to the Study of Political Power," *Political Science Quarterly*, vol. 65, no. 2, pp. 161–180, June, 1950.

    This is a generalized discussion of the sociological roots of political power. It deals trenchantly with the problem of related physical to political controls. There is in this field also a considerable literature to be examined.

4. Rosenfarb, Joseph: *Freedom and the Administrative State,* New York: Harper & Brothers, 1948.
This is cited as a good demonstration of the kind of thoughtful research and speculation that is going on among statesmen and social planners. The list is enormous, and the range extends from careful appraisal such as this to shouting insistence upon some particular conception of the "true" role of government.

CHAPTER 12

1. "Wool's Battle with the Synthetics," *Fortune,* vol. 45, no. 5, pp. 128–131, May, 1952.
2. *World Energy Supplies in Selected Years 1929–1950,* p. 6, United Nations Publication, September, 1952. Statistical Papers, series J, no. 1. International Document Service, Columbia University Press, N. Y.
3. *Energy Resources of the World,* State Department Publication 3428, June, 1949.
4. Compare, for example, *Energy Resources of the World, cited,* with Ayres and Scarlott, *cited;* and Putnam, Palmer Coslett: *Energy in the Future,* New York: D. Van Nostrand Company, Inc., 1953.
5. United Nations Publication, World Energy Supplies, *previously cited,* pp. 4 and 5.
6. Yugow, Aaron: "Thirty-five Years of Economic Progress," *New World Review,* Nov. '52, pp. 22–29; and C. J. V. Murphy, "New Strategy for NATO," *Fortune,* vol. 47, no. 1, pp. 80–85, January, 1953.
7. Solow, Herbert: "The Congo Is in Business," *Fortune,* vol. 45, no. 11, pp. 106–115, November, 1952.

Index

Africa, 35
Agriculture, effect of price system on, 158–164
  industrialization of, 155–158
  productivity of, compared with other industries, 118
  spread of, by Romans, 67
  use of horses in, Russian state farms, 121
  in United States, 120
Animals as converters, 19, 20
Antwerp, 90
Argentina, land use in, 163, 301

Bantu, 36, 37
Belgian Congo, 307
Bengal, agricultural productivity and population, 128
Birth rate, decline in, and industrialization, 167
Bottlenecks in production, 143
Bureaucracy, growth of, 265, 266

Capital, British, historic sources of, 185–190
  definition of, 183
Capitalism, theory of, 182, 185
Cheops pyramid, 33
China, land utilization in, 35
  location of villages in, 83

China, position of trader in, 190, 203
  United States aid to, 306
Clipper ships, 50
Coal, energy cost of, in United States, 147
  reserves of, world distribution, 295–297
  surplus energy from, 94
  at tidewater, influence of, on British economy, 124
Coal miners, productivity of, in England, 86
  in Russia, 145
  in United States, 87
Columbus, Ohio, 91
Cominform, 299, 300
Communism, primitive, 243
  (See also Marxism)
Comparative advantage, law of, 58
Congestion resulting from use of steam engine, 81
Control, concentration of, in high-energy society, 207–208
Corn, energy costs and surplus derived from, in United States and Mexico, 142
Corporation, revival of, in modern times, 222, 223
  and Roman law, 222, 223
Cost, development of concept, 173

Cost, instrumental, of high-energy technology, 175, 176
(*See also* Price)
Critical ratio, between rate of population growth and accumulation of converters, 172
result of failure to attain, 177

Danube River, 90
Dayton, Ohio, 91
Denmark, farm workers per acre and productivity, 128
Diesel engine, field, limit, and gradient of, 107, 108
Division of labor, effect of, 209–212
Draft animals, energy yield from, 20, 21
Due process of law and rapid technological change, 275

Economic, meaning of, 53, 54
Economic funtions, in British experience, 89
in medieval world, 244
Economics, British theory, 173–175
Manchester school, 125
and morals, 54, 55
and politics, 270
Efficiency defined, 8
Egypt, as example of food-raising culture, 33
use of sailing ships in, 48, 66
Electricity, field, limit, and gradient of generators, 98, 102
hydro-, as compared with thermal, 105, 106
social effects of, 99–104
transmission of, 103, 104
Emigration from Europe, 125, 126
Energy defined, 5
Energy costs, of coal in United States, 147
of corn in Tepoztlán, 141

Energy costs, effect of, on employment, 143–147
of industrialized agriculture, 148–152
and petroleum surplus, 94–96
of rice, in Arkansas, 139
in Japan, 140
role of, in history, 113–116
of wheat, in China, 141
in Idaho, 141
English common, 217
Euphrates River, 41

Fair return, 75
Family, decline of, following use of price system, 256
as exploiter of individual, 257, 259
and government, in high-energy societies, 257, 266
in low-energy societies, 37
values, and subsequent behavior, 239, 240
Farms, size of, in Denmark, 128
in United States, 122, 129
in Yunnan, 138
Feudal production, 146
Field defined, 9
Food gatherers, 24
Food raisers, 28, 30
Food supply and mechanization, 166
Forde, Daryll P., 23, 26–28, 31
Free trade, British espousal of, 89
France, and trader, 69
use of surplus energy by, 192, 193
Full employment, 290

Germany, use by, of railroads, 90
of surplus, 127, 191, 192
Government, effect of war on, 268–269
expanding functions of, in high-energy society, 259–264
family functions taken on by, 266

Government, interstate relations and, 279–282
  legitimacy and, in practice, 273–277, 294
  in Western theory, 272–273
  local, decline of, 262
  modern, administrative law in, 266–267
  nationalism and, 281–284
  pressure politics and, 274
  as value creator, 269–271
  and welfare state, 301–303
Gradient defined, 10
Greek ships, nature of, 49
  use and effect of, 64–67

Hart, Hornell, 5
Hoe culture, energy yields of, 22, 135, 136, 142
Horsepower defined, 7
Horses, effect of, on Plains Indians, 26
  energy yield and efficiency of, 21
  use of, in United States agriculture, 120
Hydroelectric power, 105, 106

Idaho, energy cost of wheat in, 141
Ideology and technology, 299, 304–307
Immigration, effect of, in United States, 123
Imperialism, effect of, in energy terms, 170, 171
India, cultivated area and population, 36
  trader in, 190
Indiamen, 50
Indianapolis, Indiana, 91
Internal-combustion engine, field, limit, gradient, and efficiency of, 106–108
  social effect of, 108, 109

Investment bankers, 303
Iowa City, Iowa, 91
Iran, 44, 45
Italy, farm workers per acre in, 128

Japan, energy cost of rice in, 140
  rise to power, 193–194
  use by, of Manchuria, 118
  of surplus energy, 193–194
Just price concept, 188, 246

Keynsianism and use of surplus energy, 197
Kilowatt-hour defined, 7
Kinship groups and production, 202, 234–236
Korea, 300

Legitimate use of power (*see* Government, legitimacy and)
Lewis, Oscar, 135
Limit defined, 8
Los Angeles, California, 297
Low Countries and trade, 69

Mahan, Admiral, 65
Malaya, 292
Manitoba, 58
Maori, 285
Market (*see* Price)
Marxism, explanation of social change in, 194–195, 220, 248, 300, 308
Mercantilism, 72–76
Mesabi, 291
Minoans, 64
Mississippi River, 42
Monroe Doctrine, 282
Morrison, F. B., 21
Mumford, Lewis, 5

Napoleonic Wars, 71
Nationalism and democracy, 279–284
New England, early industry in, 122
Nile River, 42, 66
Norse ships, character of, 49
  use of, 64
North Atlantic Treaty Organization
  (NATO), 301
Nuclear fuel, effect of, 97, 98

Occupational codes, 210, 213, 231
Occupational groups, increased
  power of, 254
Occupational roles and sailing ships,
  202
Occupations restricted by govern-
  ment, 263
Ogburn, W. F., 5
Opportunity costs defined, 53

Paiute Indians, 25
Peak load, effect of, 120
Periclean age, 64
Petroleum, energy costs and surplus
  of, 94–96
  location of reserves, effect of, 96,
  97
Phoenician ships, character of, 48, 49
  use of, 65, 66
Plains Indians, 25
  and railroads, 203
Plants as converters, field, limits, and
  gradients of, 17
Population, capitalist theory and, 184
  increase in, and difficulty of transition, 166–167
  movements of, accompanying
  transition, 167
Portugal, growth of empire, 69
Price, consequences of fluctuation in,
  250, 251
  measurement of productivity by,
  89

Price, values mediated by, 243–250
Price system, decline of family fol-
  lowing use of, 256
Primary groups, use of, in low-energy
  society, 238
Primogeniture and entail, effect of,
  in transition, 189
"Production for use," meaning of,
  233
Production unit, size of, as function
  of technology, 204, 205
Productivity of United States in
  World War II, 252
Property, meaning of, changes in,
  214–220
  and values, concept of, 178
Puritanism and the trader, 190

Railroad usage, by British, 88, 89
  by Germans, 90
  by United States, 91, 93
Reaper, effect of invention and use
  of, 120, 121
Rents in Asia, 187
  basis for, 174, 187
Rice production, in Arkansas, 140
  in Japan, 138, 139
Rivers, conditions affecting use of, 59
  (See also specific names of rivers)
Roman law and corporation, 222,
  223
Roman ships, characteristics of, 49
  use of, 67, 68
Rubber, 292
Russia, accumulation of converters
  in, 196, 197
  agriculture in, 208
  coal miners, productivity of, 145
  ideology and technology, 308, 309
  population of, and production, 132
  state farms, 121
  use by, of Siberia, 118
  of surplus energy, 195
Russian mir, 217, 219

Sailing ships as converters, field, gradient, and limits of, 47, 50
  and occupational roles, 202
  and river towns, 60
  steam engines in, 79
  use of, in Egypt, 48, 66
    by English, 70, 71
    by French, 69
    by Greeks, 64
    by Romans, 67
Sante, early petroleum site, 93
Slavery, 40
Socialized medicine, 260
Sovereignty in modern world, 278
Spain, growth of empire, 69
Spices, trade in, 60
State (*see* Government)
Status, effect of change on, 228, 229
Steam engines, efficiency of, 100
  field, limit, and gradient of, 81–85
  fuel for, 85
  use of, in agriculture, 93
    in coal mines, 79
    congestion from, 81
  effect of, 83–86
    on sailing ships, 79
Stewart, J. K., 5, 161
Surplus energy, claims on, nature of, 152–155
  definition of, 11, 12
  derived from coal, 94
  use of, by France, 192, 193
    by Japan, 193–194
    and Keynesianism, 197
    by Russia, 195
Swiss pastures, 217

Tawney, R. H., 185
Technological change not inevitable, 117
Tepoztlán, 136, 137
  energy cost of corn in, 141
Thompson, Warren S., 124

Thurnwald, Richard, 22, 29
Tigris River, 42
Trade and transportation, 44, 57, 71
Trade winds, 80
Traders, changing position of, 74, 153
Transition to high-energy society, and birth rate, 166–167
  cost of, 117, 118, 149, 150, 176, 177
Transmission of electricity, 103, 104
Trieste, 90
Trolley cars, 100

United Nations, 310
Universal Postal Union, 284
Universities, changing curriculum of, 55
Uranium, 98
Uruguay, 301
Utah, 297
Utilization of land, in Argentina, 163, 301
  in China, 35

Value, definition of, 236
  theory of, 177, 178
Veblen, Thorstein, 185, 186, 191

War, effect of, on accumulation of converters, 198
War of 1812, 71
Water wheels, effect of, 44
  field, limits, and gradient of, 43
Weber, Max, 185
Welfare state, 301–303
Westward movement, 190
Wheat, energy cost of, in China, 141
  in United States, 141
  energy yield of, in form of meat, 20
White, Leslie, 5

Willcox, O. W., 15–17
Windmills, effect of, 46
  field, limits, and gradient of, 45
Wool, in China, 156
  in early trade, 60, 70
  replaced by coal products, 88
World War I, 121

Yunnan, population and productivity,
  35, 37, 129, 138
  size of farms in, 138

Zipf, G. K., 5
  and principle of least effort, 6